The War against
Regulation

STUDIES IN GOVERNMENT
AND PUBLIC POLICY

The War against Regulation

FROM JIMMY CARTER TO GEORGE W. BUSH

Phillip J. Cooper

 University Press of Kansas

Published by the University Press of Kansas (Lawrence, Kansas 66045),
which was organized by the Kansas Board of Regents and is operated
and funded by Emporia State University, Fort Hays State University,
Kansas State University, Pittsburg State University, the University of
Kansas, and Wichita State University

Library of Congress Cataloging-in-Publication Data
Cooper, Phillip J.
The war against regulation : from Jimmy Carter to George W. Bush /
Phillip J. Cooper.
p. cm. — (Studies in government and public policy)
Includes bibliographical references and index.
ISBN 978-0-7006-1681-7 (cloth : alk. paper)
1. Trade regulation—United States. 2. Industrial policy—United
States. 3. Administrative law—United States. 4. Industrial laws and
legislation—United States. 5. United States—Politics and
government—20th century. I. Title.
KF1600.C66   2009
343.73'08—dc22   2009028365

British Library Cataloguing-in-Publication Data is available.

Printed in the United States of America

10 9 8 7 6 5 4 3 2 1

The paper used in this publication is recycled and contains 30 percent
postconsumer waste. It is acid free and meets the minimum
requirements of the American National Standard for Permanence
of Paper for Printed Library Materials z39.48-1992.

For Rosslyn S. Kleeman,
who has taught so many of us by her example
what public service professionalism truly is

Contents

Preface

Defend regulation? Someone must be kidding! That is exactly what I thought as I hung up the phone one morning in 1981 after speaking with a student who invited me to participate in a debate his group was sponsoring on the subject of regulation. What a ridiculous idea. I wondered what preposterous cause I would be asked to defend next. But, as time passed, I grew to regret that visceral response as it became clear that there was a growing group-think, not only in the United States, but around the world, on this subject. Ironically, the mantra of deregulation was often accompanied by dramatic demonstrations of hypocrisy, as some of the most vocal leaders in the debate behaved in ways that suggested a clear willingness to use power—political, military, economic, or social—to impose controls on a wide variety of behavior by people in their own countries and abroad. On the other hand, some politicians ran for office campaigning against what they considered were attacks on critical regulation in such areas as the environment and health and safety, only to make deregulation a central element of their agendas once in office. The rhetoric of protection was loud, but the policy action ran in a very different direction. In the process of these political games, a good deal of bad policy and destructive politics have been visited upon us all.

Perhaps the situation might not have reached such extremes if, in all these years, analysts who were motivated by neither ideology nor partisanship had offered another side to the debate. And it may also have happened that the wholesale attack on regulation that also led to an equally dramatic assault on public institutions associated, accurately or not, with the dreaded idea of regulation could have been more effectively challenged, though perhaps not prevented. There were some voices raised,[1] but they were often dismissed as ideologues, partisans, or defenders of particular policies or regulatory agencies. The fact that such charges were generally not true was of little consequence. It may simply have been that it was too much to ask society to think seriously about the subject in a time when the idea of sweeping away burdensome regulatory requirements was a mantra and in an era dominated by grand rhetoric, proclaiming dramatic visions of a new day of freedom, ease, and plenty without limit. Although it is a truism that when virtually everyone agrees about something, it is probably time to ask hard questions, such questioning is rarely welcome. That is particularly true where a great many people stand to gain a good deal politically, economically, or socially from riding the wave of apparent public consensus in opposing regulation.

It may be, however, that now, after more than a quarter century of the deregulation drumbeat, such a discussion can take place. That is particularly true in the wake of dramatic evidence of the consequences from the lack of effective regulation in a host of fields from corporate governance, financial services, and banking to food and drug safety and environmental protection. While this manuscript has been in preparation for a long time, it arrived at University Press of Kansas on the day that Lehman Brothers went under. After that seismic event in September 2008, of course, the number of casualties of the war against regulation and the damage that has flowed from it escalated dramatically. The massive failures of financial and industrial organizations and the growing evidence of misconduct up to and including outright fraud have caused many to ask: "Where were the regulators?" The damage assessments are continuing and efforts to understand the consequences of the war against regulation systematically will be under way for years.

Clearly, the need for a careful assessment is well past due. In support of that idea, the chapters to follow analyze the war against regulation that has been waged by both Republican and Democratic administrations and present arguments that recall the reasons for regulation that remain valid and have even taken on new urgency. It is also not merely a retrospective analysis, for, if contemporary history is any indication, it is probable that once the immediate crises have passed, the economy has begun a significant recovery, and the memory of some highly publicized abuses has faded, the battle against regulation is very likely to resume. The motivations of those who have waged the war, whether in the political arena or in regulated organizations, will remain.

The conclusion that emerges from the analysis presented in this book is that the war against regulation has been, to quote General Omar Bradley, "the wrong war, at the wrong place, at the wrong time and with the wrong enemy."[2] It has left a host of casualties in its wake, not only in this country but around the world. The thesis that arises from this study is that ultimately the war against regulation has been a self-defeating and damaging conflict that has undermined the effective use of an important policy tool.

This book focuses on the war against regulation as it was waged from the James Earl Carter administration through the Ronald Reagan, George Herbert Walker Bush, William Jefferson Clinton, and George Walker Bush years.

That is not to suggest that regulation has not been a subject of controversy over the nation's history. Indeed, as Chapter 5 explains, the framers were quite clear that one of the reasons that the Constitution was needed was to ensure that the regulatory powers not available before would be provided to address problems fundamental to development of the new nation. Certainly in the years leading up to the Civil War, various states rejected regulatory authority of the federal government. However, after the war, as industrialization and urban growth became the focus of change, the nation saw the rise of the era of the spoilsmen, when corruption and abuse of concentrated economic power brought demands for reform. Populists in the rural areas and Progressives in urban centers demanded and got change that included regulatory policies. Thus, states pioneered in the regulatory arena with the creation of what are now known as public utility commissions in the form of independent regulatory commissions intended to minimize political interference. That model was copied at the federal level as the Interstate Commerce Commission and other independent regulators were created. Antitrust legislation was enacted to address abuses by those known as robber barons.

But then came the era of the gospel of wealth and, with it, the social Darwinist attitudes that rejected the idea that government should play a key role in the protection of citizens and workers. Of course, life in the economic jungle also was a major factor in the Great Depression that followed. And, as it has tended to over time, the private sector promptly demanded that the government take action to address the mess. Indeed, most of the first New Deal was focused on the restoration of the marketplace.

The New Deal was followed by World War II, which brought its own regulatory requirements. In the years since then, there has been an ebb and flow between demands for and reaction against regulation. By the late 1960s and early 1970s, new awareness of problems in health, safety, the environment, and civil rights all brought calls for action.

While it was clear that Richard Nixon had his own fights with federal agencies, he was more concerned with controlling them and using them for his own purposes than eliminating them. Ford launched his "Whip Inflation Now" campaign and did have people in the administration who pressed hard for an emphasis on deregulation, but the fact is that the administration did little of any significant effect toward that end. However, Carter came to the White House as the one of a string of presidents who would run against Washington, and indeed against the government he sought to lead. Like

Reagan, Clinton, and George W. Bush to follow, Carter was a governor who offered a message and promised action that was far different in ideology, politics, and policy than what had come before.

As Chapters 2 and 3 explain in great detail, President Carter and his successors of both political parties, however, were committed to a serious fight against regulation, and they prosecuted it tenaciously with a wide range of weapons, forces, strategies, and tactics over an extended period of time and with historic levels of success. In the end, of course, that success actually meant losses on a variety of fronts for the many Americans, and even those in other countries, who became casualties of the war against regulation.

While the sources and methods used to research this study are discussed in more detail in an appendix to this volume, it should be noted that it emphasizes policy tools research. There is a treasure trove of information available on the behavior of the administrations studied here in a range of policy tools, including not only the specific legal instruments through which the policies are put into operation, but also the large quantity of material in the form of investigative reports prepared by legislative and executive institutions as well as those developed in connection with litigation. There is also a significant body of correspondence and other internal communications available from a variety of sources. Additionally, this study used a content analysis of newspaper articles for the period from the beginning of the Carter administration through the summer of 2008 to track public statements by participants in the war against regulation in addition to those provided in official documents.

The argument advanced in the pages to come is not focused on any one regulatory program or policy or on any particular sector or policy domain. Neither is it grounded in a particular ideology or political party. Indeed, it criticizes both major U.S. parties, since both came to embrace the cause of deregulation, though in different ways and, in some instances, for different reasons. Finally, it does not assume that governments hold the answers to all problems or that any one government at any level operates in the way that even its most ardent advocates would like. That said, I would ask the reader to try to suspend visceral reactions to the topic and to put on the table during the reading some of his or her own assumptions that may underlie those intuitive reactions until the end of the argument.

Let it be clear at the outset that most people come to a discussion of regulation with firmly established perspectives. For those who are just opposed to regulation on ideological grounds, there may simply be no room for a careful consideration of the argument to follow. Others are ardent foes of regulation because they have a self-interest at stake in ridding themselves of regulation under which they operate on a daily basis and which, they are convinced, gets in the way of their personal and business goals. Self-interest has long been a driver of opposition to regulation. They may at least consider the argument with the question in mind as to what would happen if others in the society were also able to rid themselves of regulation. Still others come to the discussion with a view that any discussion of regulation must be conducted and even defined according to the terms and modes of debate drawn from economics, and any argument that does not proceed in that manner is simply not legitimate, or at least not credible. These readers would do well, if they cannot entertain this discussion, to engage the arguments of Joseph E. Stiglitz in such works as *The Roaring Nineties.*[3]

The chapters that follow assess different aspects of the challenge to regulation. Chapter 1 explains the strategies, tactics, and forces arrayed in the war against regulation. Chapter 2 examines how Presidents Carter, Reagan, and George H. W. Bush prosecuted that war. Chapter 3 considers the Clinton and George W. Bush administrations, which, while they differed dramatically in many ways, both continued the fight against regulation through a variety of strategies and tactics. Chapter 4 considers the battle in the courts. It examines the Supreme Court attack on regulation during the Burger and Rehnquist eras and also explores the problems with the effort to use lawsuits as an alternative to regulation through administrative agencies. The battle in the courts is another of those fronts in the war that has been extremely important even if it attracted little public attention. Chapter 6 imagines a possible post-conflict future in which regulation is seen in a less charged and more realistic and fruitful light and offers suggestions as to some of the steps needed to move in that direction.

This project proved to be considerably more complex and took a great deal longer than anticipated when it was originally conceived. In part that was a result of the increasing complexity and intensity of the war against regulation. There was also the challenging political, economic, and legal context within which it has been waged. To a considerable extent the difficulty emerged from the challenge of trying to present the complex story of this conflict in a clear, understandable, and, hopefully, interesting manner. As a result, the shape and content of the material has evolved considerably from the initial design.

I am particularly grateful to Michael Briggs, Editor-in-Chief of the University Press of Kansas, who demonstrated patience above and beyond any reasonable expectation as I worked through this challenging project. He cares not only about producing books that will be successful in the marketplace, but that will add substance to the public discourse and works to assist authors in meeting both challenges. Perhaps that is why he enjoys a well-deserved reputation among scholars.

Indeed, the entire staff at the University Press of Kansas has been extremely helpful, from Publisher Fred Woodward, to Marketing Director Susan Schott, to Production Editor Jennifer A. Dropkin. They have a way of reminding authors that we are not just "content providers," as the jargon of the publishing profession describes us, but committed scholars whose work is to be respected even as they do all they can to make it better. I am grateful for their efforts.

I am especially grateful to Claudia María Vargas. On one level, she is a first-rate editor who asks excellent questions and whose blue pencil helped a great deal to make this manuscript more readable. She dislikes public acknowledgments, but her help and support in this and all other things are too important not to mention.

Phillip J. Cooper
Portland, Oregon

Abbreviations Used in This Book

ADA	Americans with Disabilities Act
ADEA	Age Discrimination in Employment Act
APA	Administrative Procedure Act
BSE	bovine spongiform encephalopathy
CAB	Civil Aeronautics Board
CERCLA	Comprehensive Environmental Response, Compensation, and Liability Act
COP	Congressional Oversight Panel
CPSC	Consumer Product Safety Commission
CRA	Congressional Review Act
CRS	Congressional Research Service
DHS	Department of Homeland Security
DoD	Department of Defense
DOJ	Department of Justice
EO	Executive Order
EPA	Environmental Protection Agency
ERISA	Employee Retirement Income Security Act
FAA	Federal Aviation Administration
FAR	Federal Acquisition Regulations
FCC	Federal Communications Commission
FDA	Food and Drug Administration
FERC	Federal Energy Regulatory Commission
FLSA	Fair Labor Standards Act
FMC	Federal Maritime Commission
FOIA	Freedom of Information Act
FTC	Federal Trade Commission
GAO	General Accounting Office; [later] Government Accountability Office
GATT	General Agreement on Tariffs and Trade
ICC	Interstate Commerce Commission
IG	Inspector General
MACT	Maximum Achievable Control Technology
NAFTA	North American Free Trade Agreement

NEPDG	National Energy Policy Development Group
NHTSA	National Highway Traffic Safety Administration
NPR	National Performance Review
OIRA	Office of Information and Regulatory Affairs
OMB	Office of Management and Budget
PRA	Paperwork Reduction Act
RARG	Regulatory Analysis Review Group
RCRA	Resource Conservation and Recovery Act
Reg. Flex Act	Regulatory Flexibility Act
SARA	Superfund Amendments and Reauthorization Act
SEC	Securities and Exchange Commission
TARP	Troubled Assets Relief Program
USDA	U.S. Department of Agriculture

1. Can There Really Be an Attack on Regulation When There Is So Much of It? The War, the Weapons, and Modes of Attack

It may seem strange to talk about an attack on regulation when there appears to be so much of it. Many Americans would immediately reject the idea that such an assault has been under way by pointing to some particularly onerous or nettlesome rules—and the agencies that enforce them—as ongoing barriers to their accomplishment of important personal and business goals. Still others who are involved in one way or another in the regulatory arena will suggest that the world of regulation has never been more complex and challenging than it is today.[1] They will talk about what they refer to as new techniques and types of regulation. Then there will be those for whom almost any regulation is too much. Their ideology is simply at war with the concept of public regulation under all but the most extreme circumstances.[2] Finally, others might claim, since the fall of 2008, that although such attacks on regulation might have been in progress before, they ended with the massive downturn in the economy with the attendant bank failures, collapse of financial firms, and foreclosure on home mortgages as many voices were suddenly raised in a chorus of demands for regulation.

Even so, there has in fact been an ongoing attack on regulation for a considerable period—at least since the late 1970s. Indeed, it is not too much to say that these assaults are better described as an ongoing war against regulation. This war has been fought across several administrations, under both Democrats and Republicans, as well as by congresses controlled by both political parties, and with widespread public support. It has had serious consequences for the environment, health and safety, telecommunications, and banking and financial services fields, to name but a few of the many policy domains affected. Although there is at the time of this writing a temporary cessation of hostilities because of recent disasters discussed in detail in Chapter 3, it is an open question whether there will in fact be serious action to address regulatory needs as compared to the rhetoric that has in the past so often been unaccompanied by resources and effective policy. Moreover, if recent history is any indication (again, see Chapter 3), it is very possible, and indeed probable, that as soon as the worst circumstances of the current emergency have calmed, the temporary peace will end, and the war against regulation will resume.

The conclusion that emerges from this analysis is that the war against regulation is, to quote General Omar Bradley, "the wrong war, at the wrong place, at the wrong time and with the wrong enemy."[3] It has left a host of casualties in its wake in this country and abroad. The thesis is that ultimately the war against regulation has been a self-defeating and damaging conflict that has undermined the effective use of an important policy tool.

This chapter describes the war, its weapons, and its strategies and tactics, while Chapters 2 and 3 analyze several of its major campaigns from the 1970s to the present. Like many conflicts that have been waged for many years, the ideas and terms central to the discourse on the war may—and in several cases have already—become politically loaded, confused, devalued, and, like the term "reform," even seem to have lost their meaning. For now, consider the ways in which an assault on regulation has been conducted from within the government and from outside it, as well.

A WAR MORE REAL THAN APPARENT: THE ATTACK FROM WITHIN

Like most wars, the assault on regulation has been waged with many strategies and tactics, fought on a variety of fronts, and has involved a range of weapons. Sometimes the strategies have employed a series of frontal assaults with heavy weapons, while, in other campaigns, the techniques of choice have been stealth and guile, using light, but nevertheless effective, weapons. The fact that battles have often been waged as what are known in contemporary military parlance as "low-intensity conflicts" does not mean that they lack serious consequences. Indeed, the war is sometimes fought by what is referred to in the more polite arena of foreign policy as public diplomacy. In some settings, outright disinformation and propaganda have been employed.

To begin, then, attacks have often been direct broadsides against the general concept of regulation, even when the intended targets and objectives are far clearer and more specific. Still more common is the claim that the real objective is regulatory reform when the actual purpose is regulatory reduction or elimination. So common is this gambit that the term "reform" has, in reality, all but lost its meaning. Those who often have used this term, insisting that they want better regulation, have often, like the Clinton administration, measured success by counting the number of pages of regulations eliminated from the Code of Federal Regulation (see Chapter 3) rather than by measures of improvement in quality.

Direct Attacks on Regulation: Legislative and Administrative Approaches

Consider just a few of these types of assault on regulation. First, there are direct attacks, which have included outright deregulation policies centered on passage of legislation to eliminate various types of regulation and, if possible, the agencies charged with their implementation. It is difficult now to remember the Civil Aeronautics Board or the Interstate Commerce Commission, though airline passengers, stranded in flights delayed for five or more hours without food or clean restrooms, and relocating families, who have fought moving companies for loss or damage to their goods with little meaningful recourse, might wish those agencies were still in operation.[4] Ironically perhaps, this direct attack approach has been pursued with particular success under Democratic administrations, like the Carter and Clinton years.

Second, there is the direct, but far less visible, assault by way of administrative deregulation in which congressional (or state legislative) action is not sought, but political appointees in executive branch departments or independent regulatory commissions take it as their task to use their powers to reduce an agency's involvement in or even seek to withdraw from existing areas of regulation. Perhaps ironically, given traditional tendencies to criticize major policymaking decisions by administrative agencies rather than legislative bodies, administrative deregulation has been the strategy of choice for some Republican presidents, as in the Reagan administration's efforts to eliminate rules mandating automobile airbags and to eliminate requirements on broadcasters through action by the Federal Communications Commission.[5]

A third direct assault is the preemption attack, in which federal deregulation policy includes either a direct or implied prohibition against later state or local government attempts to step into the breach. Thus, following airline deregulation state governments were blocked from providing protections for consumers against deceptive or abusive trade practices.[6] And when the state of Washington reacted against the lack of effective protection of the Puget Sound's fragile ecosystem from dangerous operation of oil tankers by understaffed federal administrative agencies operating under weak international agreements and national policies, the state's efforts were preempted in litigation led by the same Clinton administration that proclaimed itself to be an ardent advocate of the environment.[7]

Indirect Attacks on Regulation and Regulatory Agencies

Beyond these direct modes of attack, there have been a number of commonly marshaled techniques that are less direct and far less obvious—and therefore faster, more certain, and less politically risky—that have been used by administrations of both parties. They include antipersonnel weapons, strategic resources attacks, the blame-the-casualties approach, and the burden-loading attack. These are sometimes employed strategically for broad purposes to be achieved over the long term. In other cases, these attacks can be used for tactical pinpoint strikes against discrete targets.

First, there is the use of antipersonnel weapons, the downsizing of the staff, or, more commonly, the effort to reduce overall government human resources, often accomplished by changes in human resource policies designed to encourage staff to remove themselves from the field by early retirement or by resignation, or through policies intended to make it easier to transfer, discipline, or terminate employees. In some circumstances, these efforts have included attacks on agency experts whose research, publications, and legislative testimony supported the need for regulation in the face of an administration's political and ideological predispositions against it. This is a tactic that has drawn serious criticism during the George W. Bush administration in such issue areas as global climate change and health policy issues, where testimony by government scientists was controlled or reports modified for political reasons (see Chapter 3).

Another such approach is the strategic resources attack, a form of assault designed for attrition of the opponent. It is intended to reduce the capacity of regulatory agencies to perform their responsibilities, sometimes to the point where they are largely ineffective, no matter how dedicated their professionals may be. Off the record, and in some partisan political circles, this is known as the "starve the beast" campaign. The ongoing failure to ensure resources adequate to a regulator's assigned mission surfaced in the public eye in the later years of the George W. Bush administration when widespread sicknesses and deaths to family pets resulted from pet food containing imported products, and subsequent discoveries of tainted health care and food products destined for human use led to the revelation that the FDA had the capacity to inspect only 1.3 percent of imported food products.[8]

Common strategic resource tactics have included decisions to devolve functions to the state or local level without accompanying resources, to privatize, or to contract out—processes referred to in the public administration literature as "hollowing out" of government.[9] These techniques have the advantage that they can be publicly defended as moving authority closer to the state and local level, reducing layers of bureaucracy, or enhancing efficiency. Such claims form the basis for what was once termed in Washington "plausible deniability," since it is easy to argue that these are not attacks on regulation at all.[10]

Notwithstanding the public explanations, these tactics can be and have been used to weaken agencies and programs. If agencies have legislative mandates to regulate and are deprived of the minimum organizational capital and operating resources required to perform those mandated functions, they are doomed to regulate badly or not to be able to regulate effectively at any minimally acceptable level. The hollowing out has, for some agencies at least, meant not merely an inability to enforce existing policies but a reduction of expertise required for effective regulatory policy development, even when Congress has required new regulatory policymaking.

It is no answer to say that these agencies can contract out for expertise. First, the evidence is, and has for some time been, clear that many federal agencies, not to mention states, lack the trained contract management personnel and resources required to ensure effective contract operations from the decision to contract through contract administration.[11] Beyond that, though, this process undermines the stature of the agencies and effectively disposes of the idea that these agencies are repositories of expertise utilized in the public interest. Historically, deference has been accorded to regulatory agencies in significant part at least because they were designed and staffed to be repositories of expertise in their field, but the hollowing out process has dramatically undermined that capacity.[12] The ability to hire consultants does not respond to that problem and may exacerbate it. Indeed, the same experts employed by a regulatory agency one month may be hired by the regulated industry the next.

Few states have the resources to build their own repositories of expertise sufficient to match the resources of the firms or industries they are supposed to regulate and, in the absence of national capacity, states operate at a distinct disadvantage in formulating policies in the first instance and later in defending those policies against the legal attacks that are commonplace. Moreover, even if the states can build these agencies, federal preemption and the fact that their jurisdiction is limited may prevent them from utilizing their expertise effectively in the public interest. In addition, the increase in the transfer of day-to-day operational responsibilities for regulatory enforcement has come to states from the federal government without the resources needed to carry out those functions. It is clear to those waging the battle against regulation that few state legislatures want to take the political risks of appropriating the resources necessary at that level, particularly when that means shifting resources from other far more popular programs and agencies. Such support is all the more unlikely in times when those legislatures must cut programs or services because of budget shortfalls.

The resource attack has an even more subtle variant; one that is a more passive but very effective tactic of starving the opposition into submission. It is not really necessary to mount a full-scale siege of a program or agency through direct budget-cutting. In contexts where agencies already have inadequate resources to carry out their missions, it is enough to let them languish with what is known as flat-funding (budgets that allocate the same number of dollars as in the previous year), without increases adequate even to keep pace with rising operating costs, let alone enough to build the real capacity required to do their job. If an agency is operating in a field where costs are increasing dramatically, such as health care–related regulation or complex environmental toxic chemical regulation, even a few years of funding at the previous level will result in dramatic decreases in real purchasing power, whether it is for human resources or other needs. This approach takes time, but over the medium or long term, it is very effective. An intermediate and even less obvious approach is to provide for extremely limited increases where the burdens and costs of the regulator's obligations are growing significantly as a result of new legislative demands or simply changing circumstances as in the case of the dramatically increasing level of importation of products without funds to support increased availability of inspectors and testing facilities. This technique has the added attractiveness of permitting an administration to reject the criticism that it is deliberately cutting an agency's resources, while it is effectively doing precisely that. The George W. Bush administration has employed the full range of such resource attack options.

These attacks aimed at weakening and hollowing out regulatory capabilities have an additional benefit for those leading them that is best described as the "blame the casualties" approach. It is inevitable that, as the regulators lose capacity relative to the scope and complexity of the obligations assigned to them, they will increasingly fail in their obligations, and those shortcomings will become more obvious and troublesome with each passing year. They are then vulnerable to attacks justified on the argument that these regulatory programs are failed programs operated by ineffective agencies. Ironically, then, it is possible to break the agencies, disable the programs, and then attack them for being broken, an approach that found some of its most effective practitioners in the Reagan administration.

These weapons work even more effectively when they are paired with assault by increased burdens. It has been common to add procedural and substantive burdens to agency policymaking and enforcement over time, from increased procedural steps to complex analytic requirements to reduced time limits to issue rules in increasingly complex fields, even as agency capacity has been weakened (see Chapters 2 and 3). This is a variant on the old legal tactic of "inundation" or, in less polite terms, "kitchen sinking the opposition."[13] That is, the strategy is to pile obligations on organizations with inadequate resources, knowing full well that they will either have to abandon the fight or drown under the growing burden of work and political opposition.

The weapons of choice in this kind of attack have most often been presidential directives, including executive orders, presidential memoranda, and presidential signing statements, or Office of Management and Budget (OMB) circulars, all of which have been implemented by the OMB and particularly by its Office of Information and Regulatory Affairs (see Chapters 2 and 3). At the state level, these burdens often come in the form of unfunded mandates. These attacks have been employed by both Democrats and Republicans.

The process that federal regulators are required to meet in order to issue what is formally known as a substantive or legislative rule (a rule having the force of law),[14] even if it is mandated by statute, have been made so onerous that agencies have been driven to try to evade them by referring to their actions as interpretations or policy statements, not subject to the statutory rulemaking requirements.[15] Recently efforts have been made to launch countermeasures against any agency that seeks to use this tactic.[16] The development and nature of these weapons are considered in Chapters 2 and 3. They began with basic, and quite understandable, requirements for regulatory analysis before an agency could issue a rule and moved from there to mandatory positive cost/benefit calculations, to conditions on cost/benefit calculations that were strongly biased against regulations—even if rules were mandated by Congress—to risk assessments with a range of uncertainties and imponderables, to, most recently, demands for external peer review of proposals.[17] Like the other capacity attacks, this burden-loading approach has the added benefits to the aggressor of the "break the agency and then attack it for being ineffective" assault described above.

With all of these techniques in mind, there is an additional quiet but effective attack based on change in mission priority and exploitation of conflicting missions. While regulatory bodies and the programs they administer were created for the purpose of regulation, recent administrations, both Democratic and Republican, have made a key standard of performance in their governments the number of rules eliminated, public service positions cut, resources reduced, or functions contracted out. This was certainly true of the Clinton administration's reinventing government efforts and the George W. Bush administration's President's Management Agenda (see Chapter 3). Where agencies have been assigned conflicting missions by Congress, such as the Federal Aviation Administration's simultaneous obligations to promote the air transport system and its regulation of the safety of the air transport industry, promotional efforts have sometimes been stressed and the regulatory role de-emphasized or even undermined. The events leading up to and surrounding the 1996 Valujet crash in the Florida Everglades provided abundant evidence of the problem.[18] Support for deregulation and development of start-up airlines was made the clear priority, with regulation under-resourced, undervalued, and inadequately executed.

Other examples arose when bovine spongiform encephalopathy (BSE), otherwise known as "mad cow disease," identified in a Washington state cow in the winter of 2003, raised serious questions as to the willingness and ability of the U.S. Department of Agriculture (USDA) to respond adequately when the department's primary role is support for agricultural producers, even as it has simultaneous responsibilities to protect consumers. Quick assurances that everything was under control and the food supply was safe soon gave way to recognitions that the USDA did not have policies in place adequate to regulate for the protection of consumers against the presence of tainted meat, the use of so-called downer cattle, or the ability to track and identify the source of disease. It had to scramble to address the problem.[19] (Chapter 3 provides another example with regard to the regulation of agrochemicals.)

Even agencies with clear mandates for regulation have found themselves with politically, if not legally assigned, promotional responsibilities. Criticisms of this sort have been rampant during investigations of the corporate and market scandals in which the Securities and Exchange Commission (SEC) had clearly failed in its regulatory responsibilities in the 1990s and early years of the twenty-first century. And yet, as Chapter 3 explains, as soon as the market began to recover and less attention was being paid by the media, the Bush administration moved quickly to renew the attack on the SEC for excessive aggressiveness and reminded it of its obligation to help the firms in the marketplace and the economy more generally.

THE ATTACK FROM THE OUTSIDE: THE OTHER SIDE OF THE TWO-FRONT WAR

These, then, are some of the standard weapons in the arsenal of those who have waged the war on regulation along with some of the general strategies and tactics according to which these weapons have been deployed. In particular, they represent the approaches taken by opponents within government; more specifically by elected officials and their political appointees. There are a number of strategies and tactics that have long been employed by those outside government, in the regulated community, who, not surprisingly, often do not wish to be regulated or at least want to be able to use regulation for their own purposes—such as to hold off competition or reduce their own liability—rather than to permit it to be used to control them or render them accountable.

Political Money: The Use of Strategic Resources to Maintain Alliances

Among the standard strategies is the deployment of strategic resources, better known as political money. Political officeholders and candidates are addicted to political contributions, either direct support for their campaigns or indirect assistance, in the form of issue ads or other so-called soft-money uses.

Neither the passage of the McCain-Feingold legislation nor state campaign spending statutes have resolved the problem of changing types of spending on political campaigns designed to avoid regulatory limits. And those statutes have been under a withering legal barrage since their enactment.[20] The Supreme Court struck down the McCain-Feingold regulation of issue ads in 2007.[21]

At the heart of the money contest is the battleground of contemporary political media. As campaign media costs escalate, the need for financial contributions also grows. As regulated groups have found that issue-oriented political media buys (campaign jargon for the purchase of political ads and airtime to broadcast them) intended not only to elect sympathetic officials but also to influence policymaking efforts are effective, they have employed public relations firms and broadcasters to staff their media campaigns. They have also used media campaigns against regulatory policy and candidates perceived as supportive of those programs.

Another related strategy is to support nonprofit organizations that have a program of continued criticisms of regulatory agencies and programs or organizations that advance ideological perspectives opposed to regulation and make it a point to produce publications and speakers ready to appear on television to press their group's positions, such as the Heritage Foundation and the American Enterprise Institute. At a more tactical level, regulated companies have developed a host of techniques to counter or evade regulatory efforts, such as supporting publications that are expected to counter the work done by regulatory agencies.

Among the more obvious examples in contemporary history has been the effectiveness of the tobacco and pharmaceutical industries to constrain policy change and, until relatively recently, efforts by regulatory opponents in the energy industries to deny the role of greenhouse gas emissions in the rapidly intensifying problem of global warming. Notwithstanding all that was made public about the behavior of tobacco companies, there was still little enthusiasm in Congress to submit the industry to serious regulation, even after the FDA developed a well-documented case of deliberate behavior leading to increased addiction to smoking and marketing of those products to young people. Indeed, while accepting the soundness of the findings, the Supreme Court pointed to the apparent unwillingness of Congress to support regulation as the basis for rejecting FDA rules aimed at preventing advertising directed at children and young people.[22]

The pharmaceutical industry has continued to avoid a serious tightening of controls in many areas to address highly publicized problems, apart from technical drug approval requirements, and it has also been able to maintain constraints on the marketplace as well through various devices used to avoid expansion of generic versions of profitable drugs. Even with respect to licensing requirements, pharmaceutical companies have discovered the tactic of purchasing large quantities of articles from journals that provide supportive findings for uses of drugs outside those specific applications for which the drug has been approved by the Food and Drug Administration (FDA) for distribution to doctors.[23] The firms cannot advertise the off-label uses, but large purchases support journals that publish articles that deliver findings on such applications, thereby indirectly promoting uses that cannot be advertised directly.

The Environmental Protection Agency (EPA) rejected petitions for rule-making from states and public interest groups to issue rules with respect to automotive greenhouse gas emissions that exacerbate global warming.[24] When the U.S. Supreme Court ruled against the EPA's assertions that it lacked authority to issue the rules and, even if it did have authority, it could exercise discretion not to do so, the Bush administration promptly made it clear that there would be no regulations if having them meant limitations on economic growth. These uses of political money to challenge or avoid regulation or to challenge regulatory proposals as damaging to economic growth do not always defeat the adversary, but the resource battle has often been an effective rear-guard action that has kept highly profitable products and market conditions in place for years before regulatory action was taken.[25]

Regulatory Capture: The Attempt to Turn the Adversary

Another well-known mechanism is known as regulatory capture.[26] The simplistic version of capture suggests that the regulated industry simply takes control of the regulatory agency through a variety of means such that, as journalists frequently put it, the "watchdog" becomes a "lapdog." Put in such crude terms, the idea of capture is a dramatic overstatement or even simply inaccurate and also an insult that impugns the integrity of many good people who have spent their careers working for the public interest in regulatory agencies. It also fails to explain the fact that the opponents do not always prevail.[27] Some scholars have labeled this capture charge, at least when put in such bald terms, as a myth.[28]

That said, regulated firms have ongoing relationships with their regulators simply by virtue of the work that must be done. There are often shared interests in the regulated field, such as aviation, the financial services, or nuclear power. Agencies that regulate, but that have responsibility of promoting the well-being of producers, like the USDA, are in a particularly vulnerable position. For these and other reasons, the regulated sector is in a unique position to affect, constrain, or even prevent regulatory action even if they do not capture the regulators in the simplistic sense of that term.

Still other regulated organizations seek to capture regulators in a very direct sense through concerted efforts to shape appointments to regulatory commissions and by providing tempting opportunities for lucrative employment when regulatory policymakers choose to leave elective or appointed office. Examples discussed in Chapter 3 include direct efforts by Ken Lay of Enron to shape George W. Bush's appointments to the Federal Energy Regulatory Commission and the movement of key regulatory policymaker Representative Billy Tozen (R-La.) from the Congress to head the pharmaceutical industry's leading lobbying organization.

Legal Attack: A Different but Effective Arena of Combat

Then there is the highly developed strategy of legal attack, with a host of tactics that can be employed against the adversary; a strategy that is sometimes very visible, but more often largely unseen by the public and even policymakers. The practice of what is termed "power law" operates most often in the background.[29] When it is practiced with greatest skill and effectiveness, the matter never reaches a courtroom. It is more often fought out in meeting rooms during rulemaking processes or negotiated enforcement procedures. Except in the most dramatic cases, these operations are never even noticed by the news media, and, if they are, the attention is most often extraordinarily thin and fleeting.

Even when legal skirmishes are lost in the agency setting, the battle can be shifted to the courts where the option exists for victories, partial victories (remands in which a court upholds part of a regulatory agency action but sends other aspects back for correction),[30] or delaying actions. Often, in the regulatory context, delay can be a victory, where, for example, a firm can keep a profitable drug on the market for months or years with legal fees representing only a small fraction of that addition to the bottom line.[31] The level of legal resources that the regulated groups can bring to bear, the technical expertise they can hire to support the legal campaign, and the risks of defeat can provide strong encouragement for regulatory agencies to constrain their efforts. These factors represent a form of strategic deterrence.

These outside forces, their strategies, tactics, and weapons, are not new, but they have grown in sophistication and effectiveness. More important, though, is the fact that they have joined with the opponents of regulation among the elected political leaders and their appointees to shape a far more effective assault than ever before—a two-front war. The primary focus throughout this book will be on the attack from within, but the fact that the war is being fought on two fronts is important. It was one thing when the battle was waged principally by those who were regulated, but quite another when the leadership in the fight has been provided by presidents and their administrations along with the Congress.

CONCLUSION

Thus, it should be clear that there is a range of weapons that have been used against regulators and regulatory policy both from outside government as well as from within. Some are direct and obvious, while others are generally not seen by the general public and in many cases even by people in the public arena. However, it is essential to move beyond cataloging the arms and doctrine to consider the specific manner in which they have been developed and employed by both Democratic and Republican administrations from Jimmy Carter through George W. Bush. That is the focus of Chapters 2 and 3.

2. The War against Regulation from Jimmy Carter to George H. W. Bush: The Commanders in Chief and Their Attacks on Regulation

As Chapter 1 explained, an impressive arsenal of weaponry has been developed over time with which to press the attack on regulation. Even so, no war can be adequately understood simply by touring an armory. The commanders in chief who have led the fight through both Democratic and Republican administrations have deployed their forces and their weapons in a variety of effective and, to most Americans, not always visible ways. Like any long war, the attacks on regulation have taken a toll and have weakened both policy and the national regulatory infrastructure needed to develop, maintain, and implement effective regulatory programs.

This chapter will focus on the action at the federal government level under the leadership of presidents Jimmy Carter, Ronald Reagan, and George H. W. Bush. The war under William Clinton and George W. Bush will be considered in Chapter 3. The theme that emerges is that despite very different rhetoric and personalities, there is a surprising degree of similarity in the behavior of these presidents and their administrations in their effort to constrain regulation.

CARTER LEADS THE ATTACK ON REGULATION

President James Earl Carter was on the leading edge of a wave of governors who would successfully run for president as outsiders against what they referred to as the Washington establishment. Carter ran as a contemporary southern populist. The "contemporary" qualifier came from the fact that he was, in a number of respects, more liberal on social and environmental issues than many other southern populists. Put differently, he was an earlier version of what came, during the Clinton years, to be called a New Democrat; one who saw himself as more conservative on economic and regulatory issues than most post–New Deal Democrats, but very much in that tradition in some areas of social policy.

Whatever the label, there were two things that were clear about Jimmy Carter from the outset. First, he ran against Washington and, more generally, the federal government. Second, although he was later pictured differently by his Republican adversaries, Carter was committed to deregulation, and it was a commitment that he moved aggressively to transform into policy.

This second point may come as a surprise to many who are accustomed to the picture that was created of Carter, in no small part by his adversaries in the Reagan campaign and after as well as by Democratic supporters, who have compared the Carter administration to the far more dramatic and obvious attacks on regulation of the Reagan and Bush administrations. Further, in the decade of the 1980s, at a high point of the war against regulation, there was a tendency to point to a modest number of people appointed by Carter who were strong supporters of regulation, such as Joan Claybrook at the National Highway Traffic Safety Administration (NHTSA) and Michael Pertschuk at the Federal Trade Commission (FTC). Others referenced important environmental and safety legislation. Still, that was a limited part of a much larger and quite different picture.

First, it should be said that much of the major federal environmental and safety legislation was enacted during the Nixon era, not during the Carter era. In truth, much of the pressure for increased regulation in these areas came, not from the White House, but from Congress throughout the 1970s and 1980s. Second, it is true that Carter was not Reagan or George H. W. Bush. It is also true that the Carter administration did not oppose all regulation. However, the appointment of some active regulators to a few agencies is far from the full picture and those appointments must be viewed against the other actions taken by the administration in a very different direction.

Carter's Aggressive Legislative and Administrative Action

In fact, President Carter was largely responsible for the most dramatic and most active deregulation efforts that had been taken in decades, steps that were the forerunners of the battle against regulation that is still in progress today. Jimmy Carter not only staged a frontal assault with major deregulation legislation, but also developed and employed many of the other administrative weapons that have been used by what President George H. W. Bush would later term "generals in the war" on regulation ever since.[1] Finally, and something that is in many ways just as important as any of the other efforts, Carter was largely responsible for changing the character of the discussion and policymaking efforts on regulation such that economists came to occupy a central if not dominant importance.

The Legislative Attack in the Carter Years:
Who Said Government Organizations Are Immortal?
In many important respects, President Carter launched the war on regulation, and he was fully prepared to use a full-scale direct attack in the Congress to prosecute it. Even before he took office, during his 1976 campaign for the presidency, Carter wrote to the governors of Texas and Oklahoma, indicating that one of the factors contributing to growing natural gas problems could be traced to regulation and that he would support deregulation.[2] However, it quickly became apparent that Carter's interest in pressing deregulation legislation was not limited to energy issues. Before he left office he could claim credit for supporting deregulation legislation with respect to airlines,[3] railroads,[4] and the trucking industry.[5]

Within his first weeks in office, Carter indicated his intention to press for "deregulation of the transportation industry as much as possible."[6] He quickly announced his support for airline deregulation and then indicated that this effort would be followed by proposals to deregulate trucking. Carter saw victories quickly, signing the Airline Deregulation Act in October 1978 and, a month after that, a bill partially deregulating natural gas.[7] True to Carter's early commitment, within a month of signing the airline bill, the administration formally announced that it would be moving forward immediately on trucking deregulation. The administration joined forces with Senator Edward Kennedy (D-Mass.) on the trucking deregulation effort. While that legislation was in development, in March 1979, the Carter White House proposed railroad deregulation as well. The trucking bill was ultimately signed in July 1980 and the Staggers Rail Act became law in October of that year.

If Carter had stopped there, his administration could have claimed more major deregulation legislation than that of any of his predecessors (or successors as of the time of this writing), all the more impressive since he was a one-term president. But since he had been so successful with deregulation in the transportation sector, he was ready to move on. In particular, the administration sought to deregulate financial services and, had he had more time, to reduce regulation in the rapidly developing telecommunications industry as well. He did manage major change in the banking industry that would have serious consequences across the range of financial services.[8] Press reports at the time put the matter in blunt terms: "They deregulated airlines last year, they are working on trucking and new members of Congress are wrapped up in a real Pier Six brawl on the whopper of them all—banking deregulation. . . . Cheered on by the Carter administration, which calls reform essential, the Senate this month passed a major 'depository institutions' deregulation bill designed to put an entirely new face on the thrift industry."[9] It was a dramatic shift that eliminated ceilings on interest rates, preempted state usury laws (laws that set upper limits on loan and mortgage interest rates), and relaxed a variety of other controls that put banks and savings and loan institutions into head-to-head—and often cut-throat—competition, with dire consequences to follow.

In some of these legislative efforts, the administration was in the lead, while in others it joined forces with members of the legislature who had been pressing for deregulation. However, the administration could and did claim credit for this record-setting legislative program of deregulation.

While these specific, sector-by-sector deregulation policies captured the headlines, Carter was also at work on other far less visible legislation that would have a major impact not only during his term, but from that day to this. His actions were part of an effort to change the administrative processes by which regulations were adopted and implemented. The administration managed to get two of the three major pieces of legislation that it sought in this area. Congress adopted the Regulatory Flexibility Act[10] in September 1980 and the Paperwork Reduction Act (PRA)[11] in December. The third piece of legislation was a sweeping proposal broadly labeled as a regulatory reform act that would have given the president wide-ranging powers to intervene in agency rulemaking processes. However, even without this dramatic third piece of legislation, the PRA and the Regulatory Flexibility Act were extremely important in their own right for reasons that will be explained below.

The Administrative Attack: Carter Administration
Development of Weapons and Forces
These two pieces of legislation that were aimed at the regulatory process did not stand alone. They were part of a broader attack on regulation that

employed less visible weapons, offensives that relied on changing administrative processes to alter fundamentally the assumptions about the role of administrative agencies and that weakened their ability to pursue aggressively their regulatory missions as well as their ability to withstand political challenges from regulated industries. Moreover, once developed and deployed, these weapons and tactics would prove extremely effective in the hands of the administrations that followed Carter.

The administrative attack was based on several elements. First, the Carter administration employed what later came to be known as counterstaffing; the appointment of officials in regulatory agencies who were committed to deregulation. Second, it used the strategy of administrative deregulation. Third, the administration advanced what it termed the "innovative techniques" program to press regulators into choosing alternative approaches, largely market-oriented and incentive-based alternatives, to traditional regulatory techniques or to explain why they had not done so. Fourth, the administration created mechanisms of regulatory review that put the burden on agencies to justify their actions and ensured that their policies would be more easily subject to challenge. Fifth, the administrative assault involved creation of institutions, as explained below, that would conduct oversight of regulatory agencies, using requirements for regulatory analysis as the principal vehicle for intervention. Sixth, regulatory agencies were weakened by increasing demands for work and analysis and declining resources to meet the challenge, which limited and indeed weakened their capabilities to be aggressive regulators. Finally, the administration sought ways by which to obtain greater influence over independent regulatory commissions.

Counterstaffing: Challenging the Regulatory Agency from Within.—Before Carter, most presidents paid relatively little attention to appointments to the regulatory agencies.[12] For a long time, the assumption was that "neither the patronage value that the president attaches to individual appointments in particular nor the public importance he attaches to agency appointments in general outweighs the substantial political costs incurred by selecting an appointee who is too controversial."[13] However, that is not true if a president wants appointees who will take the lead—and therefore the political heat—in advancing controversial policies. Hence, the administration practiced counterstaffing; the deliberate appointment of people who have views and commitments contrary to the prevailing culture of the organization into which they are being appointed.[14] In less formal terms, it is the practice of appointing people who will shake up an organization and take it in a very different direction from its current path.

For the Carter administration, the lead example, though by no means the only one, was the appointment of Cornell University economist and committed opponent of regulation Alfred Kahn as chair of the Civil Aeronautics Board (CAB). The CAB was the independent regulatory commission whose job it was to regulate routes, rates, and business practices for the airline industry (as compared to the Federal Aviation Administration, which is primarily responsible for air safety). Kahn had developed a scholarly reputation for his criticism of regulation, but had also become a practitioner of the art of deregulation as the chair of the New York Public Service Commission.[15] While his appointment was announced at the beginning of May 1977, the president had wanted to name him earlier. Kahn resisted at first, but the president met with him, as did Senator Kennedy, and convinced him to take the job. Kahn went on to become the public point man for the Carter administration's deregulation effort. That is true despite the fact that he headed an independent regulatory commission; a type of agency originally created to be independent of presidential control. Although Kahn was the best-known spokesperson for deregulation, he was by no means Carter's only counterstaffed appointee.

Dan O'Neal was appointed chair of the venerable Interstate Commerce Commission (ICC). One of the first independent regulatory commissions, the ICC was designed to regulate railroads and, later, the trucking industry.[16] In November 1978, O'Neal reportedly circulated a paper on how the ICC could begin deregulating trucking, leading some in the industry to respond: "We're seriously thinking of suing the ICC for trying to deregulate without benefit of law."[17] Three months later, when Carter got the opportunity to name four additional members of the ICC, he made sure to include people who were supporters of deregulation.

Carter is often remembered, and frequently chastised, for appointing some very visible and active regulatory players such as Michael Pertschuk, chair of the FTC, and for the apparent aggressiveness of the Environmental Protection Agency (EPA) and the Occupational Safety and Health Administration (OSHA), but the fact is that other appointees were key players in the administration's assault on regulation.

Administrative Deregulation and the Innovative Techniques Program.—As these descriptions would suggest, the new appointees did not wait for legislative change to take action. They used administrative techniques to begin steps toward deregulation while the broader proposals were pending in Congress. Indeed, Carter encouraged administrators to take the initiative to relax what he saw as the regulatory burden imposed on various industries. He wrote to agencies seeking that kind of innovation and, in 1980, held a government conference to both publicize the effort and to pressure agencies to come on board. Eventually, this campaign was formalized into something the Carter White House called the "innovative techniques" program.[18] "The Administration's reform program emphasizes the use of innovative regulatory techniques as an alternative to traditional command-and-control regulation; these techniques are generally less likely to interfere with competition. Many work by structuring incentives that will resolve regulatory problems through market mechanisms. These innovative regulatory techniques move away from centralized decision-making and allow industry and consumers more freedom of choice."[19]

The innovative techniques program encouraged regulatory agencies to avoid traditional techniques of regulation, thereafter known by the dreaded epithet "command and control" policies, in favor of such alternatives as marketable rights (now best known popularly through such programs as emissions trading or carbon offsets), economic incentives, use of competition, performance standards instead of engineering standards (meet the targets any way one can rather than specifying precisely what must be done by a regulated industry), information disclosure through labeling and advertising, use of voluntary standards or self-regulation by industry groups, and tiering (development of different types of standards better suited to different sizes of businesses or types of industries). For reasons that will be discussed later, some of these were not really regulation at all, but primarily alternatives that allowed and encouraged agencies to avoid, reduce, or relax regulation. Later administrations, like Al Gore's reinventing government effort during the Clinton years, would claim credit for these techniques, but they were in fact creations of the Carter administration.

Hybrid Rulemaking and Regulatory Review Requirements: Effective Burden Loading Attacks.—For those who did not get the message and insisted upon issuing regulations, the administration had two answers. First, these agencies would have a more complex process to follow if they really intended to issue rules having the force of law, known formally in administrative law as legislative or substantive rules.[20] Second, there would be a set of institutions in place within the White House to conduct oversight of agency rulemaking. The process changes had two primary elements, the broad purposes of which could hardly be criticized by anyone reasonably familiar with the regulatory process as it had been operating to that point. These consisted of a general mandate for what was known as hybrid rulemaking and an obligation to conduct regulatory analyses before issuing rules.

Hybrid rulemaking is a complex-sounding process, but one that started with a relatively simple and straightforward idea, originally developed by the courts and later picked up by Congress and the White House. The Administrative Procedure Act (APA), the basic statute governing rulemaking by federal agencies, required that when agencies engaged in rulemaking they had to do so in a manner that was open, orderly, and participative.[21] That is, they were required to give notice of their intentions, permit public participation in this important process (carried out by unelected officials), consider the input provided, and provide notice of the rule that was being issued and the date by which it would become effective. However, the APA did not say what type of notice must be provided, what kind of participation agencies must permit, or just what is meant by a requirement that agencies consider the input provided during the public participation process.

The judicial development of hybrid rulemaking was led by the U.S. Circuit Court of Appeals for the D.C. Circuit. This court, which is the one most often responsible for important decisions on the operation of regulatory agencies, indicated in a series of decisions in the late 1960s and early 1970s that the APA meant what it said and that rulemakers must honor the APA's rulemaking requirements in substance as well as in form.[22] Notice that provided only days, or at most a few weeks, before important action was to be taken could hardly be regarded as adequate to ensure that those affected would truly be informed or have the opportunity to prepare comments and recommendations. Mere publication in the *Federal Register* may meet a technical requirement of notice, but it is plainly not calculated to ensure the maximum participation by those likely to be affected by the new rule. Simply permitting those interested to submit comments that would be placed into a file, with no evidence that they had actually been considered by decision makers, was not sufficient either to satisfy participation requirements or to meet the requirement for consideration by the agency mandated by the APA. Agencies would be required to provide evidence that notice, participation, and consideration procedures were serious, realistic, and meaningful as compared to empty and formalistic. The courts would look to the rulemaking record established by agencies to ensure that these steps had been taken.

While the Supreme Court eventually struck down demands by reviewing courts for increased procedural requirements on administrative agencies, the idea had taken on a life of its own.[23] Congress began mandating, in one form or another, in virtually all regulatory legislation adopted from the early 1970s on that hybrid rulemaking was to be the mode of policymaking. For those executive branch agencies and programs not already covered by that legislation, the Carter administration mandated hybrid rulemaking by executive order.[24] In fact, the administration went beyond what the courts had previously mandated to include a range of enhancements on the idea of hybrid rulemaking such as the production of an annual regulatory calendar that would announce planned rulemaking efforts as well as expanded notice requirements to include the use of advanced notice of proposed rulemaking (ANPRM) and publication of notice in places other than the *Federal Register,* such as trade group publications.

The second major set of procedures that agencies would have to face was more complex and, ultimately, more controversial. Agencies that wished to issue substantive rules would be required to conduct regulatory analyses. Again, the basic idea that regulatory agencies should give consideration to the impact of planned regulations before issuing them is a reasonable request with which few people could disagree. However, there was a great deal of disagreement when it came to the specific mandates to agencies as to just what kind of regulatory analysis would be required, what the burdens presented by these procedures would entail, and who would oversee the process.

To his credit, and unlike most other administrations, Carter opened up the creation of the regulatory-process policy, ultimately issued as Executive Order 12044, to public comment and also solicited comments from relevant agencies. As a result, the policy that was eventually issued was less dramatic than what had originally been contemplated. Then EPA Administrator Douglas Costle, for example, noted a number of key issues in the early form of the policy that were eventually changed. He objected to setting a requirement that any regulation with an annual impact of more than $25 million should require a regulatory analysis, noting that such a low limit would mean that even relatively minor changes in regulations would trigger a time- and resource-consuming process. While he lauded the idea of regulatory analysis in general for major rules and boasted that EPA was a leader in providing such analyses for its own rulemaking, he raised concerns about initial suggestions as to what would be required as part of those reviews. He said, for example: "We believe that an analysis of realistic and practical alternatives is appropriate for inclusion, but that an analysis of *all* the major alternatives would in some cases b[e] unduly resource consuming and could delay regulations more than is intended."[25] (Emphasis in original.) Castle was also concerned about the loss of control over the rulemaking process to the Office of Management and Budget (OMB). He noted, for instance, that: "[I]f interpretation is left to the Agency, as we believe it should be, this would satisfy the spirit of the order. However, if interpretation is delegated to OMB, flexibility would probably be lost and unreasonable resource burden and delay could result."[26] Castle's suggestions were accepted in the final version of EO 12044 issued in 1978.[27]

New Institutions to Oversee Regulators.—As Castle noted, movement of discretion and authority out of regulatory agencies and into the Executive Office of the President would raise significant issues. Although the regulatory-process executive order was softened in this respect, Carter had taken already significant steps to provide a greater role for the White House in centralized oversight of rulemaking. The two mechanisms best known outside the administration at the time were Carter's U.S. Regulatory Council and the Regulatory Analysis Review Group (RARG). The council was made up of three dozen representatives of various agencies, including the regulatory agencies, both executive and independent, and what were known as the "economic representatives" from the Council of Economic Advisers, Office of Management and Budget, and the Departments of Commerce, Labor, and Treasury. Its mandate was to examine the regulatory policies and processes currently in place in order to bring them into line with the president's commitment to reducing regulation, streamlining the regulatory programs that remained, and lightening the burdens on the economy that came from regulation.[28] The RARG conducted its own analyses of proposed agency rules, with staff work coming from Council on Wage and Price Stability analysts. The criteria for when and in what circumstances a regulatory analysis would be probed were broad and open-textured.

> The reasons for selecting a Regulatory Analysis can reflect a variety of considerations, but in general the following criteria seem dominant:
> * large total cost—relative to other regulations being proposed by that same agency within a year or so, the total burden associated with compliance (including capital outlays, operating and maintenance costs, government expense, etc.) is substantial; and in absolute terms, this total cost exceeds $100 million in any one year.

- large sectoral impact—overall costs or average prices for some industry, level of government or geographic region would increase by a substantial percentage, perhaps 3 percent or more, as a result of compliance, and this percentage is large relative to that associated with other regulations being proposed by that same agency within a year or so.
- deficient Regulatory Analysis—incomplete or inadequate analysis particularly with respect to alternatives, costs or benefits.
- precedential importance—the regulation sets a noteworthy precedent that will influence subsequent rulemakings.
- broad policy issues—the regulation raises important methodological or other broad questions encountered in a variety of rulemakings.[29]

The administration also created a less well known focal point within OMB for its regulatory oversight and analysis program called the Office of Regulatory and Information Policy, initially headed by James Tozzi (formerly a budget official responsible for the EPA), the forerunner to the Office of Information and Regulatory Affairs (OIRA) that has been the command post for the White House wars against regulation ever since.

Increasing Burdens and Declining Resources.—Not surprisingly, while members of Congress and various interest groups were not opposed to ensuring improved quality regulation, they were concerned that the message was clear that what was happening was the development of a series of procedures that would burden regulatory agencies and interfere with their obligations to regulate aggressively and actively according to the statutory mandates under which they were supposed to operate. One of the problems that agencies faced was that their mandates were increasing, but their resources were not. In fact, though it is often forgotten today, these were years of fiscal stringency in which the Carter administration moved the country to a balanced budget. In those days of double-digit inflation, even modest increases in agency budgets represented a serious loss in resources in real terms as the cost of so many things skyrocketed.

However, the administration was not through yet. In January 1980, the administration convened the White House Conference on Small Business. Participants argued for additional obligations on the part of agencies to reduce the paperwork and implementation burdens for regulations and called for the OMB to have more authority to oversee compliance with these requirements. There were two aspects to the small business leaders' criticisms. For one thing, they argued, regulators needed to take into consideration the special regulatory burdens that fall on small businesses. They demanded, in addition to existing regulatory analysis requirements, that agencies perform what came to be known as regulatory flexibility analyses, to be reviewed by OMB, which demonstrated attention to the burdens on small businesses and set forth the techniques used to reduce or mitigate those burdens. They also attacked the general issue of excessive paperwork requirements imposed by regulatory agencies and demanded that OMB should provide a clearance process designed to constrain agency information demands.

The report of the conference recommended that "the Office of Management and Budget should be designated the lead agency for both Federal regulations and paperwork of all agencies and programs, . . . with responsibility for forms clearance, paperwork reduction, simplification and elimination; coordinating regulations and cost control oversight; requiring agencies to submit to OMB an economic analysis measuring administrative and compliance costs, particularly for small business, of all proposed regulations and paperwork."[30]

Much of this came to pass with the enactment in the fall of the Regulatory Flexibility Act and PRA.[31] The PRA formally created the OIRA within OMB. Agencies were thenceforth required to prepare Regulatory Flexibility Analyses and address the special burdens on small businesses, small nonprofits, and small local government units, and small units of government. The Small Business Administration's advocacy office was also given a role with respect to participation in and oversight of the regulatory flexibility requirements. The PRA required clearance of agency requests for information from regulated entities and development of new compliance forms. While the PRA may have been intended to reduce paperwork outside government, it certainly did not do so within it.

The Effort to Constrain Independent Agency Action.—Of course, one of the key differences between the steps that could be taken administratively and those pursued through legislation was that the Congress could ensure application of these regulatory policies to independent commissions as well as executive agencies while the president could not do so by executive order. Even so, the Carter White House was not waiting for legislation in its battle against regulation and took steps intended to extend its deregulation efforts to these independent bodies. Presidents have the authority to appoint heads of independent commissions, even if they cannot appoint all of the members who serve in fixed and usually relatively lengthy terms. Carter demonstrated—and his successors learned the lesson—that these commission chairs are often in a position, even in what is by statute an independent and collegial institution, to exert considerable influence over the work of these regulatory bodies. As the earlier discussion indicated, Carter used his appointment powers effectively to put into place people who were committed to deregulation, led, of course, by CAB chair Alfred Kahn. However, the administration considered how, in the battle against regulation, it might apply its other administrative tactics to independent commissions.

On June 6, 1977, Sam Lazarus, associate director of Carter's Domestic Council, wrote the Department of Justice (DOJ) about the possibility of direct control of independent agency action. In July, the DOJ responded to Lazarus's inquiry as to "(a) whether the president by Executive order has the authority to extend to the independent regulatory agencies proposals designed to improve administrative processes within the executive branch; and (b) whether individual work plans contemplated by the proposals would be subject to compulsory disclosure under the Freedom of Information Act."[32]

While the White House clearly wanted to extend its authority, it quickly encountered opposition to the involvement by the administration in rulemaking in executive branch agencies, let alone independent bodies. The OMB General Counsel indicated in a memorandum in February 1977 that there were dangers involved in attempting to intensify the use of administrative deregulation tactics.

> The recent increased concern within the Executive Office of the President (EOP) about major and potentially costly regulations and the reform of the regulatory process in general, has focused attention on the authority of the President and his advisers and assistants to involve themselves in agency rulemaking. The activities of members of the Council of Economic Advisers (CEA) attracted considerable attention during the promulgation of the cotton dust regulations by the Department of Labor. Recently a suit was filed (and dismissed as premature) against CEA and Secretary Andrus pertaining to communications between CEA and Interior on the strip mining regulations which will be issued by the Office of Surface Mining. Other important rulemakings are imminent. One proposed element in a strategy for regulatory reform is communication by EOP officials with the agencies to ensure that a full range of options (including the most cost effective) are presented in the record of the rulemaking and that the options are appropriately evaluated. In part, this is the purpose of the Regulatory Analysis Review Group (RARG) process. There are, however, limits to and risks attendant to involvement by EOP officials in agency rulemaking.[33]

The administration continued to jawbone, but backed off efforts to include independent agencies in what became EO 12044. However, the White

House did seek specific statutory authority to intervene in rulemaking in its regulatory reform act proposal that was ultimately unsuccessful.

Carter Moves Economists to the Forefront
in the Battle against Regulation

One of the most important strategic moves against regulation of the Carter presidency was a matter of force posture. It was as dramatic in regulatory terms as President Kennedy's support for the enhanced development and increased deployment of special forces troops was to the military.[34] Before Carter, regulatory policy was dominated by law and politics, but he dramatically increased the role and importance of economists to the point where, by the time Reagan came to office, the field was dominated—and in many important respects defined by—economists. Economists had certainly been involved with the regulatory arena in a variety of ways since the rise of utilities regulation and other rate-setting policies. However, Carter dramatically expanded the role and influence of economics as a field in regulatory policy and the agencies that designed and implemented it.

Consider just some of Carter's moves in this area. Despite the image with which Republican opponents were able to define him in the 1980 campaign, the fact was that Carter, as an early incarnation of what came to be known as New Democrats, was a devotee of the marketplace and not nearly the advocate of big government solutions to every national problem that he has since been portrayed. He repeated what was fast becoming a mantra; that the increased attention to the marketplace offered to reduce regulatory burdens on the economy and cut "red tape" as well. "We must cut inflationary costs which private industry bears as a result of government regulation. . . . I am determined to eliminate unnecessary regulations and to ensure that future regulations do not impose unnecessary costs to the American economy."[35] Upon signing the airline deregulation legislation he said: "With this legislation we achieve two critical national objectives: controlling inflation and, at the same time, cutting unnecessary bureaucratic red tape."[36] "Calling himself a 'product of our free enterprise system,' Carter said the government must have 'a constant recommitment to competition.'"[37] In signing the railroad deregulation bill, he added: "By stripping away needless and costly regulation in favor of marketplace forces wherever possible, this act will help assure a strong and healthy future for our nation's railroads and the men and women who work for them."[38]

Second, the economy was, until near the end of his administration (when the Iran hostage crisis commanded the nation's attention), the defining issue of the Carter years, though he clearly would have preferred the Camp David accords to have provided that focus. While his policies may have presented their own difficulties for the nation's economic well-being, the fact is that he inherited two sets of problems that would have challenged any president. As he came to office, the nation was experiencing the long-festering economic impacts of the years of war in Southeast Asia, and then it was hit by the dramatic inflationary pressure brought on by the OPEC oil embargo. Thus, double-digit inflation became one of the most pressing problems Carter faced. It was therefore not surprising that so much attention was given to economics.

Third, Carter was favorably disposed to the growing focus on analytic devices and market-oriented public policy tools, particularly microeconomic tools. Cost/benefit analysis was coming to occupy center stage. Given Carter's education and interests, it was not surprising that he came to be seen as a technocrat in the White House. Many of the techniques and designs to counter traditional regulation were being developed by economists. Carter's advocacy of the alternative techniques of regulation fit perfectly with his own predilections and the prevailing policy trends from academic and practitioner economists.

Finally, and most important, the Carter administration appointed economists to a variety of key positions. It was journalists covering regulatory beats who noticed before most others that Carter "relied more than his predecessors on the appointment of economists, rather than lawyers, to regulatory boards, and they in turn have been more market-oriented in their approach to regulation."[39] Those economists tended to bring with them a set of strong assumptions and biases with respect to regulation and, more important, to deregulation. Carter's lead general in the battle against regulation, Alfred Kahn, stated one of the premises in no uncertain terms. "I have more faith in greed than in regulation."[40] Kahn made no apologies for making economic criteria more important than any other dimension. Speaking of airline deregulation, he said: "Frankly, I don't know one airplane from another. To me, they are all marginal costs with wings."[41] Economists concerned with economic efficiency and market alternatives to regulations would be key forces not only during the Carter years, but from that time on through both Democratic and Republican administrations to follow.

THE REAGAN ADMINISTRATION AND THE
IDEOLOGICAL ASSAULT ON REGULATION

The Reagan administration declared war on regulation long before inaugura-
tion day. Indeed, Reagan's attack on government deliberately made Carter
look like a raging liberal and a rabid regulator. The Reagan Republicans characterized the EPA and OSHA as the quintessential exemplars of overly aggressive and intrusive regulatory agencies that had to be reined in. Some large
agencies with regulatory programs, including the Department of Education
(whose regulatory programs came in the form of grants with regulatory requirements attached) and the recently created Department of Energy, were
targeted for elimination. Above all, the intensity of the Reagan antiregulation
warriors was greater than their predecessors in significant part at least because, for these players, the battle was ideological—for some even visceral. Indeed, it was perhaps because of this depth and strength of commitment that
some later left the administration, convinced that the administration had not
accomplished as much deregulation as it might have. In fact, the Reagan team
scored a host of victories, even if its antiregulation warriors did not achieve
total defeat of their adversaries.[42]

Direct Attack in the Reagan Years: The Choice of
Administrative Weapons over Legislation

While it was prepared to fight the battle on all fronts, the Reagan team chose
carefully from the weapons developed by the Carter administration those
likely to be most effective in the Reagan administration's political context.
They then dramatically enhanced those weapons and deployed them with a
palpable seriousness of purpose. Thus, they chose not to fight their major battles in the Congress, which was controlled, initially at least, by Democrats. It is
true that they found themselves embroiled in legislative conflicts because
some statutes, such as the Clean Air Act, had to be reauthorized, but legislative
battle was clearly not the preferred mode of operation. Instead they focused
on the administrative weapons. In many instances they employed those
weapons to fight a wide range of perhaps less visible and less dramatic conflicts, but many important ones that left the regulatory landscape far different
from what it had been when they arrived. In other situations, however, the

battles were public and hotly contested. One very direct mode of attack was both visible and controversial; the attack by counterstaffing.

Reagan Counterstaffing: Attack across the Regulatory Landscape

The Reagan administration appointed any number of officials whose job it was to take on the prevailing direction and culture in regulatory agencies. They were people who, by virtue of their backgrounds and experiences, could be counted on to be steadfast warriors. Carter had employed the counterstaffing concept as a significant part of his deregulation strategy, but the Reagan White House went far beyond its predecessor in naming those who would take the battle into the regulatory agencies themselves. These Reagan appointees, referred to by Robert Durant as "Ronald Reagan's 'happy band of deregulators,'"[43] included many who had more than adequately established their deregulation credentials.

Thus, Murray Weidenbaum was appointed chair of the Council of Economic Advisors. Weidenbaum, an economist who headed the Reagan transition group on regulation, was a well-established author whose work focused on criticism of regulation and presented dramatic figures that purported to be actual calculations of the economic impacts of regulation.[44] Then OMB Director David Stockman, a former Michigan congressman, who had a well-known disdain for regulatory agencies, had become the head of the agency that was to have central oversight authority within the White House of regulation and of the budgets that would be presented to Congress to fund those agencies. James Miller, another economist with well-known professional experience as a regulatory critic, was named initially to head what became the OIRA, which was in charge of regulatory review of agency proposals. Miller was later named chair of the FTC, one of the leading Reagan administration regulatory targets.

James Watt, one of the administration's mostly widely known deregulation warriors, came to his post as Secretary of the Interior from his position as head of the Mountain States Legal Foundation with a clear commitment to deregulation of many areas of western land and resources policy. Watt also recommended two other stalwarts of the Reagan war on regulation: Anne Gorsuch, who became one of the most controversial appointees when she took on the EPA as its new administrator; and John Burford, soon to be Gorsuch's husband, a long-standing opponent of federal land management, who was named to head the Bureau of Land Management in the Department of the Interior. Then there was James Harris, named director of the Office of Surface Mining at Interior, who, in his previous position as an Indiana Senator, had called for state challenges to the constitutionality of the strip mine bill, a policy the enforcement of which he would control in his new post at Interior.

John Van de Water was named chair of the National Labor Relations Board, but his confirmation was effectively blocked on grounds that his past antilabor work rendered him unsuited to this position. Two construction company executives moved into key positions at Labor, with Raymond Donovan named secretary and Thorne Auchter appointed to head OSHA. Raymond Peck was appointed administrator of the NHTSA, a priority target of Reagan administration deregulators. Peck, who had honed his antiregulatory skills during the Ford administration, had played a key role in a fight to block strip mine legislation and later worked with the National Coal Association. He admitted at the time of his appointment to the NHTSA post that he had no expertise in highway safety. However he was reported to have said shortly after that: "I'm the best damned deregulation lawyer in town"[45] and demonstrated that commitment in his deregulatory efforts in his new role.[46] There were many others.

The list of these top-level appointees intended to counterstaff the regulatory agencies, both executive branch and independent commission, was long. However, that was only part of the effort. The administration worked with the Heritage Foundation to train other political appointees below the level of agency head to ensure that they would challenge prevailing policies and programs.[47] In fact, the administration sought to use temporary civil service appointments to push political appointees well into agencies at as many levels as possible.[48] The administration took the position that it had been elected with a clear commitment to remove what it termed "excessive regulatory burden" and it made no apologies for putting in place people who were ardently committed to accomplishing that task.

Administrative Direct Action:

Deregulation without Benefit of Congress

The dedicated deregulators in the administration were of the view that they were appointed to eliminate regulations and they were going to do it without waiting for Congress. Carter's deregulators, led by Alfred Kahn, had done some of this work, but often in conjunction with simultaneous proposals to

Congress for new legislation. Many of the Reagan deregulators had little expectation that the administration could move that kind of legislation successfully—given the rapidly increasing levels of conflict between the two ends of
the avenue—and they were not disposed to wait until they could do so. There
were any number of regulatory appointees who sought to use administrative
deregulation to achieve their goals, but consider just two as exemplars: Mark
Fowler, chair of the Federal Communications Commission (FCC), and Raymond Peck, administrator of the NHTSA.

When Reagan's first FCC chair took office, deregulation efforts launched
during the Carter years were already under way. Indeed, just the week before
the new administration came to office the commission had removed time
limits on the amount of commercials that could be run in a given period on
radio stations and relaxed requirements for radio stations to provide public
affairs broadcasting and conduct community surveys to show that their pro-
gramming met community needs. Then chair Charles Ferris, appointed to
that seat by Carter, announced that "no longer will radio broadcasters be required to follow empty governmentally required procedures and compile
stacks of paperwork. . . . Instead they will be able to follow their own path in
determining how to serve their community's needs and interests in ways that
reflect the realities of today's radio markets."[49]

But his Reagan administration successor, Mark Fowler, a lawyer who specialized in communications and had worked in a number of jobs in radio,
took the commitment to administrative deregulation to a new level. Fowler
attacked existing regulations with enthusiasm, reducing records to be used for
oversight during renewal processes, removing a number of limits on radio
station operations, and attacking, with the help of Congress, the limits on the
number of radio and television stations that could be owned by the same
company. There were any number of other areas that he wanted to attack, including the so-called fairness doctrine, that he was unable to eliminate before
his term ended, but it was not for lack of dedication to the task. By the time he
resigned from his position in 1987, Fowler felt justified in proclaiming himself
"Mr. Deregulation."[50]

Raymond Peck came to the NHTSA with no background in that field but
established his antiregulation credentials in the Ford administration. Immediately upon taking office he moved to block the NHTSA rules mandating
airbags in automobiles. Like a number of other things the administration
wanted to do, there was attention to procedural requirements when it was

useful to constrain administrative agencies but not when process got in the way of deregulation. Hence, Peck moved precipitously, without any serious effort to study the long history of the passive restraint rule in that agency, a fact that ultimately led to the reversal of that action.

The passive restraint rule can be traced back to the early years of the agency and originally focused on seatbelts. The NHTSA rules survived two rounds of challenges in court and various delays in implementation.[51] They were slated for implementation as the Reagan administration came to office. Peck immediately moved to block the rules on grounds of economic hardships in the automobile industry, publishing notice of that action in the *Federal Register* in February 1981.[52] Two months after that, the agency called for a delay in implementation of the rules and indicated that the NHTSA would likely rescind them.[53] It was clear that the administrator was moving to kill the regulations; and that was what followed.

In making the case for the rescission of the airbags rule, the administration not only set out to uphold the NHTSA action, but to gain legal support for administrative deregulation. The argument was that the courts should take an extremely deferential approach to regulatory agency decisions to withdraw regulations, requiring far less justification than would be required if the agency were creating new regulations. Indeed, the administration argued, the court should review this decision to draw back as if the agency simply was not acting at all rather than as an assertion of agency authority. The administration made this argument even though it was clear from the NHTSA's basic statute and from the APA that rescinding a rule was to be treated like rulemaking in terms of the procedures required under the law. The administration's argument was clearly a reach, but it was a bold effort to make administrative deregulation a far more potent weapon, one that would be extremely difficult to challenge in court.

The U.S. Supreme Court resoundingly rejected that attack on well-understood principles of administrative law. In so doing, the Court made it clear that deregulation enjoyed no presumptive validity. While recognizing that there must be flexibility for change when administrative agencies find good reasons for it and take action in the proper manner, the Court cautioned:

> But the forces of change do not always or necessarily point in the direction of deregulation. In the abstract, there is no more reason to presume that changing circumstances require the rescission of prior action, instead of a revision in or even the extension of current regulation. If Congress established a presumption

from which judicial review should start, that presumption—contrary to petitioners' views—is not against safety regulation, but against changes in current policy that are not justified by the rulemaking record. While the removal of a regulation may not entail the monetary expenditures and other costs of enacting a new standard, and, accordingly, it may be easier for an agency to justify a deregulatory action, the direction in which an agency chooses to move does not alter the standard of judicial review established by law.[54]

The Court rejected the NHTSA action as arbitrary and capricious. While Justice Rehnquist, writing for himself and Justices Powell and O'Connor, found that the agency had justified one part of the change, even these three strong conservatives had to agree with the majority that, with respect to its elimination of the requirements for airbags and continuous spool seatbelts, "the agency gave no explanation at all."[55]

At the same time the administration was making a number of other bold assertions of authority and offering a range of arguments to avoid, defeat, or lessen their burdens in legal challenges that were sure to grow as Reagan deregulators pursued their strategies. A number of these came with the administration's dramatic moves to get centralized control over regulatory policy.

Centralization of Regulatory Policy in the Reagan White House

The political appointees counterstaffed into key positions were to be the "tip of the spear," in military parlance, but the administration was not prepared to adopt a cabinet government model that sent its people into the field and left them free to operate according to their best lights. The deregulation battles were to be led from the White House and, given the work of deregulators like Murray Weidenbaum during the transition, the general battle plan was ready when the administration took office. There would be none of the "notice and comment" style discussions and no solicitation of inputs from the affected agencies as there had been when the Carter administration developed EO 12044. The administration, as James Miller, head of the newly created Vice President's Task Force on Regulatory Relief, put it, "would not have guerilla warfare from agencies that don't want to follow Reagan's prescription for regulatory relaxation."[56]

The offensive featured a three-pronged attack that was substantive, institutional, and procedural. Substantively, nine days after taking office, Reagan imposed a sixty-day delay in the effective date of new regulations.[57] The idea was to prevent rules that came from the Carter era but had not yet gone into effect from moving to implementation and to block any pending actions that might be issued by regulatory agencies while new political appointees were taking control. It would also give the administration time to push forward its offensive.

Institutionally, the administration moved immediately to put in place its command staff, first sweeping away the Regulatory Council and RARG of the Carter years. The new structure featured a Vice President's Task Force on Regulatory Relief, whose title made plain its mission, and a seriously empowered OIRA within OMB. The operational chief, James Miller, would be the director of OIRA and would double as the director of the Vice President's Task Force. The day-to-day operations would be conducted out of OIRA, originally created by the Carter administration as part of the PRA. With his two regulatory relief task force colleagues, Richard Williamson and C. Boyden Gray, Miller set about creating a structure that would make it clear to the agencies that they would be expected to comply with the administration's deregulatory policy and that, if they sought to evade those dictates, there was a counterinsurgency program and structure to respond. They set about crafting procedural mechanisms to ensure that they had the authority and the opportunity to prosecute the offensive against regulation.

The tool that they chose was an executive order. Miller and his colleagues worked to craft the policy in a way that used the Carter EO 12044 as a base, but then dramatically altered the earlier approach to regulatory analysis and hybrid rulemaking, turning the new order into a significantly more effective weapon against regulation. The order both communicated the Reagan administration's policy to regulatory agencies in no uncertain terms and indicated what could—and probably would—happen if agencies persisted in generating rules that were not consistent with that policy. Consider the following features of Executive Order 12291.[58]

Where Carter's rulemaking order 12044 had mandated that a regulatory impact analysis be accomplished, Reagan's went much further to demand that there be a successful cost/benefit analysis, and successful analysis was to be defined in the most demanding terms. Reagan's order required that:

Section 2. General Requirements. In promulgating new regulations, reviewing existing regulations, and developing legislative proposals concerning regulations, all agencies, to the extent permitted by law, shall adhere to the following requirements:

(a) Administrative decisions shall be based on adequate information concerning the need for and consequences of proposed government action;

(b) *Regulatory action shall not be undertaken unless the potential benefits to society for the regulation outweigh the potential costs to society;*

(c) *Regulatory objectives shall be chosen to maximize the net benefits to society;*

(d) *Among alternative approaches to any given regulatory objective, the alternative involving the least net cost to society shall be chosen;* and

(e) *Agencies shall set regulatory priorities with the aim of maximizing the aggregate net benefits to society, taking into account the condition of the particular industries affected by regulations, the condition of the national economy, and other regulatory actions contemplated for the future.* (Emphasis added.)

In the regulatory impact analysis to be submitted by the agency producing a rule, the order required:

(1) A description of the potential benefits of the rule, including any beneficial effects that cannot be quantified in monetary terms, and the identification of those likely to receive the benefits;

(2) A description of the potential costs of the rule, including any adverse effects that cannot be quantified in monetary terms, and the identification of those likely to bear the costs;

(3) A determination of the potential net benefits of the rule, including an evaluation of effects that cannot be quantified in monetary terms;

(4) A description of alternative approaches that could substantially achieve the same regulatory goal at lower cost, together with an analysis of this potential benefit and costs and a brief explanation of the legal reasons why such alternatives, if proposed, could not be adopted; and

(5) Unless covered by the description required under paragraph (4) of this subsection, an explanation of any legal reasons why the rule cannot be based on the requirements set forth in Section 2 of this Order.

These obligations were to be met not only when the agency issued its final rule, but also at the time that the agency sought to publish its notice of proposed rulemaking on the front end of the process. And while the agencies were doing all of that, they were obliged under the executive order to "initiate reviews of currently effective rules in accordance with the purposes of this Order, and perform Regulatory Impact Analyses of currently effective major rules." In addition, the order imposed the requirement that:

(a) Each agency shall publish in October and April of each year, an agenda of proposed regulations that the agency has issued or expects to issue, and currently effective rules that are under agency review pursuant to this Order. These agendas may be incorporated with the agendas published under 5 U.S. §602, and must contain at the minimum:

(1) A summary of the nature of each major rule being considered, the objectives and legal basis for the issuance of the rule, and an approximate schedule for completing action on any major rule for which the agency has issued a notice of proposed rulemaking;

(2) The name and telephone number of a knowledgeable agency official for each item on the agenda; and

(3) A list of existing regulations to be reviewed under the terms of this Order, and a brief discussion of each such regulation.

If the administration meant what it said—and it did—then any major rule, whether mandated by Congress or not, would have to meet a heavy burden.[59] At the time, the common barb around Washington was that this order should have been entitled the Economists' Full Employment Act of 1981.

The proof that the Reagan White House meant to implement these requirements was not merely the fact that it was one of the priority actions taken by the administration in its early days or the choice of the well-known and highly committed foes of regulation appointed to key positions, but was clear from the mechanisms and authority provided by EO 12291 itself. The order authorized the director of the OMB to

(1) Designate any proposed or existing rule as a major rule in accordance with Section 1(b) of this Order;

(2) Prepare and promulgate uniform standards for the identification of major rules and the development of Regulatory Impact Analyses;

(3) Require an agency to obtain and evaluate, in connection with a regulation, any additional relevant data from any appropriate source;

(4) Waive the requirements of Sections 3, 4, or 7 of this Order with respect to any proposed or existing major rule;

(5) Identify duplicative, overlapping and conflicting rules, existing or proposed, and existing or proposed rules that are inconsistent with the policies underlying statutes governing agencies other than the issuing agency or with the purposes of this Order, and, in each such case, require appropriate interagency consultation to minimize or eliminate such duplication, overlap, or conflict;

(6) Develop procedures for estimating the annual benefits and costs of agency regulations, on both an aggregate and economic or industrial sector basis, for purposes of compiling a regulatory budget;

(7) In consultation with interested agencies, prepare for consideration by the President recommendations for changes in the agencies' statutes; and

(8) Monitor agency compliance with the requirements of this Order and advise the President with respect to such compliance.

The OMB could also cause agencies to delay publication of their planned notices of proposed rulemaking or of final rules. It could require the agencies to provide further information or analyses. Although the order recognized that the actions mandated by the order could be pursued only "to the extent permitted by law" and that agencies could not violate statutory obligations in complying with the order, the reality was that, in a number of important situations, targeted agencies found themselves caught squarely between a legislative mandate to issue regulations within a particular time period and pressures from the OMB to constrain their rulemaking or face delays or outright barriers. When agencies tried to deal with the squeeze by using interim rules, policy statements, or other devices to meet their statutory deadlines, Miller's successor as OIRA administrator accused them of attempting to "end run" the process and warned them to back off.[60]

The EPA was a classic case of an agency caught in this bind. In fact, the squeeze was so obvious that some officials within EPA started keeping logs of the delays in OMB preclearance. In enjoining the White House from violating statutory rulemaking requirements mandated by the 1984 amendments to the Resource Conservation and Recovery Act (RCRA—the law providing for the regulation of toxic and hazardous wastes), Judge Flannery presented the problem in terms that merit quotation at some length.

> OMB did contribute to the delay in the promulgation of the regulations by insisting on certain substantive changes. . . .
>
>   A certain degree of deference must be given to the authority of the President to control and supervise executive policymaking. *Sierra Club v. Costle*, 657 F.2d 298, 405 (D.C. Cir. 1981). . . . Yet, the use of EO 12291 to create delays and to impose substantive changes raises some constitutional concerns. Congress enacts environmental legislation after years of study and deliberation, and then delegates to the expert judgment of the EPA Administrator the authority to issue regulations carrying out the aims of the law. Under EO 12291, if used improperly, OMB could withhold approval until the acceptance of certain content in the promulgation of any new EPA regulation, thereby encroaching upon the independence and expertise of EPA. . . . This is incompatible with the will of Congress and cannot be sustained as a valid exercise of the President's Article II powers.
>
>   This court has previously found that in certain egregious situations, statutory delay caused by OMB review is in contravention to applicable law . . . and therefore that no further OMB review could occur. *NRDC v. Ruckelshaus*, . . . 14 ELR 20817, 20818 (D.D.C. 1984). . . .

... Through answers to interrogatories, plaintiffs show that EPA submitted
169 regulations to OMB which were subject to statutory or judicial deadlines, and
on 86 occasions OMB extended its review beyond the time periods outlined in
EO 12291. OMB's propensity to extend review has become so great that EPA keeps
a running record of the number of its rulemaking actions under extended review
by OMB and the resulting delays. ...

This court declares that OMB has no authority to use its regulatory review
under EO 12291 to delay promulgation of EPA regulations arising from the 1984
Amendments of the RCRA beyond the date of a statutory deadline. Thus, if a
deadline already has expired, OMB has no authority to delay regulations subject
to the deadline in order to review them under the executive order. If the deadline
is about to expire, OMB may review the regulations only until the time at which
OMB review will result in the deadline being missed.[61]

The EO 12291 requirements also rendered regulators more vulnerable to
attack by antiregulation forces outside government. On the one hand, the order sought to avoid making OMB subject to judicial challenge by stating:
"This Order is intended only to improve the internal management of the Federal government, and is not intended to create any right or benefit, substantive or procedural, enforceable at law by a party against the United States, its
agencies, its officers or any person." However, the additional analyses required
for the agencies generating rules were to "be made part of the whole record of
agency action in connection with the rule." As such, they could be used in efforts to argue that an agency was acting in a manner that violated the arbitrary and capricious or substantial evidence standards under the APA. The
issue is not that the challenge would prevail, but that agencies faced some degree of increased exposure.

The key player in this process was to be the director of the OIRA within
the OMB. In theory at least, agencies that disagreed with the OIRA's use or
abuse of power under EO 12291 could appeal to the Vice President's Task Force
on Regulatory Relief. However, the task force mission was contained within its
title and, beyond that, the person in the task force responsible for managing
such appeals was the executive director whose other title was director of the
OIRA.

While there was widespread criticism of the Reagan White House policies
and those implementing them, the administration pressed forward and intensified its efforts to exercise central control. In fact, at the beginning of the second term, the administration expanded the OMB's power to constrain the

agencies with the issuance of Executive Order 12498.[62] On its face, the order was a requirement that agencies prepare a regulatory agenda and stick to it. The idea of a regulatory calendar was not new, and indeed the previous rulemaking orders called for one. Not surprisingly, therefore, EO 12498 attracted little public attention. However, if one read that order carefully in conjunction with a presidential memorandum about how it was to be implemented that was issued on the same day as the executive order, it became clear that this new attack on the regulatory process was serious and substantive.

The new executive order did not simply call for an agency to publish notice of the regulations it intended to address. Section 2 of EO 12498 contained language that went largely unnoticed except by those intimately involved in regulatory policy. It commanded:

> The head of each agency shall submit to the Director an overview of the agency's regulatory policies, goals, and objectives for the program year and such information concerning all significant regulatory actions of the agency, planned or underway, *including actions taken to consider whether to initiate rulemaking; requests for public comment; and the development of documents that may influence, anticipate, or could lead to the commencement of rulemaking proceedings at a later date,* as the Director deems necessary to develop the Administration's Regulatory Program. (Emphasis added.)

The memorandum made clear that the seemingly innocuous language emphasized in this part of the executive order was a core point. The object was to interdict the regulatory process at its start. As Reagan put it in the presidential memorandum:

> With your help and active support, this Administration has substantially reduced the burden and intrusiveness of Federal regulatory programs. In the past three years, we have eliminated many needless rules, revised ill-conceived ones, and held the number of new rules to the minimum necessary. The policies and procedures of Executive Order No. 12291 have imposed long needed discipline on the rulemaking process.
>
> Today, I have signed an Executive Order to establish a regulatory planning process by which we will develop and publish the Administration's Regulatory Program for each year. Under this process, it will be the personal responsibility of the head of each agency to determine—at the beginning of the regulatory process, not at the end—whether a given regulatory venture is consistent with the goals of the Administration and whether agency resources should be committed to it.[63]

The operative term mentioned only once in the middle of the memorandum to heads of departments was "prerulemaking" activities. These were any activities that involved research into or serious consideration of the possibility of developing rules, including the gathering of information. These activities, like all other parts of the process, were to be judged by one standard. Agencies considering the possibility of developing regulations were required to "explain how each new activity will carry out the regulatory policies of this Administration and specify the agency's plan for reviewing and revising existing regulatory programs to bring them into accord with Administration policies."

Most importantly, the order and accompanying memorandum gave full authority to the OMB to regulate these "preregulation" activities and to do whatever was necessary to discipline the agencies. Perhaps least noticed but in some respects most important was the ability to block agencies in their efforts to acquire information needed to begin rulemaking proceedings. In addition, the administration had another potent tool that the OMB had learned to use in new ways. The PRA required agencies to acquire permission to collect various types of data. It also provided a statutory foundation for the OIRA. When Congress, the courts, and numerous critics battled back against the administration's attack on regulatory policies and the agencies that administered them, the Reagan White House, and later the George H. W. Bush administration, turned to the OIRA and its authority under the PRA to continue with the work launched under the two executive orders. The reaction was swift and strong in several arenas, leading, for example, to an admonition by the U.S. Supreme Court that the OMB should not attempt to use its authority under the PRA as a general regulatory control device as opposed to the specific purposes for which it was enacted.[64] Even so, the Reagan administration used the OIRA as its headquarters for centralized control over rulemakers, and the George H. W. Bush administration followed suit.

The Reagan White House and the Tactics of Indirect Attack:
Antipersonnel Warfare, Strategic Resources Attack, and
Psychological Warfare

While the Reagan White House was very public and direct in its assault on regulation, the administration also employed a variety of tactics of indirect attack that, while less visible, were extremely effective in pursuing its objectives and overcoming its adversaries. These included attack with antipersonnel weapons, strategic resources attacks, and psychological warfare.

The Antipersonnel Attack during the 1980s

While there were advisers in the Reagan White House who counseled respect for professionals in the civil service, it was no secret that other Reagan insiders saw people in government as adversaries likely to scuttle, or at least delay, deregulation efforts and other administration priorities. The administration's first days in office demonstrated that antipersonnel weapons would be deployed with a vengeance in order to convey the strong message that people in government should be aware that there should be less of them, and those who planned to remain had better be prepared to accept a disciplined approach to their work. In his inaugural address, Reagan declared that "government is not the solution to our problem; government is the problem."[65] Immediately after this address, Reagan signed a presidential memorandum imposing a federal hiring freeze.[66] The same training sessions for new political appointees by the Heritage Foundation mentioned above also included training on dealing with the presumptively recalcitrant bureaucracy.[67]

While all this was in progress, Reagan's newly named director of the Office of Personnel Management, Donald Devine, addressed the national conference of the American Society for Public Administration in Detroit. Devine, a Reagan campaign leader in Maryland and University of Maryland political science professor, served notice in no uncertain terms that civil servants were going to be kept "on tap, not on top." He left those assembled (including the author) with little doubt as to his contempt for the audience and his intention to threaten anyone who failed to toe the new administration's line.

Devine and the other political appointees in the regulatory agencies went at the task of radically redirecting their organizations with a vengeance. Soon thereafter it became clear that longtime careerists were opting to leave or were facing obvious encouragement to leave. For those who did not get the message, the next step was a round of reductions in force (RIFs). "For example, during 1981 and 1982 alone, nearly twelve thousand federal employees lost their jobs through RIFs, with the total loss soaring to ninety-two thousand by the end of 1983."[68]

Strategic Resource Attacks on Already Weakened Agencies

For those who remained, life got more complex and challenging as the administration moved forward with a strategic resource attack. The loss of personnel from regulatory agencies had a magnified effect since, contrary to common assumptions, they had already been hard hit by budget cuts during the Carter era as well as increasing legislative demands to implement new policies. There were also demands to provide greater accountability for ongoing operations, to meet intensified demands in an increasingly complex environment, and to do so with limited resources. David Stockman moved at lightning speed with a new round of domestic budget cuts during 1981, with ideology a significant driving force. It was clear to Stockman and others in the administration that increasing defense expenditures and tax cuts would create pressure to cut spending that would allow the administration to go after domestic programs and expenditures that would otherwise have been untouchable.[69] Regulatory agencies that had been the target of Reagan deregulators quickly saw that their budgets would be significantly reduced.

These were not simply tactical cuts in nominal dollars for a given year aimed at particular agencies. They were strategic in a number of senses. First, while it is common to think of deregulation in terms of legislation of the sort passed during the Carter years or the blocking of new rules that agencies sought to promulgate, in real terms significant cuts in agency budgets drastically limited the ability of agencies to conduct enforcement proceedings and curtailed their ability to do the research and other work needed to generate rules (including those required by statute). It also meant that less time and energy could be devoted to particular cases, leading to the possibility of procedural or record-keeping errors that could make regulatory actions more vulnerable to legal challenge. Legal challenges, in turn, also consumed considerable amounts of agency resources.[70] The dangers of losing, of course, increased if the agencies could not dedicate the necessary resources to the defense of their policies and administration, especially when those changes in rules and procedures were dramatic and controversial. Even in other contexts, the reduced capacity of regulators limited their reputation for expertise and authority. Finally, inflation rates were—and are—a deregulator's ally, since the effective cuts because of decreased spending power came on top of cuts in real resources.

One of the claims made by the administration was that it would create a "new federalism" that would transfer authority back to the states. After all, a significant contingent of Reagan's appointees and supporters included leaders of the western "sagebrush rebellion," people who had vehemently objected to federal regulation of land and resources in the western states. Several of these players, like Burford, were now in leadership roles in those regulatory agencies.

However, the term "new federalism" was actually a Nixon-era concept, and the Reagan version proved to be quite different from its predecessor.[71] The Nixon administration had worked to move some program authority back to the states and localities but had sent along with that increased responsibility a considerable body of resources in the form of block grants, categorical and project funding, and revenue sharing. During the Reagan years, revenue sharing was eliminated. Block grants and some of the categorical grants were consolidated, but with a cut of approximately 12 percent across the board.[72] The dollar loss and burden shift were substantial, such that while in 1980 federal grants supported 25 percent of state and local expenditures, by 1988 that support level had dropped to 18.2 percent.[73] The state governments pointed out that the federal mandates did not stop or decline as the funds dried up.

All of this made the working lives of those in the regulatory arena much more difficult at both the federal and the state and local levels. In fact, in many areas, the combination of counterstaffing, resource deprivation, antipersonnel attacks, and burden-loading bogged regulators down dramatically. Of course, for those who are regulated, delay or no action at all is often victory.[74] For the deregulation warriors in the administration, the breakdowns had the added benefit of the "break the system and then attack it for being broken" tactic. In due course, the administration could truthfully say that much of the regulatory machinery just was not working properly. They had made sure of that.

The irony of those problems in regulatory operations was that they led to what has been described as the policy failure syndrome in which the legislature reacted to failed or inadequate policy implementation by producing new and significantly increased regulatory mandates with more details in an attempt to force agency action.[75] If the responsible agencies had been unable to meet the previous version of the legislation, they were virtually assured of failure in the implementation of the second. That happened, for example, in the Superfund program designed to address the need for cleanup of abandoned toxic waste sites. The attacks on environmental agencies by the administration ensured that the recently adopted Comprehensive Environmental Response, Compensation, and Liability Act (CERCLA) would not be adequately implemented in a timely manner. That, in turn, prompted Congress to adopt a more demanding, complex, and specific set of requirements in the Superfund Amendments and Reauthorization Act (SARA) a few years later.[76]

The EPA, NHTSA, and other obvious administration targets were not the only regulators hit with budgetary weapons. Even the agencies that regulated banking were under attack in the midst of a major banking crisis by the simple OMB tactic of including these agencies under the budget-cutting requirements of the Gramm-Rudman-Hollings budget deficit reduction act.[77] This move to limit the enforcement capacity of the bank regulators was not only strange in light of the political timing and public visibility of bank problems, but also because most of these agencies were largely self-funded, receiving their revenues from various kinds of fees gathered from the regulated industries. Even so committed a conservative Republican as Utah Senator Jake Garn, chair of the banking committee, complained to reporters: "I can't believe O.M.B. has any brains. . . . When we have this many banks in trouble, it's not the time to cut back the banking agencies. That is just plain stupid."[78]

Shifting the Presumption to Deregulation: Ideological Attack

At root, one of the most important Reagan administration attacks on regulation was carried out using what is commonly known as psychological warfare or, in the softer language of international conflict, as public diplomacy. It was an effort to infuse an ideological perspective into middle America where it did not already exist and to strengthen and deepen those attitudes where they were already present. The effort was to convince Americans that their natural inclinations to resist regulation were not simply egocentric reactions, but principled behavior that was to be rewarded in the marketplace and that would, in the end, be good for the nation. The level of materialism and expectations grew and intensified. Conspicuous consumption and hypermaterialism were, as portrayed by the administration, good for the nation. The argument about limits to growth and consumption were, as the Reagan administration saw it, simply wrong and, more than that, wrong-headed. The marketplace would provide for the nation's needs, now and in the future.

Second, and related to the first argument, individualism was to be the dominant value. There had long been a tension in the United States between individual discretion and the community's ability to protect itself from individual behavior that threatened the well-being of others. There was no question that, with few exceptions, Americans had long since rejected extreme limitations of individual liberty such as that presented by socialism on the left, but it had also been the case that libertarianism had also been rejected as too dramatic a position on the right. The Reagan administration, while not adopting outright a libertarian position, nevertheless campaigned continuously for significant movement of the nation toward the individualism end of the continuum. It was a campaign that struck a responsive chord in the public and, from that point on, deregulation was, in general terms at least, presumptively good and regulation was assumed to be both wrong and potentially damaging to the nation's bright future. Regulations that appeared to stand in the way were to be fought—and they were. Indeed, by the time Reagan's successor, George H. W. Bush, took the presidential oath, the only question was whether he would be adamant enough in his own command of the war against regulation.

GEORGE H. W. BUSH AND HIS "GENERALS" IN THE WAR ON REGULATION

When George H. W. Bush came to office, it was commonly expected that the new administration would take a quite different approach to governing as compared to the Reagan White House. After all, unlike his two predecessors, Bush was not a governor who had made his way to Washington by running against government. Bush was an insider who was, in a number of respects, very different from Reagan. Beyond that, the context was different when Bush took office than when his predecessor had been elected. In fact, the reaction in many quarters from former Reagan appointees to the media suggested that the Bush administration was inclined toward increasing regulation; more like a Democratic administration than the successor of the Reagan era.

Indeed, Reagan warriors in the battle against regulation bemoaned the fact that the Bush administration appeared to be re-regulating at a level not seen since the 1970s. Christopher DeMuth, who became Reagan's operational leader in the battle against regulation from his position as head of OIRA, observed: "There is a great growth in regulation these days all over the Federal Government. It is being led by Bush appointees."[79] Such criticisms continued throughout 1989 and 1990. This picture was so widely accepted that the coverage of a reinvigorated offensive against regulation in early 1992 was viewed largely as an election year effort to add punch to a flagging reelection campaign.

But while it is true that the regulatory situation in the early years of the Bush administration was different than the dramatic intensity of deregulatory warfare during the Reagan years, the battle continued. Although George Bush may not have been Ronald Reagan or Jimmy Carter, the Bush administration opened a number of new fronts in the fight against regulation, an offensive largely ignored or at least underestimated by the press and other observers. Moreover, Bush stayed on the attack despite the fact that it created stresses within the administration and outside it, both domestically and internationally.

A Limited Suspension of Hostilities?
The Appearance and Reality

Following the Reagan administration, virtually any administration that could have been elected would likely have paled by comparison with the fervent ideological attacks on regulation of its predecessors. Even some Reaganites recognized that there was an emerging backlash based on the view that some deregulation had simply gone too far. That backlash continued throughout the Bush years and into the Clinton administration in such areas as airlines, banks, and energy. Second, there were also reactions against the attitude and behavior of some of the most extreme of the Reagan era deregulators like James Watt and Anne Gorsuch Burford. Hence, Bush was faced with pressure not to engage in the kind of dramatic counterstaffing that had been the hallmark of the Reagan administration. A third argument recognized by some in the business community was the claim that most of the easy targets had been hit during the previous eight years and by deregulation legislation during the Carter years. The fight would be for consolidation of those victories against the counterattacks noted above.

A fourth factor was the reality that there were legislative and judicial mandates extant that required rulemaking. The critics later pointed to the Clean Air Act, the Civil Rights Act of 1991, and the Americans with Disabilities Act as culprits in causing additions to the Code of Federal Regulations. However, the Bush administration did not create the Clean Air Act and there was no likelihood that the legislation would be refused reauthorization. As for the two other statutes, there was strong bipartisan support for the Civil Rights Act of 1991.[80] Even so, Bush had vetoed the version of the bill passed in 1990 to avoid what he saw as excessive pressures on employers and ultimately issued a presidential signing statement for the 1991 legislation that had the same intention.[81] The ADA also had strong support, and the Bush White House was very positive about the idea that, while it gave some existing agencies implementation responsibilities in their sectors, it avoided creating a major new regulatory agency and relied primarily on suits to be brought by victims of discrimination as the vehicle for enforcement.[82] Bush attempted to use these laws as evidence of what his son George W. Bush would later call "compassionate conservatism."

Quite apart from the new legislation, however, part of the limits on the numbers of rules published during the Reagan years had came from deliberate delaying tactics that would not remain effective indefinitely. Those delaying tactics used by the administration were challenged in litigation that dragged on for some time. Ultimately, though, these cases established that agencies were required to meet their statutory obligations notwithstanding any regulatory review processes imposed by the administration, and the Bush administration would have to produce some of the delayed rules.

Finally, and of major importance, was the context in which President Bush found his administration. Cornelius M. Kerwin, then dean of the School of Public Affairs at American University and the nation's leading scholar on administrative rulemaking,[83] put the matter in direct terms: "The volume of rule-making in this country is a reflection of the demands made on our political system by the American people, and they now want the Government to take an active role in solving a broad swath of problems."[84] There were a number of such problems that meant that there were demands on the Bush administration for action by both business leaders and the public. The dramatic downturn in the stock market that came to be known as Black Monday had occurred just the year before he was elected and the savings and loan meltdown was an economic nightmare (due in no small part to the deregulation of that sector launched during the Carter years). As had often been the case in the past during dramatic economic downturns, traditionally antiregulation conservative Republicans joined with liberal Democrats to demand an active government response. Moreover, there were reactions against the perceived deregulation excesses of the Reagan years, with demands for Bush not to oppose regulation in such areas as advertising directed at children—legislation that he let become law without his signature in October 1990.

George H. W. Bush, a New General Staff,
and Direct Attack Tactics

For all these reasons, the war against regulation was different, though real and more effective than some might have imagined during the Bush years. While he did not pursue the direct legislative assault of the Clinton years or create anything as dramatic as EO 12291 of the Reagan era, Bush was fully prepared to commission his own "generals" in the war on regulation and take action in his own way.

Notwithstanding the criticisms by some on the far right and others in the media who thought otherwise, George Bush was no liberal. Neither was he a supporter of regulation. During the Reagan administration, Bush had been the chair of the Vice President's Task Force on Regulatory Relief created by EO 12291. His work in that role drew fire from Democratic candidates during the 1988 election and again in 1992, though some of Reagan's other deregulatory warriors were not sure that Bush's heart was in it. Even so, one of these, Martin Anderson, predicted that Bush would continue the fight if elected and that he would commit his vice presidential running mate, Dan Quayle, to a leadership role in the battle, just as Bush had been assigned to the fight by Reagan.[85] That is just what Bush did. That was but one of several modes of attack on regulation during his watch, four of them domestic and another beyond U.S. borders. At home there was first the creation of the Council on Competitiveness, better known as the Quayle Commission. Second, and related to it, there was the continued and expanded use of PRA to provide a foundation for the internal fight against regulation led by the OIRA, after the use of EOs 12291 and 12498 had been constrained by judicial opinions and legislative threats. Third, beginning in early 1992, there was a full-blown frontal assault, grounded in a moratorium on rulemaking declared by the president and led by the men he termed his "generals" in the war against regulation. Fourth, the Bush White House also pushed a far less visible, but very important initiative to constrain efforts at regulation by way of private lawsuit through what the administration termed "civil justice reform." Finally, there was the effort, largely unpublicized in the United States, to deregulate in the international arena. Consider each of these in turn.

The Council on Competitiveness and the OIRA
Unlike the Reagan White House, which struck hard and fast with an institutional structure and procedures to attack regulations in its highly publicized EO 12291, the Bush effort was initiated with far less fanfare, but it ultimately produced major battles against regulation. His message to Congress on February 9, 1989, outlining the goals of his administration, devoted only one line to the creation of the new council: "I've asked Vice President Quayle to chair a

new Task Force on Competitiveness."[86] Even though it was mentioned as one of the administration's priorities, there was little emphasis on the Quayle task force in the early months of the new president's term.[87] At the time the council was created, Quayle was not being taken seriously in many circles, and it was a period when a variety of new advisory groups and other bodies were being installed by the new administration.

Although the task force was actually announced early in 1989, it really did not become a focus of activity until more than a year later, in June 1990, when President Bush issued a press release indicating that the council would be responsible to "review issues raised in conjunction with the regulatory program under Executive Order 12498. The president has also directed the Council on Competitiveness to exercise the same authority over regulatory issues as did the Presidential Task Force on Regulatory Relief under Executive Order 12291, which established the administration's regulatory review process."[88] Also in June 1990, the cabinet secretary issued a memorandum directing executive branch agencies as to how they were to work with what was coming to be known as the Quayle Council.[89]

However, national attention was soon drawn away from domestic issues as Operation Desert Shield was launched in August and American troops prepared for possible combat in Kuwait and Iraq. By December, Desert Shield became Desert Storm and the United States was engaged in full-scale combat in the region.

By 1991, as attention shifted back to domestic matters, it was becoming clear that the Council on Competitiveness would become a serious force for fighting regulations. It was able to do so because the council was made up of key officials in the administration (the president's chief of staff, OMB director, Council of Economic Advisors chair, cabinet secretaries, and the attorney general), because the president supported their efforts—illustrated by the fact that there was an understanding that appeals from the council would not be welcome—and because there was little public awareness of just what the council was doing and what difference it made. Quayle appointed a businessman from Indiana, Allan Hubbard, as the executive director, and the council was off and running.

The Quayle council turned out to be an aggressive antiregulatory body that acted through the vice president and his staff. The initial claim was that the council was an interagency coordinating committee and not an agency. As such, it could exempt itself from compliance with a variety of federal administrative laws. The vice president and his colleagues were ready to pressure agencies to back off of controversial regulatory proposals, despite the fact that the council had no statutory or executive order authority. The council participated in the OIRA meetings and took decisions about pending rulemaking proposals totally away from the public eye.[90] Quayle also demanded that agencies offer deregulation proposals.[91] This reminded some of Murray Weidenbaum's dictum that when officials were in doubt as to what to do, "undo."[92] The council defined its scope of authority broadly, claiming that it could review agency materials even beyond those covered by EO 12291. Quayle asserted that the council could review "strategy statements, guidelines, policy manuals, grant and loan procedures, Advance Notices of Proposed Rulemaking, press releases, and other documents announcing or implementing regulatory policy that affects the public."[93]

The council weighed in on environmental, occupational health, and other favorite targets of deregulators of the period, but it did not stop there, addressing issues from energy to transportation. In some cases, the Quayle council gave suggestions (which were in reality orders) to the OIRA as that agency conducted reviews of proposed rules under EOs 12291 and 12498. In other instances, Quayle went to agency heads or cabinet secretaries directly. Quayle made it obvious that there was no serious opportunity for these officials to appeal the council's decisions to President Bush. These activities resulted in a number of highly publicized battles on issues like the regulation of wetlands. Another such battle went international, as Quayle put EPA Administrator William Reilly (who was representing the United States at the Rio Earth Summit in the summer of 1992) and, for that matter, the reputation of the nation into serious difficulty by moving to block from Washington Reilly's ability to sign the biodiversity treaty and take other important steps at the Earth Summit.

Members of Congress were outraged by what many saw as a power grab as well as the methods, the secrecy, and the substantive policy changes forced by the council. Congressman David Skaggs (D-Colo.) insisted that "the Council has become an off-the-record, no-fingerprints operation for subverting necessary and appropriate regulatory activity of the Federal Government."[94] California Representative Henry Waxman (D) charged: "There is unmistakable evidence that White House officials, spearheaded by Vice President Dan Quayle . . . are working with industry to undermine implementation of the new clean air law. . . . This is not only horrible policy, it is clearly illegal."[95]

There were some ironic and rather strange aspects to the tactics employed by the administration at the time. The Bush administration asserted executive privilege over the information about the operation of the council that Congress sought.[96] Still, details about the modes of intervention and the kinds of impacts that the council had on rulemaking in such areas as the environment and health were leaked to reporters. That included such revelations as Quayle's role in the embarrassing fumbles by the United States at the Rio Earth Summit in 1992.

Despite the efforts at secrecy and public denials in some quarters, it was widely known that the council was operating as a kind of political appeal body in which regulated groups could attack proposed agency regulations in a forum that was off the record and outside of the public process that was required by the APA. Council executive director Allan Hubbard admitted that "when [businesses] feel like they are being treated unfairly, they come to us."[97] As a former chief economist of the U.S. Chamber of Commerce, Richard Rahn, put it: "Quayle has gotten into the deregulation battle more substantively than anyone else. He has done his homework. He's forceful. And he's made a difference in the eyes of American business."[98] As Barry D. Friedman pointed out, the OIRA director James B. MacRae, Jr., actually admitted to reporters that:

> Yes, the [Council on Competitiveness] does advise [OIRA] on regulatory matters.
> No, [MacRae] cannot think of an instance when his staff turned down the advice.
> Yes, his staff communicates regularly with the council.
> No, these communications are not recorded in any form.[99]

The OIRA was the operational body that was responsible for processing regulatory reviews under EOs 12291 and 12498. However, as noted earlier, litigation during the Reagan years had indicated that there were boundaries to how those presidential orders could be applied and particularly so in situations where there was a statutory mandate to issue regulations. As the Bush administration ran up against those constraints, its antiregulation warriors shifted toward a greater use of the PRA to continue the fight against new rules.

This use—or, as congressional critics contended, misuse—of the PRA was in addition to the view that the OIRA was significantly and inappropriately controlled by the Council on Competitiveness. Congress had by then had enough and moved to block funding for the OIRA, ultimately holding up the needed reauthorization of the PRA. The frustration of members of Congress when they concluded that OIRA was having off-the-record communications about rulemaking reviews and other issues with key players, both in the administration and in the regulated communities, led to a limited agreement on disclosure of some of the communications. However, the Bush antiregulation warriors pushed the envelope on that agreement and the Council on Competitiveness simply rejected any such requirement.

In order to deal with growing anger on the Hill and to find a way to move reauthorization of the PRA, a so-called sidebar agreement was worked out between the OMB and the House Government Operations Committee. The agreement, entitled "Administrative Agreement: Procedures Governing OIRA Review of Regulations under Executive Order Nos. 12291 and 12498," would have assured Congress that the OIRA would disclose contacts with parties from outside government and critical communications between the OMB and regulatory agencies concerning pending rulemaking matters. However, White House Counsel C. Boyden Gray not only repudiated the agreement that had already been approved by OMB Director Richard Darman but threatened that the White House would impose sweeping executive privilege claims to withhold information that was already being disclosed to Congress by the administration.[100] The PRA was ultimately not reauthorized and, in defiance of that fact, the OIRA continued to operate without legal authority until well into President Clinton's first term, at which time an agreement was reached with Clinton's new OIRA director to address the problems that created so much bad blood earlier.[101]

Bush's Use of Presidential Direct Action to Block Regulation and Order New Offensives

While it was far from clear in 1991 that a youthful former governor from Arkansas would unseat President Bush, a president who had been basking in the political glow of Gulf War military victory, it was obvious by early 1992 that Bush's popularity had lost its wartime luster. He was being criticized at the time by both the Democrats and many within his own party for lacking a clear focus and direction for his administration. A *New York Times*/CBS News Poll in April 1992 found that "fifty-eight percent of the 1,151 registered voters questioned April 20–23 said the Administration was drifting without clear policies."[102] Yet Quayle and his council had been rallying the conservative base

of the Republican Party with his fight against regulation in addition to his efforts to be the standard-bearer for traditional values (recall the famous—or
infamous—"Murphy Brown" debate concerning the vice president's criticism
of the lifestyle of a character in a television program).

For his part, Bush determined to make it clear that he was the commander
in chief in the war against regulation and that Quayle was but one of his commanders. The president made the point firmly in his 1992 State of the Union
address, in which he announced a ninety-day moratorium on new regulations. The operational order went out to the troops in the form of a presidential memorandum to executive branch agencies that ordered them to respond
to the leadership of the Quayle council and report to that body on their
progress.[103] Like his predecessors, Bush attempted to enlist the independent
regulatory commissions in his fight, though legally, of course, they did not report to the president and had been designed to be independent of political
control from the White House. Still, Bush's memorandum included the independent commissions.

Bush's moratorium memorandum ordered agencies to "work with the
public, other interested agencies, the OIRA, and the Council on Competitiveness to (1) identify each of your agency's regulations and programs that impose a substantial cost on the economy and (2) determine whether each such
regulation or program adheres" to the Bush administration's regulatory policies. In addition, agencies were to "designate, in consultation with the Council
on Competitiveness, a senior official to serve as your agency's permanent regulatory oversight official."

The president sought to capitalize on the controversy that had been generated by the clashes between congressional Democrats on one side and the
OIRA and the Council on Competitiveness on the other. Bush issued a second
memorandum at the same time as his moratorium order in which he insisted:
"Although the Congress has created the regulatory schemes within which we
must operate, I am confident that, with your help, the executive branch can
do much to create conditions conducive to a healthy and robust economy."[104]
This offensive would help to sharpen the distinctions between his administration and the Democrats and solidify his leadership in his own party.

Having highlighted the fight against regulation as a campaign theme, Bush
announced an extension of the moratorium for an additional 120 days in
April 1992.[105] In so doing, the president announced his extension with a
"salute [to] the three generals in the war for regulatory reforms: our Vice

President, Dan Quayle, Boyden Gray, and Dr. Michael Boskin," members of the Council on Competitiveness.[106] Bush ordered that "the Competitiveness Council [would] take the lead in implementing these reforms."

Of course, in sharpening the issue positions of the candidates, Bush also helped Bill Clinton and Al Gore rally Democrats and independents in defense of the environment, health rules, and workplace safety. Ironically, these two Democrats, who credited their fight against the Bush antiregulators as one of the reasons for their victory, would themselves quickly launch attacks on regulation.

Civil Justice "Reform" and Pressure for Deregulation Abroad: Less Direct, but Nevertheless Important Operations

There were two far less visible fronts along which the Bush White House pressed the war—one domestic and the other international. Neither was really recognized outside of a limited number of directly interested parties at the time, but both created arenas of conflict for years to come, including, ultimately, the administration of George W. Bush.

The Civil Justice Reform Attack: An Effort to Block Pro-regulation Litigation

Before widespread government regulation expanded during the twentieth century, the common mode of addressing problems that are today seen as targets for regulation was by private lawsuits (see Chapter 4). In addition, following the rise of interest-group litigation, first in the civil rights field and then expanding into such areas as environmental protection, litigation was seen as a vehicle to move public policy where government either would not or could not act.[107] In addition, specialized practice in fields such as products liability, various types of malpractice, and tort liability claims against government was growing in the 1980s and 1990s. All of these provided privately driven, litigation-based regulatory mechanisms. As the war against regulation developed from the Carter years through the Reagan era and into the Bush administration, advocates outside government saw litigation as a way to address some of the issues that government deregulation had either abandoned or problems in areas in which government agencies were so weakened that they could not act effectively.

Many regulated industries that had been seeing victories against regulation feared growing losses from civil litigation. Hence, it was not surprising that foes of regulation joined the nascent movement for what came to be known as "civil justice reform." To some of its early advocates, civil justice reform was about avoiding litigation when possible through the use of tools such as alternative dispute resolution and enhanced efficiency of litigation that did go to court through improved case management and procedural improvements. For the deregulation forces, however, it was a way to constrain litigation, put caps on its scope, and limit liability.

The Reagan administration had wanted action to block what many conservative Republicans denounced as regulation by lawsuit, but it was the Bush White House, again with Quayle as a point person, that made it an issue of some importance.[108] The administration supported the Civil Justice Reform Act passed in 1990.[109] The Council on Competitiveness formed its own working group on civil justice reform to press further on the issue. President Bush, in October 1991, ultimately issued Executive Order 12778 on civil justice reform, ordering government attorneys to apply civil justice reform principles in cases in which suit was brought by or against the government.[110] Ironically, the Bush DOJ took until January 1993 to develop a guidance document for implementation of the executive order, by which time the Clinton administration was taking power.[111] However, George W. Bush would later take up the fight in this arena.

Taking the Fight into Other Theaters of Operations
There was another campaign that was considerably more successful in the short term, at least when judged according to the goals of Bush-era deregulators. The president was a supporter of what came to be termed "free trade" and, later, "globalization." Like the Reagan administration of which he had been a part, Bush wanted to export the commitment to deregulation, privatization, and free trade. Of course, in practice and in many important respects, privatization and free trade were, for the Bush administration, about deregulation.

The administration was able to use its leverage over developing countries to force movement in these areas. One of the obvious examples of this effort was what the Bush White House referred to as the Enterprise for the Americas initiative. Among other things, the policy repackaged existing foreign aid dollars going to Latin American countries and conditioned receipt of assistance on moves by those governments to privatize, deregulate, and move toward free trade.[112] Coming as it did on top of pressures of the 1980s by the International Monetary Fund and World Bank for similar moves and for structural adjustment of the economies of these developing nations, a number of countries felt the pressure to deregulate in the several ways in which the Bush program demanded.

The Clinton administration later pursued some of the same approaches abroad. Clinton's chair of the Council of Economic Advisors, Nobel Prize–winning economist Joseph E. Stiglitz, would later write of this campaign:

> Acting as if we had come up with a unique, guaranteed formula for prosperity, we ... bullied other nations into doing things our way. ... Uncle Sam became Dr. Sam, dispensing prescriptions to the rest of the world. ... Like some physicians, we were too busy—and too sure of ourselves—to listen to patients with their own ideas. Too busy, sometimes, even to look at individual countries and their circumstances. ... The deregulation mantra that we pushed too far at home we pushed even further abroad.[113]

CONCLUSION

Although it is often forgotten now, the battle against regulation extends back to the mid-1970s and has been fought by Democrats as well as Republicans. Though he is remembered as a liberal, President Carter was an active deregulator. From his campaign for office through a range of successful direct assaults on long-standing regulatory agencies and policies, he was clearly committed to the fight. His efforts led to more deregulation than any of his predecessors. In fact, his administration changed administrative agencies and regulatory procedures in a manner very different from the picture that was painted by his successor. While Carter employed direct strategies and tactics in his campaign against regulation, he also developed many of the indirect attacks that would later be adopted by his Republican successors.

Ronald Reagan took the strategies and tactics of the Carter years and brought to their expanded and intensified use a no-holds-barred ideological approach with a particular emphasis on administrative weapons and tactics. His administration made dramatic use of such weapons as counterstaffing, strategic resources attack, and antipersonnel tactics, coupled with the development of a command post for the battle against regulation in the OIRA as part of the OMB within the Executive Office of the President. And, to ensure that all were aware of the orders, his White House began the practice, continued by his successors, of placing the vice president in charge of what the Reagan administration called the Task Force on Regulatory Relief.

Though he was not as ideologically committed as Reagan, leading some within his own party to criticize what they saw as an inadequately combative approach to regulation, George H. W. Bush fought the battle in his own way. Working with and through his "generals in the battle against regulation," Bush continued the Reagan-era use of administrative weapons against regulation. Vice President Dan Quayle's Council on Competitiveness more than made up for Bush's lack of personal ideological fervor and pressed the battle in ways often unseen by the public, but effective nevertheless.

However, new energy and a variety of new battle plans were about to come from, of all places, a Democratic successor and then from George H. W. Bush's son, George W. Bush, fully the heir of the Reagan ideological tradition—and then some. Some of the troops were about to change, and the context within which the battles developed would be new and different, but the fight would continue and even intensify. That next phase of the battle against regulation under the William Clinton and George W. Bush administrations is the subject of Chapter 3.

3. The William Clinton and George W. Bush Administrations: New Warriors in the Ongoing Battle against Regulation

The administrations of William Clinton and George W. Bush differed in many respects from their predecessors and from each other, but when it came to the war against regulation, both enthusiastically chose to continue on the attack. While their styles and political approaches certainly differed from each other, both chose to pursue the attack on regulation. They employed weapons that were surprisingly similar in some respects and dramatically different in others through their respective eight years in office.

THE CLINTON PARADOX: SPEAKING OUT FOR REGULATION WHILE WARRING AGAINST IT

Just as the Reagan campaign machine was effective in picturing the Carter administration as supporters of excessive and intrusive regulation, the George W. Bush campaign was able to portray the Clinton administration along with his vice president and would-be successor, Al Gore, as rabid regulators. Of course, that image-creating effort was aided by the fact that Clinton and Gore had come to office charging that the Reagan and Bush administrations had been hostile to health, safety, and environmental regulation. Even so, the picture painted of the Clinton administration by partisan opponents was far from accurate. In fact, the portrait that the Clinton White House painted of itself with respect to regulation was often far from complete, accurate, or consistent. In truth, the Clinton administration continued the war against regulation both in ways that were visible and others that were less obvious.

It is no small irony that Clinton and Gore used their attack on the Bush administration's deregulation efforts and the work of Bush's "three generals in the war"[1] against regulation as a stepping stone to the White House, only to make the fight against rules and, more broadly, against regulation a core element of their government on both the international and the domestic fronts. While it is true that there were some areas in which the Clinton White House rejected the positions of its Bush and Reagan predecessors, it is also the case that even in these areas, the new administration often sought to avoid regulation in favor of market-based alternatives and implementation by negotiated agreements as compared to enforcement approaches. And in its program to take the nation "From Red Tape to Results," as its reinventing government effort entitled its manifesto, the Clinton White House would employ the full panoply of weapons developed by its predecessors and add a few of its own.

While sometimes less obvious to the general public and much of the mass media than its predecessors, the Clinton administration push against regulation was real and sustained. It must be understood at quite different levels. First, there was the combination of ideology and context that drove the effort. Then there was the reinventing government campaign, with battles against regulations and regulatory program design. Finally, there was the effort to implement regulatory programs so as to constrain the use of full regulatory authority. Throughout, the administration was prepared to deploy both the direct and indirect weapons used by its predecessors in their campaigns against regulation.

The Foundations of Deregulation in the Clinton White House: "We Were All Deregulators"

Joseph Stiglitz was not merely a critic of U.S. deregulation mandates abroad. He had won his Nobel prize in economics for his work in the field of regulation. In his critique of the Clinton era, *The Roaring Nineties,* Stiglitz argued that the battles against regulation under previous presidents and in the Clinton administration, of which he was a part, were responsible for many of the problems of recent history, including some that have developed—and that were exacerbated in—the George W. Bush years that followed.

> If there was ever a time not to pursue deregulation, or to manage it particularly gingerly, the Roaring Nineties were it. The Democrats had always provided a check on the mindless pursuit of deregulation. Now, we joined in the fray—sometimes pushing things even further than under the Reagan administration. . . .

"We are all Berliners" was the sentiment of President Kennedy's declaration. Thirty years later, we were all deregulators. The distinction in the parties lay only in the degree of their enthusiasm.[2]

There were at least two major forces behind the Clinton administration's deregulation drive—one ideological and another pragmatic. Clinton was the New Democrat candidate, the standard-bearer for a new combination of modern southern populism (though he did not like that term) and what might be termed new progressivism.[3] On the national level, these were political players who saw the future as one in which they could have moderate to liberal social policy with a brand of economic conservatism that would make them attractive to middle-class suburban voters and independents without losing the Democratic base who expected active government to address pressing problems.

They were ready to use public policy to achieve their ends but not particularly willing to trust government agencies and employees to carry out those policies. The theme was not that government was "the problem" as Reagan had argued, but instead that the government was populated by good people trapped in a bad system. We have created a system, said the administration's "National Performance Review" document, that "makes it hard for our civil servants to do what we pay them for, and frustrates taxpayers who rightfully expect their money's worth. . . . Hamstrung by rules and regulations, federal managers simply do not have the power to shape their organizations enjoyed by private sector managers."[4] The administration declared that "effective, entrepreneurial governments cast aside red tape, shifting from systems in which people are accountable for following rules to systems in which they are accountable for achieving results."[5] In attempting to achieve their new vision of entrepreneurial government, the Clinton White House announced a set of principles in which it declared that it would "replace regulations with incentives" and "search for market, not administrative solutions."[6]

Notwithstanding the rhetoric about concern for the good people in government, it was clear that many Clintonites held little trust or confidence in the public service to make the changes they sought. That lack of confidence—and for some a very real suspicion—was manifest in part by a focus on policy formulation that emphasized the creation of policies that relied as much as possible on incentives and other market dynamics and not primarily on implementation and administration by public administrators. Lurking in the

background, and despite the public rhetoric to the contrary, was a strong
sense that those in the bureaucracy were likely engaged in what Eugene Bardach has termed "Implementation Games" to block needed changes.[7] Further,
the new administration quickly committed itself to antipersonnel warfare
tactics with highly touted major reductions in public service positions after
years during which the federal service had already suffered dramatic losses
from reductions in force (RIFs) and other attacks outlined earlier in Chapter
2. Indeed, cutting more than 377,000 civil servants would, at the end of the
day, be one of the accomplishments of which Clinton and Gore would boast
most often and on which Gore campaigned in 2000.

While much was made of the Clintons' New Year's trips to Hilton Head Island to gather with their policy "wonk" ("know" spelled backwards) friends at
the so-called Renaissance Weekends, the real significance of those gatherings
was often missed. Many of those assembled were involved in an organization
known as the Progressive Policy Institute. Its members and their ideas surfaced often in key Clinton administration policies, and its members were later
found in significant appointed positions.[8] They were among the policy de-
signers who would attempt to wage the battle against "red tape."

This group of policy wonks came to the White House under a campaign
theme driven in large part by the context in which Clinton found himself. The
now well-known slogan for the campaign, purportedly originated by Clinton's campaign ramrod James Carville—"It's the economy, stupid!"—
responded to the set of conditions that had a great deal to do with George
H. W. Bush's downfall.[9] Once in office, it meant that the marketplace would
become not only the primary, but the overriding focus of the Clinton administration, rhetoric to the contrary notwithstanding.[10] That, in turn, meant a
heavy reliance on the admonitions and support of the chair of the Federal Reserve, the secretary of the treasury, the national economic advisor (a post
Clinton created to mirror the national security advisor), and a number of
economists who were members of the domestic policy staff. In fact, although
early press reports touted the selection of a wide range of economic advisors
and policymakers selected for appointment as Clinton entered office,[11]
Stiglitz explained how quickly and thoroughly the pro-market and antiregulatory forces became the key cadre of policy-shapers for the administration.[12]
That orientation fueled a driving emphasis within the administration for
budget cuts to achieve deficit reduction—quite dramatic cuts in fact—and
deregulation, both domestically and in the arena of international trade.

Smile When You Make That Regulation:
Polite Language, Real Constraints

Despite the effort to use language that spoke of balance and commitment to the consumer, safety, and environmental protections that had been provided through regulations, the new administration's actions demonstrated that the Clinton administration's people would, in truth, become the deregulators that Stiglitz described. The new administration's early actions indicated that fresh forces had entered the field to fight in the battle against regulation.

On February 10, 1993, Clinton issued Executive Order 12839 commanding a reduction of 100,000 positions in the federal government, specifying that "each executive department or agency with over 100 employees shall eliminate not less than 4 percent of its civilian personnel positions . . . over the next 3 fiscal years. . . . At least 10 percent of the reductions shall come from the Senior Executive Service, GS-15 and GS-14 levels or equivalent."[13] The requirement for 10 percent of reductions to come from the top ranks of the civil service would mean the loss of some 10,000 experienced leaders and managers.

Also in February, the new Environmental Protection Agency (EPA) administrator, Carol Browner, announced plans to ask Congress to eliminate the Delaney Clause, a provision of law that required that substances that caused cancer in laboratory animals be banned in products for human consumption, prompting criticism from environmental and health groups. The following month, the administration announced its intentions to ease banking regulations. In August, the Clinton White House indicated its intention to reduce controls on the export of computers. These are but a few of the introductory steps that signaled a much wider campaign that was about to begin.

The Weapons and the Tactics: Simultaneous Pursuit
of Direct and Indirect Attacks

With this general introduction in mind, it is useful to turn to the administration's specific attacks on regulation over the course of Clinton's two terms. Like their predecessors, the Clinton administration would employ the full panoply of weapons and tactics.

Direct Attacks: Both Legislative and Administrative
Once again, and notwithstanding the George W. Bush–era revisionism and the rhetoric that President Clinton and Vice President Gore tended to use to

differentiate their administrations from what had come before, the fact was that the battle against regulation was waged with direct weapons in a series of well-publicized campaigns, both on the domestic front and internationally. Both legislative and administrative weapons were employed in the effort.

The Clinton Administration's Ongoing Legislative Offensives: Direct Attacks on Regulatory Programs.—It became clear early on that the administration would go to Congress for deregulation action even in health, safety, and environmental matters when the White House thought the targets worthwhile, much to the consternation of many of those who had supported Clinton for election. Thus, the February 1993 announcement by the EPA administrator that she would ask Congress to eliminate the Delaney Clause led to responses in the press from people like Albert H. Meyerhoff of the Natural Resources Defense Council, who replied to a reporter who told him of the legislative initiative: "Say it ain't so. . . . This is an Administration that ran a campaign based upon a promise to enhance protection of public health and the environment. We will fight diligently to insure that promise is kept."[14]

Much of the rest of that year was spent in a deficit reduction effort, followed by a campaign to ensure ratification of the North American Free Trade Agreement (NAFTA) and, later, the General Agreement on Tariffs and Trade (GATT), both of which were part of a free trade agenda that would place pressure from the global marketplace on domestic regulatory programs, which could and would be challenged under these agreements as illegal trade barriers. The Clinton administration seemed to be behaving more like a conservative Republican White House rather than the group that had campaigned for office the previous year.

By 1994 it became clear that the administration intended, with respect to deregulation at least, to pick up where its predecessors, dating back to the Carter administration, had left off. In January, Vice President Gore began a campaign on behalf of the administration that he would maintain over time to press for deregulation legislation for the telecommunications sector to be matched by efforts to ensure that the rapidly evolving Internet would be protected from regulatory legislation, all part of his advocacy of the "information superhighway."[15] Gore called corporate executives from cable television and telephone firms to a meeting at UCLA to assist in the development of and support for the deregulation package that the vice president announced in his speech on January 11.[16] In keeping with the administration's penchant for showmanship, Gore added the theatrical touch of having comedian Lily Tomlin, in character as Ernestine the Operator, do a brief exchange with the vice president as part of the presentation.[17] Like others of the Clinton-era campaign-style deregulation speeches, the vice president's speech was long on slogans and short on details of precisely how the deregulation would be designed and implemented. While the bill favored by the administration passed the House in the summer, it was later blocked in the Senate. The administration promised to return with a similar effort at a later date.

While there had been proposals in Congress offered by John Dingell (D-Mich.) and others, it was obvious from that point on that the initiative for telecommunications deregulation was something the administration wanted for its own agenda. These efforts on telecommunications were followed in April by the administration's announcement of its plans for changes in the Federal Insecticide, Fungicide, and Rodenticide Act (FIFRA) that would, among other things, end the so-called Delaney Clause, which banned any residual in food products that had been identified as causing cancer, a move that had been initially revealed shortly after the administration took office.

August and September 1994 saw two major steps accomplished in the administration's deregulation agenda in the legislature. In August the president signed legislation intended to complete work on trucking deregulation, a process that had begun during the Carter years, in what seemed to be an unlikely context, the Federal Aviation Authorization Act of 1994.[18] Title VI of the Federal Aviation Administration (FAA) authorization legislation prohibited states from attempting to "enact or enforce a law, regulation, or other provision having the force and effect of law related to a price, route, or service of any motor carrier (other than a carrier affiliated with a direct air carrier covered by section 41713(b)(4) of this title) or any motor private carrier with respect to the transportation of property." It also barred a state or any of its subdivisions from efforts to "enact or enforce a law, regulation, or other provision having the force and effect of law related to a price, route, or service of an air carrier or carrier affiliated with a direct air carrier through common controlling ownership when such carrier is transporting property by aircraft or by motor vehicle (whether or not such property has had or will have a prior or subsequent air movement)."[19] The Carter-era airline deregulation legislation not only eliminated federal regulation, but also blocked state regulation as well.[20] That had not been the case with respect to trucking in earlier congressional action. It was not at all clear what the impact of the further deregulation of the trucking industry would be with respect to service, prices, or safety, though the legislation did leave open to state governments their traditional authority to enact laws as to vehicle and driver safety. For their part, the administration and its congressional supporters assumed that prices would go down and competition would increase with resulting efficiencies.

September saw the president sign new legislation, another step in the continuing effort, originally launched during the Carter years, to deregulate the banking industry. The Riegle-Neal Interstate Banking and Branching Efficiency Act amended the Bank Holding Company Act of 1956. Section 101 of the legislation provided that "the Board may approve an application under this section by a bank holding company that is adequately capitalized and adequately managed to acquire control of, or acquire all or substantially all of the assets of, a bank located in a State other than the home State of such bank holding company, without regard to whether such transaction is prohibited under the law of any State."[21] Section 102 added: "Beginning on June 1, 1997, the responsible agency may approve a merger transaction under section 18(c) between insured banks with different home States, without regard to whether such transaction is prohibited under the law of any State." The president was following the lead of Secretary of the Treasury Lloyd Bentsen and others on his economic team, but he made it clear that the deregulation agenda was his and that he regarded it as both good government and good politics. In signing the statute Clinton said, "Under this law . . . banks will be able to operate in more States with less trouble. We wipe away obsolete Government-created restrictions, something I'm determined to do in many other areas. And you'd be amazed how many areas these exist in."[22]

In October, President Clinton underscored the importance of the administration's deregulation agenda, both by legislative and administrative means, in a speech he delivered to the City Club of Cleveland. In language that would have been expected from a Republican president, Clinton outlined the effort.

> The key elements of the strategy are simple and direct and important. First, reduce the deficit. Second, expand trade and intensify the efforts of the United States government to be a partner with American business in doing business beyond our borders. Third, increase our investment in education and training, in technology and defense conversion. Fourth, bring the benefits of free enterprise to areas which have been isolated from it, in our inner cities and rural areas, with new strategies, including, but not limited, to welfare reform. Fifth, reinvent the federal government. Make it smaller, more effective, less regulatory, more efficient.[23]

He closed by promising that the administration would pursue an important goal that had been a key to the administration's efforts in 1993 and 1994. "We've tried to make government a better partner with deregulation of banking and trucking and exports of high-tech products." In fact, Clinton was so aware of and committed to what his administration was doing and why that he told reporters in November: "If I were a Republican president saying that, all these people would be running me for sainthood. . . . They'd be saying, 'Let's build this guy a statue.'"[24]

However, following the victory in November by congressional Republicans, led by Representative Newt Gingrich (R-Ga.) and based on his so-called Contract with America, it was obvious that, far from erecting a monument to Clinton, conservatives were going to demand even more deregulation. Yet the president thought he could make common cause with the Republicans. "There are a lot of areas where we can work together with the Republicans. We can finish the battle that this administration began with the last Congress to change what I would call 'yesterday's government.' We have begun the downsizing of the government, we have begun the deregulation that we need to do."[25] He continued that theme of cooperation in bringing down the size of government, eliminating bureaucracy, and pressing for more deregulation in seeking what he termed a "new social compact" in his State of the Union address in January 1995. Conservative Republican commentator William Kristol asserted that it was the "most conservative State of the Union by a Democratic president in history."[26]

The administration lost no time in announcing new initiatives on the deregulation front, recognizing that they would have to get through a Republican Congress. Most notably, the new treasury secretary, Robert Rubin, formerly head of the Clinton administration's National Economic Council and before that co-chair of the major financial firm Goldman Sachs, announced the administration's intention to seek repeal of the Glass-Steagall Act and further amendments to the Bank Holding Company Act of 1956. The Glass-Steagall law was adopted during the Great Depression in an effort to keep a protective firewall between owners of commercial banks and investment firms, while the Bank Holding Company Act placed barriers to the simultaneous control of insurance companies and commercial banks. The effect of eliminating those restrictions would be to allow financial services firms to offer a wider range of services and, presumably, to enhance efficiencies through consolidations and cost reductions. However, these long-standing laws had been adopted precisely to avoid dangerous situations that could occur when firms could control too much capital in too many sectors, breaking down institutional checks among financial institutions and perhaps establishing perverse incentives or even outright conflicts of interests. History had already demonstrated that the failure of these institutions and their proper functioning could wreak havoc on the economy as well as on individual depositors and investors.

Ironically, Rubin announced the Clinton administration's major deregulation initiative just as Barings Bank, a venerable British institution, made public the fact that a single young trader, only twenty-eight, had destroyed the bank's capital foundation by trades in the international market. The *Atlanta Journal and Constitution* editorialized on the bank disaster, warning of the dangers of "the exotic new financial system in this age of the information revolution."

> The Clinton administration has recommended that commercial banks, securities firms and insurance companies be allowed to merge into megabanks offering one-stop financial services, thereby improving their ability to compete globally.

> But the deregulation that goes with such mergers also brings increased potential for a "rogue" trader to bankrupt an entire financial institution, instead of wreaking havoc in only a single company or division.

> In an age when trillions of dollars, pesos or yen can be sent across borders merely by hitting a computer key, Congress should take this opportunity to set up an international clearinghouse to monitor such transactions.[27]

Given the positions of the key Republican committee chairs in Congress, the administration could be sure that further deregulation of the financial services industry would be forthcoming, the Barings debacle notwithstanding. It was only a matter of the precise form and scope of the legislation that would pass that was in question. While the president vetoed the first effort to get further banking deregulation later in the summer, it was clear that the question was a disagreement as to how much and what kind of deregulation rather than whether there would be deregulation at all. That would come later in the administration. The administration also came back to the Congress in June with a proposal to reduce pension regulations, particularly those affecting small businesses.

In the meantime, Congress passed and the president signed the much-heralded Unfunded Mandates Reform Act, Public Law 104-4, soon to be followed by the Paperwork Reduction Act of 1995 (PRA), Public Law 104-13. The PRA had been languishing for years because of a clash that grew out of the refusal by the George H. W. Bush administration to agree to stop off-the-record, backdoor communications that went around regulatory agencies to the Office of Information and Regulatory Affairs (OIRA) and to the Quayle Council (discussed in Chapter 2). While the Clinton administration had promised to implement safeguards against the kinds of abuses that had previously blocked reauthorization, it remained clear that the OIRA would be a focal point within the Executive Office of the President for monitoring compliance with a range of policies, imposed by both the president through executive orders and memoranda and by Congress working with the administration, that sought to control and limit the issuance of new agency regulations. Both the PRA and the Unfunded Mandates Reform Act aimed to advance those efforts.

The president ended the year by signing legislation that finally disposed of the Interstate Commerce Commission, a process that had actually begun under the Carter administration, providing at least a partial answer to Herbert Kaufman's famous question, "Are Government Organizations Immortal?"[28] There is no small irony in the fact that the venerable independent regulatory commission came under a deadly attack during one Democratic administration and was ultimately vanquished under another. As the *New York Times* put it in issuing the obituary on the agency, even though "the commission survived innumerable assassination attempts, . . . President Clinton signed the commission's death warrant on Friday night."[29]

It was clear, as the administration prepared to run its reelection campaign, that the battle for deregulation would continue in 1996 and beyond, with the foe plainly in sight and badly weakened by protracted attacks over so many years. Even though it was a presidential election year, which often limits the ability to get the kind of agreements needed to move major policies, there would be victories for the administration's deregulation warriors in the legislative and administrative arenas. Many Republican members of Congress, who loved to hate Bill Clinton, were more than happy to share in the limelight of announcements of more victories in the battle for deregulation.

In February, Clinton signed the Telecommunications Act, which passed overwhelmingly in both the House and Senate. The legislation eliminated regulatory restrictions on what had until then been local (or, more accurately, regional) telephone companies in their ability to offer long-distance services and similar restrictions on national long-distance providers in local phone services, limits on the ability of cable companies to enter the telephone market, and the ability of cable and Internet service providers to enter other communications fields.[30] It also reduced some of the restrictions on broadcasting companies as to multiple outlet ownership. While no one was really certain what changes would ultimately result in terms of services, costs, and telecommunications corporation consolidations, with the accompanying financial concentrations and job implications, it was understood that the passage of the bill meant new levels of conflict in the marketplace and, in all likelihood, in the policymaking arena in the future. The telecommunications and financial services deregulations would demonstrate to some policymakers what corporate officers already knew about such changes. The end of regulation is not the end of conflict but the beginning of new rounds of corporate warfare with casualties as well as victorious combatants. Hence, in reporting the signing of the new law, the *New York Times* observed:

> President Clinton today signed a sweeping bill to overhaul the
> telecommunications industry, starting a new round of warfare between the giant
> media and communications companies even before the ink was dry.
>
> Scores of industry executives, from Ted Turner to the chairman of AT&T,
> crowded into the signing ceremony along with politicians of both parties and the
> lobbyists, lawyers and regulators who will be the foot soldiers in the struggles
> ahead.[31]

Like the PRA reauthorization the previous year, the passage of the Small Business Regulatory Enforcement Fairness Act drew little attention, but it was part of an overall effort to ensure that small business saw some benefits from a war on regulation that had already promised to assist larger corporations. It was also a partial victory for congressional Republicans despite the fact that their attempts to pass more dramatic—even draconian—deregulation legislation that would apply across the federal government failed. The unsuccessful proposals from both the House and Senate sides would have made the already cumbersome and difficult rulemaking process all but impossible. Critics of the Republican efforts, like Vermont Senator Patrick Leahy (D), charged:

> First, this legislation claims to be a regulatory reform bill. It is not. It is a
> regulatory policy bill. Unfortunately the policy assumptions of this legislation are
> contrary to both historic and contemporary American values.
>
> Second, it does not make regulation more efficient. It is a "monkey wrench"
> bill that makes better regulations nearly impossible.

Third, this is not a bill that benefits the public or the middle class. The corporate clients of the big Washington law firms and beltway consultants, not the middle class, will be its beneficiaries. They will employ the scientists and attorneys to contest cost/benefit analyses, risk assessments, or file petitions for review of regulations.

Fourth, this bill does not protect the public from government. It is, instead, a profoundly anti-democratic, elitist bill.[32]

The Republicans had just been through a bruising budget battle that would come to be known as the "train wreck." Demands by Gingrich and other congressional leaders that the administration cave in to their policy priorities meant a partial shut-down of the federal government that would result the following year in serious losses for the GOP at the polls. It also meant that when the budget battles were resolved, must-pass bills like the debt limit extension would be vehicles that could effectively carry a host of riders, and they did.

The Small Business Regulatory Enforcement Act was one of these provisions included with the debt limit extension.[33] One of the provisions, entitled the Congressional Review Act (CRA), provided an opportunity for the rejection of regulations proposed by administrative agencies.[34] A replacement for previous types of legislative veto devices with which the Congress could strike down proposed rules which had been rejected by the federal courts,[35] the CRA provided a process by which both houses of Congress could adopt a joint resolution, with the participation of the president, that would block a proposed regulation.

Other provisions amended the Regulatory Flexibility Act (discussed earlier with respect to the Carter administration). The legislation called for "regulatory compliance simplification" and "regulatory enforcement reforms." It also amended the Equal Access to Justice Act. Under the 1996 legislation, courts could review more of the information developed during the regulatory analysis and review processes that were part of the rulemaking process. As to enforcement, the legislation called for greater agency consideration of compliance burdens and costs incurred in enforcement proceedings. Even a firm that lost its case in a regulatory proceeding could recover its litigation expenses in a case in which the final decision resulted in an excessive difference between the penalty originally demanded by federal regulators and the final sanction imposed after adjudication.[36]

As noted above, 1996 was a presidential election year, and, in addition to the challenges of the campaigns, there were two other major constraints on the deregulation efforts. First, starting in 1995, the Food and Drug Administration (FDA) administrator had issued proposed regulations that would bar tobacco advertising directed at children following disclosures of intentional efforts by the tobacco companies to entice more young people to smoke and to increase the urge of existing smokers by increasing the nicotine content of cigarettes.[37] The fact that whistleblowers from within the industry provided damning documents that supported the charges meant that ardent deregulators were temporarily quieted. Final rules were issued by the FDA in the summer of 1996.[38]

Another major challenge to deregulation came in the wake of a deadly crash of a ValuJet flight in the Florida Everglades that killed 110 people. ValuJet was one of a number of low-cost start-up airlines launched after deregulation. There were charges that, because of lax regulation by the FAA, ValuJet and others were not really fully developed airlines, but systems of rented planes and contracted operations with low-salaried crews. The FAA inspector general, Mary Schiavo, resigned. She had previously complained to Congress that the FAA was in a fundamental conflict of interest because, while its primary role was to ensure airline safety, it had in fact been under continuing pressure to support deregulation and the start-up airlines created in its wake.[39]

The deregulatory forces were on the defensive for a time, but that would not last. ValuJet would resurface under a different name, and the Supreme Court overturned the FDA tobacco regulation.[40] The forces of deregulation regrouped and both reinvigorated old offensives and opened new avenues of attack. The continuing items on the agenda were the financial services deregulation announced early in the administration and the issue of ocean shipping deregulation, the last of transportation deregulation packages. Then there was the new front that the administration was about to engage, the battle to deregulate utilities.

In March and April 1998, the Clinton administration pressed those in Congress to move legislation for the deregulation of the electric utility industry out of Capitol Hill where the effort had stalled. A number of states had already adopted deregulation legislation, but the idea of transitioning to a retail market in electricity was a complicated undertaking. Like banking, the deregulation of electric utilities sales involved a transformation from an infrastructure enterprise into a commodity-selling activity. It also represented a move from the idea that some businesses, though privately owned, are "clothed with the public interest" and therefore necessarily regulated in the public interest to ensure stable provision of essential services at reasonably controlled prices.[41] Clearly, many of the electricity providers were anxious to have access to a market worth more than $200 billion per year and to have as much uniformity and as few barriers across the states as possible. The states, on the other hand, had traditionally regulated the rates and electricity delivery within their jurisdictions through public utilities commissions, one of the oldest forms of regulatory agency.[42] Within the states, the idea was greeted with mixed reviews, including concerns by environmentalists that reduction of regulatory controls and increasing market competition would lead to the likelihood of cheap power production, using methods not likely to be sensitive to environmental concerns. Thus, David Hawkins of the Natural Resources Defense Council told reporters that the Clinton proposal "fails to deliver on the President's promise to make a significant down payment on reducing greenhouse gas emissions and other air pollutants."[43]

While that debate was pending, the president signed the Ocean Shipping Reform Act, legislation developed in a Senate commerce subcommittee chaired by Kay Bailey Hutchison (R-Tex.), which deregulated portions of maritime shipping and its relationship to other carriers.

The following year, 1999, was an important time in the battle against regulation, and the Clinton administration continued in the thick of the fight, even with all of the other difficulties the president was having, and notwithstanding the partisan divide between congressional Republicans and the White House. First, one of the impacts of the 1996 telecommunications deregulation was an end to most controls on cable television rates as of the end of March 1999. That was not a small matter, given the importance of cable as a medium of news and information, because cable providers were positioning themselves with respect to Internet services and eventually to telephone operations, and in light of the fact that previous efforts to eliminate regulation had led to reimposition of controls. Second, the Clinton administration and Congress reached the long-anticipated agreement on a deregulation bill for financial services that had been a priority for so long at both ends of the avenue. The deregulation became law with the enactment in November of the Gramm-Leach-Bliley Act, "An Act to enhance competition in the financial services industry by providing a prudential framework for the affiliation of banks, securities firms, insurance companies, and other financial service providers."[44] After many attempts over the years, the key restrictions imposed by the Glass-Steagall Act of 1933 and the Bank Holding Company Act of 1956 on combinations across the range of financial services were gone.

While it was engaged in the legislative attack, the administration was also battling on the international front.[45] Notwithstanding administration assurances about such factors as the sidebar agreement on environmental issues developed during negotiations over NAFTA, it was plain to virtually all who were involved in the issues that NAFTA and the GATT, which became major features of the Clinton foreign and economic policy, would result in pressures for further deregulation at home and abroad. Beyond that Clinton met with numerous international leaders, with particular emphasis on the Japanese, to open markets to free and unrestricted trade. That meant, among other things, elimination of a variety of regulations abroad, and by extension in the United States.

The Clinton/Gore Reinventing Government Campaign: Administrative Attacks on Regulations and Regulatory Programs.—While the Clinton administration waged its ongoing legislative campaign for deregulation, it also took action on the administrative front. The fact that it did so came as a surprise to many, both those inside the federal government and those outside it who had voted for candidates who had promised a rejection of the Reagan- and Bush-era approaches to reduction of government characterized by an uncompromising commitment to deregulation. Clinton and Gore had run on a "putting people first" platform that had criticized their predecessors' attacks on government and, in particular, on regulation.[46] However, as Stiglitz explained: "The New Democrats wanted to differentiate themselves from the Old Democrats who were seen as pro-regulation and anti-business. They wanted to wear their pro-business stripes by pushing deregulation still farther than it had gone before. They wanted to show that they too believed that the era of big government was over."[47] Then there was the fact that the administration, in its first years in office, moved to make deficit reduction, reduction in the size of government, and deregulation keys to an economic recovery and what they came to call the new economy.[48] Finally, after the Republicans took control of Congress in 1995, Stiglitz observed, "deregulation became one of the areas in which the New Democrats could join forces with the Old Republicans to show that we had moved beyond gridlock."[49]

While Clinton had the equivalent of George H. W. Bush's generals in the war on regulation on the legislative side, he also had an officer who took as his primary command the administrative battle plans and their execution—Vice President Al Gore. For Gore, the ability to provide a continuing set of announced victories in the battle against bureaucracy and deregulation not only fit his inclinations, it was a seemingly unrivaled opportunity to position himself to run for the presidency when Clinton left the scene.

Many of the operations against regulation on the administrative front under Gore's leadership involved a group of policy initiatives and people organized under the reinventing government rubric known in programmatic terms as the National Performance Review (NPR).[50] In addition to real efforts to press the deregulation agenda, the NPR provided a continuing psychological warfare operation that generated report after report designed to establish and maintain a sense of momentum in the fight. The language was the stuff of wartime propaganda and employed techniques of which any propaganda minister would be proud. Thus, for example, Gore's transmittal of his plan for action in reinventing government concluded by noting that it was a plan that would fight for the Clinton administration's vision of "a government that works for people, cleared of useless bureaucracy and freed from red tape and senseless rules."[51] Of course such simplistic and even trite language was not impressive to sophisticated professionals, but that was not the point of the campaign.

In real terms, the administration's battle for deregulation was a fight against regulations, rulemaking processes, and regulatory enforcement techniques, all of which were captured under the dreaded term "red tape" in the NPR's battle plan issued in the fall of 1993, *From Red Tape to Results: Creating a Government That Works Better and Costs Less.*[52] The rhetoric held that the administration's action was "not pro-regulation, and it is not anti-regulation; it's smart regulation," as then OMB Director Leon Panetta put it in announcing the president's executive order entitled "Eliminating Regulatory Overkill."[53] However, the fact was that the standard of performance for administrative agencies would ultimately be the degree to which they eliminated regulations, measured in terms of numbers of pages eliminated from the *Code of Federal Regulations* (CFR) and the total number of reductions in government employees who administered them.

It was in September 1993 that the White House announced its intention to move "from red tape to results" and rolled out a series of policy recommendations and presidential directives to implement a number of them. In a particularly excessive performance, Clinton and Gore marched across the White

House lawn to meet the press. They were flanked by an honor guard made up of forklifts laden with what were, purportedly, unnecessary regulations—the much-maligned "red tape" that was to be the target of the administration's new campaign. It was the public unveiling of the administration's NPR headed by Gore. The administration simultaneously launched a public relations campaign, sending CD-ROM versions of the event and accompanying materials all over the country. As was true of so many aspects of the administration, the key to understanding their use of the reinventing government initiative is an awareness that, at the heart of its efforts, the Clinton administration consisted to a large extent of one campaign after another.

The reinventing government idea was based on the book by that name by David Osborne and Ted Gaebler.[54] This book was, in turn, part of an international trend known as the New Public Management.[55] The new public management—and hence the reinventing government effort—emphasized, among other themes, deregulation, downsizing, delayering of organizations, what was termed privatization (but what was really a call for increased contracting out of government operations), reengineering of processes and organizations, and an orientation toward service to customers as compared to accountability to citizens.

While there would need to be some legislative changes to address the NPR recommendations, Gore advised publicly in *From Red Tape to Results* that the president should move quickly, using presidential directives wherever possible to avoid the delays and political constraints of legislation. The use of executive orders, presidential memoranda, and other such devices would also prevent administration change efforts from being drawn into complex rulemaking proceedings.[56] That mode of policymaking suited Clinton well, and the president and vice president immediately announced a number of new directives in the form of executive orders and presidential memoranda.

The first such order, announced at the NPR roll-out, was Executive Order 12861, mandating "Elimination of One-Half of Executive Branch Internal Regulations."[57] Like the 100,000-job reduction number, there was no real justification for the choice of "one-half" except for the political rationale. Searching out and eliminating or changing thousands of regulations was a task requiring considerable resources, far more real and complex than the simplistic political rhetoric would suggest.

In addition, Executive Order 12862, also issued on September 11, required agencies to develop "customer service standards." They were to

(a) identify the customers who are, or should be, served by the agency;

(b) survey customers to determine the kind and quality of services they want and their level of satisfaction with existing services;

(c) post service standards and measure results against them;

(d) benchmark customer service performance against the best in business;

(e) survey front-line employees on barriers to, and ideas for, matching the best in business;

(f) provide customers with choices in both the sources of service and the means of delivery;

(g) make information, services, and complaint systems easily accessible; and

(h) provide means to address customer complaints.[58]

In addition, within six months the agencies were to report on "customer service surveys" and within a year to produce a "customer service plan" based on benchmarking against the "best in the business." For obvious reasons, these requirements posed particular challenges for regulatory agencies.

Next, at the end of September came the Clinton administration's own version of the regulatory review order, Executive Order 12866.[59] The Clinton/Gore ticket ran against the Reagan/Bush era regulatory orders that imposed burdensome cost/benefit analyses and delays from OMB clearance of rulemaking, but, once in office, the new administration kept the Reagan rulemaking orders in place for an additional eight critical months. When the Clinton-era order finally was issued, it was, in a number of respects, even longer and more complex and burdensome than the Reagan/Bush version. While 12866 contained some limited changes and was accompanied with promises that it would be implemented in a more sensitive manner, the General Accounting Office (GAO, since renamed the Government Accountability Office) later concluded that, "as interpreted and administered by OIRA, the cost-benefit requirements in EO 12866 are similar to the requirements in the order it replaced."[60] The determination of the administration to constrain rulemaking was clear from the outset of the document. The language is worthy of careful attention.

Section 1. Statement of Regulatory Philosophy and Principles.

(a) The Regulatory Philosophy. Federal agencies should promulgate only such regulations as are required by law, are necessary to interpret the law, or are made necessary by compelling public need, such as material failures of private markets to protect or improve the health and safety of the public, the environment, or the well-being of the American people. In deciding whether and how to regulate, agencies should assess all costs and benefits of available regulatory alternatives, including the alternative of not regulating. Costs and benefits shall be understood to include both quantifiable measures (to the fullest extent that these can be usefully estimated) and qualitative measures of costs and benefits that are difficult to quantify, but nevertheless essential to consider. Further, in choosing among alternative regulatory approaches, agencies should select those approaches that maximize net benefits (including potential economic, environmental, public health and safety, and other advantages, distributive impacts; and equity), unless a statute requires another regulatory approach.

(b) The Principles of Regulation. To ensure that the agencies' regulatory programs are consistent with the philosophy set forth above, agencies should adhere to the following principles, to the extent permitted by law and where applicable.

(1) Each agency shall identify the problem that it intends to address (including, where applicable, the failures of private markets or public institutions that warrant new agency action) as well as assess the significance of that problem.

(2) Each agency shall examine whether existing regulations (or other law) have created, or contributed to, the problem that a new regulation is intended to correct and whether those regulations (or other law) should be modified to achieve the intended goal of regulating more effectively.

(3) Each agency shall identify and assess available alternatives to direct regulation, including providing economic incentives to encourage the desired behavior, such as user fees or marketable permits, or providing information upon which choices can be made by the public.

(4) In setting regulatory priorities, each agency shall consider, to the extent reasonable, the degree and nature of the risks posed by various substances or activities within its jurisdiction.

(5) When an agency determines that a regulation is the best available method of achieving the regulatory objective, it shall design its regulations in the most cost-effective manner to achieve the regulatory objectives. In doing so, each agency shall consider incentives for innovation, consistency, predictability, the costs of enforcement and compliance (to the government, regulated entities, and the public), flexibility, distributive impacts, and equity.

(6) Each agency shall assess both the costs and the benefits of the intended regulation and, recognizing that some costs and benefits are difficult to quantify, propose or adopt a regulation only upon a reasoned determination that the benefits of the intended regulation justify its costs.

(7) Each agency shall base its decisions on the best reasonably obtainable scientific, technical, economic, and other information concerning the need for, and consequences of, the intended regulation.

(8) Each agency shall identify and assess alternative forms of regulation and shall, to the extent feasible, specify performance objectives, rather than

specifying the behavior or manner of compliance that regulated entities must adopt.

(9) Wherever feasible, agencies shall seek views of appropriate State, local, and tribal officials before imposing regulatory requirements that might significantly or uniquely affect those governmental entities. Each agency shall assess the effects of Federal regulations on State, local, and tribal governments, including specifically the availability of resources to carry out those mandates, and seek to minimize those burdens that uniquely or significantly affect such governmental entities, consistent with achieving regulatory objectives. In addition, as appropriate, agencies shall seek to harmonize Federal regulatory actions with related State, local, and tribal regulatory and other governmental functions.

(10) Each agency shall avoid regulations that are inconsistent, incompatible, or duplicative with its other regulations or those of other Federal agencies.

(11) Each agency shall tailor its regulations to impose the least burden on society, including individuals, businesses of differing sizes, and other entities (including small communities and governmental entities), consistent with obtaining the regulatory objectives, taking into account, among other things, and to the extent practicable, the costs of cumulative regulations.

(12) Each agency shall draft its regulations to be simple and easy to understand, with the goal of minimizing the potential for uncertainty and litigation arising from such uncertainty.

The remainder of the order included a variety of reporting and process requirements that were even more detailed than before, including, for example, the call for risk assessments. Section 1 (b)(4) of the order required that: "In setting regulatory priorities, each agency shall consider, to the extent reasonable, the degree and nature of the risks posed by various substances or activities within its jurisdiction." Section 4 (c)(1)(D) also mandated "a statement of the need for each such action and, if applicable, how the action will reduce risks to public health, safety, or the environment, as well as how the magnitude of the risk addressed by the action relates to other risks within the jurisdiction of the agency." Risk assessment is a complex and often controversial enterprise (about which more will be said later) and one that was rapidly evolving during the years of the Clinton administration.[61] The assessment task mandated by the order was equally complex and difficult. Apart from methodological considerations, difficulties arose from the fact that Congress often mandated the issuance of administrative rules after having made its own decisions about risks and benefits based on political judgments and public opinion as well as on technical information offered to subcommittees and committee staff by interest groups and administrative agencies. The administration could not unilaterally change those mandates, and regulatory agencies were subject to suit under the Administrative Procedure Act (APA) for failure to comply with statutory requirements.[62]

Whatever the specifics of the executive orders, the message was clear that rules were to be avoided and that agencies that persisted in issuing them would bear a heavy burden of proof and of supporting work to generate that case. While the workload was clearly going to increase, the resources would just as plainly decrease. Administrative agencies were ordered to reduce their budget requests significantly. The NPR called for far larger personnel reductions than the president's original 100,000 figure. The new requirement would be for 252,000 jobs and that would grow to more than 300,000 by the second Clinton administration.

Even before the NPR had reported on its plan of attack, the administration was moving to blunt existing regulatory policy. Thus, in late February 1993, the administration announced its intentions to work with the Federal Reserve to trim some of the restrictions on bank loan rules imposed after the savings and loan crisis of the 1980s. The goal was to permit lenders to avoid strict requirements for collateral or credit history and to lend on the basis of the character of the borrower. This was done on the theory that there had been an overreaction to the savings and loan crisis of the 1980s and that the tendency of lenders to be conservative with respect to credit requirements was making the economic recovery slower than it would otherwise be. At the time, there were warnings by people like Charles A. Bowsher, then Comptroller of the Currency and head of the GAO, that it had been loose lending practices that had contributed to the earlier crisis and that loosening them once again could lead to similar results.[63] Of course, just as earlier efforts to relax lending rules led to the savings and loan crisis in the first instance, this and other efforts to ease loan requirements would later lead to the so-called sub-prime lending debacle and credit crunch of 2007 and 2008.

In early 1995, as President Clinton sought to make common cause with Republicans who had won control of Congress in continuing the fight against regulation, Gore issued a Vice Presidential Memorandum that announced Phase 2 of the NPR.

The President has announced his proposal for a Middle Class Bill of Rights to help the American people restore the American dream. As part of this effort, he has asked me to lead a second phase of the National Performance Review. This review will examine the basic missions of government, looking at every single government program and agency to find and eliminate things that don't need to be done by the federal government. It will also sort out how best to do the things government should continue to do.

Phase 2 of NPR will also review the federal regulatory process to find a way to get better results for the public with less interference in their lives.[64]

Gore's announcement was followed by memoranda issued by President Clinton, mandating that agencies do a better job of eliminating rules because "not all agencies have taken the steps necessary to implement regulatory reform."

Accordingly, I direct you to focus on the following four steps, which are an integral part of our ongoing Regulatory Reform Initiative.
FIRST: CUT OBSOLETE REGULATIONS. I direct you to conduct a page-by-page review of all of your agency regulations now in force and eliminate or revise those that are outdated or otherwise in need of reform. Your review should include careful consideration of at least the following issues:
• Is this regulation obsolete?
• Could its intended goal be achieved in more efficient, less intrusive ways?
• Are there better private sector alternatives, such as market mechanisms, that can better achieve the public good envisioned by the regulation?
• Could private business, setting its own standards and being subject to public accountability, do the job as well?
• Could the States or local governments do the job, making Federal regulation unnecessary? . . .
I further direct you to deliver to me by June 1 a list of regulations that you plan to eliminate or modify with a copy of the report sent to Sally Katzen, Administrator of the Office of Information and Regulatory Affairs (OIRA). . . .
SECOND: REWARD RESULTS, NOT RED TAPE. I direct you to change the way you measure the performance of both your agency and your frontline regulators so as to focus on results, not process and punishment. For example, Occupational Safety and Health Administration (OSHA) inspectors should not be evaluated by the number of citations they write, nor should officials of the Consumer Product Safety Commission be judged by the number of boxes of consumer goods that are detained in shipment. . . .
By no later than June 1, I direct you to (a) eliminate all internal personnel performance measures based on process (number of visits made, etc.) and

punishment (number of violations found, amount of fines levied, etc.), and (b) provide to the National Performance Review (NPR) staff a catalogue of the changes that you are making in existing internal performance evaluations to reward employees. You should also provide material describing shifts in resource allocation from enforcement to compliance.

THIRD: GET OUT OF WASHINGTON AND CREATE GRASSROOTS PARTNERSHIPS. I direct you to promptly convene groups consisting of frontline regulators and the people affected by their regulations. These conversations should take place around the country—at our cleanup sites, our factories, our ports.

I further direct you to submit a schedule of your planned meetings to the NPR staff by March 30 and work with NPR in following through on those meetings.

FOURTH: NEGOTIATE, DON'T DICTATE. . . . I now direct you to expand substantially your efforts to promote consensual rulemaking. To this end, you should submit to OIRA, no later than March 30, a list of upcoming rulemakings that can be converted into negotiated rulemakings. I have directed Sally Katzen to review your lists with a view toward making clear to the regulated community that we want to work together productively on even the most difficult subjects.

To facilitate our ability to learn from those affected by regulation, I will amend Executive Order No. 12838 (which requires agencies to reduce the number of advisory committees that they use and to limit the future use of such committees) to allow for advisory committees established for negotiated rulemakings.

I also . . . direct you to review all of your administrative ex parte rules and eliminate any that restrict communication prior to the publication of a proposed rule—other than rules requiring the simple disclosure of the time, place, purpose, and participants of meetings (as in Executive Order No. 12866). We will also begin drafting legislation that will carve out exemptions to the Federal Advisory Committee Act to promote a better understanding of the issues, such as exemptions for meetings with State/local/tribal governments and with scientific or technical advisors.

I also ask you to think about other ways to promote better communication, consensus building, and a less adversarial environment. . . .

As I said on Tuesday, February 21, 1995, you are to make regulatory reform a top priority.[65]

The administration wanted reports of elimination of rules prior to a June 12, 1995, White House Conference on Small Business so that the White House could report to those assembled that: "the page-by-page review effort had resulted in commitments to eliminate 16,000 pages of regulations from the 140,000 page Code of Federal Regulations (CFR), and another 31,000 pages would be modified either through administrative or legislative means."[66]

Members of Congress then tasked GAO with determining whether the administration was following through on those promises. However, in its report to Congress, GAO pointed out that merely counting the number of pages of the CFR that have been eliminated tells one very little about what has really changed. After all, the report said, one must "recognize that one sentence of a regulation can impose more burden than 100 pages of regulations that are administrative in nature." However, GAO noted, that benchmark of pages eliminated was how the administration had decided to measure progress.[67]

The fact is that the administration had already been aggressive and unrelenting in its attacks on regulation. However, Senator Robert Dole (R-Kans.), then majority leader in the upper house, was not far wrong when he charged that President Clinton was "trying to have it both ways."[68] The administration was working to demonstrate that it was effective and committed to deregulation while simultaneously claiming that it was aggressively pursuing important regulatory policy goals. But Clinton and Gore continued on what one might call the policy campaign trail, repeatedly insisting that government be smaller, and that included regulation. That, said the president, is "why we've worked hard at deregulation."[69]

Also during this period, the administration announced its intention to move from regulation to an emphasis on the use of tradeable emissions permits in the area of air pollution policy. Additionally, the FDA announced plans to streamline and speed up the processes for approval of new medicines and for medical devices.[70] Also at the same time, the Occupational Safety and Health Administration (OSHA) backed off efforts to press for new ergonomic standards in the workplace, standards that would not ultimately be issued until the Clinton administration was leaving office, only to be rejected in the first use of the Congressional Review Act during the early days of the George W. Bush administration. There were pressures from both sides to back off on this regulatory effort, since, in addition to a lack of desire to incur political costs from the administration side, there was the fact that Congress had moved to block the use of funds to create the rules.[71]

It was telling when the OIRA, the administration's central regulatory review office, issued a memorandum in January 1996 announcing new guidance on how regulatory agencies were to perform regulatory analyses under Executive Order 12866. Unlike the earlier document that it replaced, entitled "Regulatory Impact Analysis Guidance," the new explanation as to how regulatory analysis was to be done was called "Economic Analysis of Federal Regulations."

The rewrite of the policy was led not by OIRA officials but by Joseph Stiglitz, then chair of the Council of Economic Advisors. It was clear that economists were in charge of regulatory policy, a trend that began with the Carter administration. The burdens added to an agency's rulemaking processes by this document, when coupled with the executive order itself, were significant—not so much in terms of the quantity of material, although the burdens of proof required to meet these so-called best practices did suggest more in the way of quantity, but also the qualitative enhancement of the kinds of evidence and level of analysis required. Again, the message was quite clear that agencies ought to avoid regulation unless they were prepared to engage an extremely complex and resource-intensive process within their own administration, quite apart from the complexities already mandated by statute.

Preemption Attack: Constraints on State Efforts
to Go beyond Federal Regulatory Standards
Another of the areas in which the Clinton administration found criticism for talking one way and governing another with respect to regulation was in the area of federal efforts not only to attack national regulations but also to block state efforts to substitute local regulations in important fields or to provide standards more rigorous than the federal government in policy domains that states saw as important to traditional federalism concerns. President Clinton, like Presidents Reagan and Carter before him, had run as a governor against the Washington establishment. Even so, Clinton was quite prepared not only to pursue the battle against regulation in the federal government, but also to employ the substantial weapon of federal preemption to block state regulatory efforts as well.

The administration was well aware that it was not only moving in fields that had long been the province of the federal government, but also in policy domains that had historically been arenas of state action. Thus, when the administration supported further trucking deregulation, as explained above, it was moving primarily to block state regulation in that area, federal controls having previously been eliminated. Similarly, when the administration moved on banking and public utility deregulation, it plainly was seeking to bring deregulation in settings that had traditionally been dominated by state regulation.

Apart from these general constraints, the administration took more targeted and specific actions as well. Hence, when the State of Washington moved to supplement federal regulation of oil tankers operating in the Puget Sound,

the administration challenged the state. The state had acted on the basis of repeated problems and considerable evidence that the federal government was
not prepared to deploy the resources needed to prevent pollution from tankers
operating in the unique setting of the Puget Sound with its many islands, complex currents, and sensitive ecology. Neither the international agreements or
the federal government's regulatory regime were adequate to the situation. The
state looked back as far as 1852 when the U.S. Supreme Court had ruled that
states could impose some regulation—even when it had an effect on interstate
commerce—where unique circumstances raised special local concerns. That
case had concerned requirements that vessels entering the Port of Philadelphia
were required to use local pilots to bring the vessels to port.[72] In the Washington case, international tanker operators brought suit in federal court against
the state regulations,[73] and U.S. trading partners called on the Clinton administration to take the lead against the state.[74] The Clinton administration took
the case to the U.S. Supreme Court, which struck down the Washington state
action on grounds that the state's action was preempted by federal policy.[75]

Similarly, the administration moved against the Commonwealth of Massachusetts when the state sought to avoid doing business with any would-be
contractor that also did business with Myanmar, which the United States and
other countries refer to by its historic name of Burma. In this case, the claim
was that the state was a participant in the marketplace and could therefore determine whether and with whom it wished to contract. Once again, the Clinton administration moved against the state and the Supreme Court ultimately
struck down the Massachusetts policy.[76]

More generally, states were frustrated that the administration was saying
on the one hand that it was sensitive to states and concerned about federal
mandates and limitations but, on the other, was acting quite differently. Thus,
when the president issued an executive order on federalism, there was a flurry
of protest.[77] The reaction came because although the order called for consul-
tations and awareness of state concerns, it also included a list of situations in
which agencies could preempt the states. As a result, the administration was
quickly forced to suspend the order.[78]

Unilateral Disarmament: Administration Pressures
to Avoid Aggressive Enforcement
The administration did not limit its action only to rules and rulemaking processes, but went after enforcement as well, and not only by indirect methods,

but also by direct action. It goes without saying that regulatory statutes or administrative regulations without a willingness to enforce them actively, and often aggressively, meant that regulation would exist in name only. The move away from aggressive enforcement had less obvious but equally important impacts in other ways as well. The evidence was clear that effective negotiated corrections of regulatory violations were contingent on the belief by responsible parties that the federal government would not hesitate to invoke aggressive, formal, and potentially very costly enforcement actions if they did not settle the matter voluntarily.[79]

The Clinton administration made it clear from the earliest reports of the NPR that it would move away from aggressive enforcement and pushed agencies to "negotiate, don't dictate," to do so on a case-by-case basis, to discourage aggressive enforcement performance, to take a cooperative approach to enforcement with the regulated parties and even to interventions in particular regulatory actions. The NPR, EO 12866 on regulatory process, and the president's memorandum on regulatory reinvention also particularly called for an increase in the use of Alternative Dispute Resolution (ADR) techniques instead of aggressive enforcement techniques.[80] Similarly, the president's memorandum demanded that agencies shift to what is known as negotiated rulemaking whenever possible.[81]

There was nothing new about the use of ADR techniques when the Clinton administration came to office. In fact, the Administrative Dispute Resolution Act that formally encouraged the expanded use of ADR had been enacted in 1990.[82] Agencies had been using negotiated settlements for decades before that to address regulatory compliance issues. While the field of ADR continued to develop new or modified techniques, the basic concept that agencies would try initially to bring regulated parties back into compliance with regulatory requirements through some kind of alternative to litigation was a standard enforcement technique. However, many regulatory statutes call for a variety of enforcement techniques, such as inspections, and call for various types of sanctions where violations are found. Additionally, and even ironically, as deregulation took hold such that fares and rates were more subject to market forces and not protected by regulatory rate-setting, there were more incentives for regulated firms to push the envelope to reduce costs and less incentive to resolve violations quickly and informally. In fact, the message that was being sent was that regulatory agencies would likely have little support from higher-level officials in the administration, which also encouraged some degree of resistance to informal compliance resolutions. In fact, in March 1995 President Clinton ordered executive branch agencies to "eliminate all internal personnel performance measures based on process (number of visits made, etc.) and punishment (number of violations found, amount of fines levied, etc.)." They were also to provide to the NPR staff evidence of "shifts in resource allocation from enforcement to compliance."[83]

Similarly, as indicated above, the White House directed the regulatory agencies to move whenever possible to negotiated rulemaking instead of the standard rulemaking process. Negotiated rulemaking attempts to reduce conflict by crafting proposed rules through a committee made up of interested parties who enter into a facilitated negotiation process in which the agency is but one of the parties. The object is for those involved to reach consensus on a proposed rule that will then go through the remainder of the notice and comment process. That requires a process by which a group of twenty to twenty-five people will come to the table, usually in Washington, over a number of negotiation sessions to reach agreement. The process works best in cases where there is a very focused problem for which the relevant interested parties are few enough and easy enough to identify that it is possible to both ensure reasonable levels of participation without the appearance or the reality of action that nullifies the purpose of the regulatory policy at issue or seems to have the regulated parties exercising undue control over the agency that is supposed to regulate them.

Because of these dangers, the Congress warned, even as it enacted the Negotiated Rulemaking Act (also enacted before the Clinton administration),[84] that the process should only be used under certain conditions and that agencies should be free to determine for themselves, based upon their expertise and experience, whether and when such a process should be employed.[85] That decision, Congress said, would not be subject to judicial review.[86] Indeed, even the most ardent advocates of negotiated rulemaking recognized that it was a tool to be used in limited circumstances that provided the appropriate issue, context, and parties.[87] The Clinton administration, however, made it clear that it was going to mandate reduction in regular processes, rulemaking or adjudication, and expand use of alternatives.

The administration was pressing its position that government, including regulators, should be in "partnership" with business, including regulated firms. However, in addition to the issues with that approach noted above, Congress itself had recognized when it adopted the ADR Act that there are a variety of circumstances under which such alternative techniques should not be used.

An agency shall consider not using a dispute resolution proceeding if—

(1) a definitive or authoritative resolution of the matter is required for precedential value, and such a proceeding is not likely to be accepted generally as an authoritative precedent;

(2) the matter involves or may bear upon significant questions of Government policy that require additional procedures before a final resolution may be made, and such a proceeding would not likely serve to develop a recommended policy for the agency;

(3) maintaining established policies is of special importance, so that variations among individual decisions are not increased and such a proceeding would not likely reach consistent results among individual decisions;

(4) the matter significantly affects persons or organizations who are not parties to the proceeding;

(5) a full public record of the proceeding is important, and a dispute resolution proceeding cannot provide such a record; and

(6) the agency must maintain continuing jurisdiction over the matter with authority to alter the disposition of the matter in the light of changed circumstances, and a dispute resolution proceeding would interfere with the agency's fulfilling that requirement.[88]

In addition, the administration vied with Congress for bragging rights about who was more active in reducing enforcement burdens on small businesses. Among the areas in which Gore and other Clinton administration officials pressed for constraints on regulatory enforcement was in the area of small business compliance and response to violations. It was intuitively extremely attractive for the administration to stand ready to defend small business owners against the administration's own regulatory agencies. There are thousands of such businesses and they have a commercial appeal roughly equivalent to the political attractiveness of the family farm. Moreover, it was true that some legislators, executive branch policymakers, and regulatory agency officials had been insensitive to the fact that regulatory requirements developed with large corporations in mind could be particularly burdensome and onerous for small businesses. Thus, Gore announced that "the President authorized regulatory agencies to waive up to 100 percent of punitive fines on a small business if it corrects the violation within an appropriate time and/or offer the small business an opportunity to avoid punitive action by applying any fine levied towards correcting the violation leading to the fine. He also instructed agencies to cut in half the frequency of many regulatory reports required by the federal government."[89]

That said, it can also be the case that small businesses can pose serious dangers in a variety of regulatory areas precisely because they lack the capacity and size to maintain adequate environmental, health, or safety programs and may not do the kind of self-policing that some larger firms do to avoid difficulties with regulators or lawsuits that could be expected from consumers or employees. And since such businesses often run close to the margin financially and may assume that they are unlikely to be the subject of enforcement actions, their managers may sometimes be tempted to take actions that were precisely the kind of situations that regulatory policies were designed to deter, or punish if they could not be deterred. That is particularly true where, as in the program announced by Gore and Clinton, those who are cited for violations can either have fines waived or can put those same funds back into their firm in new equipment or operations that also correct the violation. Similar programs had been tried elsewhere with negative results, as in the People's Republic of China, where it was determined that they created perverse incentives because those firms caught suffered virtually no significant penalty and actually received resources and support when they eventually had to correct a problem.[90]

Both Congress and the Clinton administration competed for leadership in constraining regulatory enforcement actions on small business. Their efforts included passage of the Small Business Regulatory Enforcement Fairness Act and also administrative constraints on enforcement by regulatory agencies. Whatever their espoused purposes, these moves supported the regulated against the regulators.

In some cases, the administrative pressure was quite direct as in an intervention by Vice President Gore in EPA policymaking with respect to the process by which the agency was about to assess pesticide risks for children, beginning with evaluation of organophosphates. Gore responded to both the chemical manufacturers and to agricultural lobbies, though the administration tried to defend the effort publicly as an attempt to address opposition to the Food Quality Protection Act (FQPA), legislation that required these assessments which was enacted in 1996.[91] Gore's memorandum to EPA Administrator Carol Browner read in part:

> On behalf of President Clinton and in accordance with my responsibility for implementation of Executive Order 12866 (Sep. 30, 1993), I am requesting that the

EPA Administrator and the Secretary of Agriculture work together to ensure that implementation of the paramount public health goals of the new law is informed by a sound regulatory approach, by the expertise of the Department of Agriculture (USDA), by appropriate input from affected members of the public, and by due regard for the needs of our Nation's agricultural producers.[92]

While Gore denied attempting to weaken the law, it was clear that the administration was conditioning an environmental health and safety evaluation on the cooperation of the Department of Agriculture. That department was committed to advance agricultural interests and was clearly subject to pressure from agricultural chemical producers and distributors. Industry had lobbied the EPA directly and press reports indicated that Gore was contacted about the matter by Representative Charles W. Stenholm (D-Tex.), who was at the time the ranking member of the House Agriculture Committee.[93] Dr. Philip Landrigan, director of environmental medicine at the Mount Sinai School of Medicine, characterized the situation by observing that "I think it is fair to say that the battle is really well and truly joined."[94] The language of the memorandum suggested which forces were emerging victorious from this particular battle and what messages were being conveyed in the process:

1. Within 14 days, EPA should consult with USDA and establish a mechanism for seeking advice and consultation from affected user, producer, consumer, public health, environmental, and other interested groups, following consultation with the Council on Environmental Quality (CEQ). Representation also should reflect the diversity of interests within and among affected user groups. USDA should participate fully in this process. All facets of FQPA implementation shall include appropriate input from state and local agencies, Tribal governments, Members of Congress, and the public.

2. At appropriate points in the regulatory process, EPA and USDA should consult directly with relevant offices of the Office of Management and Budget and the Food and Drug Administration, as well as any other Federal agencies or departments that may have data or experience relevant to FQPA implementation.

3. The Office of the Secretary of Agriculture should enhance its role in coordinating USDA's pest management policy. The Office of the Secretary should provide all appropriate support to implementation of the FQPA and this memorandum.[95]

Indirect Weapons: The Continuation of the War of Attrition

The many additional requirements placed on regulatory agencies as well as the resources consumed in responding to internal administration requirements represented a major burden-loading attack on regulation to go along with the direct legislative and administrative offensives. It was ironic that the administration began by promising to do away with half the internal regulations of the federal government only to order a host of new ones by executive order and presidential and vice presidential memorandum. All of these challenges would have been difficult enough if resources had been forthcoming to address them, but precisely the reverse was true. The administration engaged a dramatic and sustained strategic resources attack and made antipersonnel attacks a centerpiece of reinventing government.

The administration had made budget cutting and reduction in the size of government priorities from the beginning. The president and his vice president embraced this agenda throughout the remaining years of the administration. In submitting his budget for fiscal year 1996, President Clinton wrote:

> Working with Congress in 1993, we enacted the largest deficit reduction package in history. We cut Federal spending by $255 billion over five years. . . . Now that we have brought the deficit down, we have no intention of turning back. My budget keeps us on the course of fiscal discipline by proposing $81 billion in additional deficit reduction through the year 2000. I am proposing to save $23 billion by reinventing three Cabinet departments and two other major agencies, to save $2 billion by ending more than 130 programs altogether, and to provide better service to Americans by consolidating more than 270 other programs. Under my plan, the deficit will continue to fall as a percentage of GDP to 2.1 percent, reaching its lowest level since 1979.[96]

And, indeed, the administration did not let up. At the end of the administration, the leading claims to accomplishments on the domestic side by both President Clinton and then candidate Al Gore were cutting the budget and reducing the number of employees in the federal government. These actions, plus tax cuts and deregulation, had, they claimed, resulted in a dramatic economic turnaround. Indeed, in submitting his last budget in early 2000, Clinton said: "We have streamlined Government, cutting the civilian Federal work force by 377,000, giving us the smallest work force in 39 years."[97]

The increased challenges and workload facing professionals in the regulatory agencies would have been challenging in any case, which made the antipersonnel offensive of the Clinton administration that much more effective as an avenue of attack on regulation. What made the assault even more devastating was the fact that these attacks were launched against the ranks of regulatory personnel already hard-hit by the continuous and withering onslaught of administrations as far back as Carter and Reagan. These attacks came both through budget cuts and also through deliberate reductions in force. Additionally, simple demographics were an ally of the antiregulation forces, since the leading edge of the baby boom who had entered public service in the late 1960s was reaching thirty years of service.

The loss of funding was not alone the result of direct budget cuts, but also flat-funding which, as Chapter 1 explained, can have dramatic impacts on the actual effective level of resources in an agency over a number of years, even though the actual number of dollars appears not to have been reduced. That is true even in years of relatively low overall inflation and especially if the particular set of challenges and burdens facing the agency has significantly increased, or if it is operating in a field in which there is increasingly sophisticated technology or levels of complexity. Those conditions were indeed what regulatory agencies were facing during this period. As Stiglitz explained, the sophistication of the accounting, financial services, banking, telecommunications, utility, and other fields was growing just at the time that the federal government was losing both authority and resources with which to address the problems and misconduct in those fields.[98]

By the beginning of Clinton's second term, even the news media were coming to see that a confluence between overt efforts at deregulation in Congress and by internal administrative means, coupled with ongoing budget reductions, had reduced the capacity of regulatory agencies to do their jobs. It was increasingly obvious that agencies as diverse as the EPA, FDA, Consumer Product Safety Commission (CPSC), Federal Communications Commission (FCC), and Securities and Exchange Commission (SEC) were not able to meet many of the regulatory challenges they faced.[99] As the investigations of the ValuJet crash in 1996 got under way, it was also evident that the FAA was one of the agencies that lacked the capacity and perhaps the willingness on the part of its top leadership to meet the many new challenges it faced as deregulation of airlines produced new business models that presented questions about the ability of regulators to ensure passenger safety.[100] Ironically, rapid economic change in various sectors, like the creation of start-up airlines, had presented additional and also novel challenges to regulators in the remaining areas in which they were to regulate.[101]

It is also more than a little ironic that even as the internal attacks on regulation produced dramatic victories, the external attacks did not abate. The attacks came both from New Democrats and traditional Republicans. As private sector executives saw more opportunities in the deregulation that had already been accomplished, they demanded more. Beyond that, weakened agencies were increasingly vulnerable to both political and legal attacks, which were indeed forthcoming.

GEORGE W. BUSH: A NEW LEVEL
OF ATTACK ON REGULATION

Ironically, the Clinton administration's campaign against regulation may not have been seen in later years for what it was (1) because there was a tendency to listen to the rhetoric of the opposition party leaders, including Bush, who were very effective at characterizing him as a liberal, rather than to watch what the administration actually did; (2) because press attention to the scandals of the Clinton administration and the rise of the Republican right overshadowed the story of the administration's deregulation efforts; and last, but certainly not least, (3) because the George W. Bush administration would take dramatic positions against regulation, though they were often not recognized as such early in his administration. Also ironic was the fact that the Bush administration's fight against regulation and others of its domestic policy actions were overwhelmed by the 9/11 attacks and all that came in the wake of those tragic events. While it was busy attacking regulation in a host of policy domains, the administration was asserting dramatic claims to authority to regulate Americans and visitors to the country in ways that, for much of his two terms, took attention away from regulatory issues.

There were other ironies as well for the Bush administration. By the time of his election to office, there was serious evidence that utility deregulation had produced disastrous results, the telecommunications industry was rife with serious abuses, airline services and operations were abysmal, the Internet was increasingly a Wild West that was producing casualties not only among the contemporary market-fighters who knowingly took risks to reap outrageous profits, but also among those who were completely innocent and, indeed, had no idea that so much of their lives and well-being were being put at risk by firms and government agencies using both domestic and off-shore contractors to move information of all types. Then there was the rapidly growing evidence of abuse by corporate executives across a range of important business sectors, with dramatic impacts on equities markets and the rest of the economy that affected millions of Americans and others around the globe. Notwithstanding all of these very public issues, the war against regulation would continue, albeit with a few temporary cease-fire episodes to address dramatic problems and an occasional counterattack against efforts to create new or enhanced regulation to address critical situations.

The Bush Administration was more than ready to continue the attack on regulation, though it did so in ways considerably different from its predecessor and with less public emphasis on the battle. In fact, while Bush had worked diligently during the campaign to build a moderate image, it became clear, once he took office, that his administration would be far more ideologically driven than most observers had anticipated. Indeed, it was soon obvious that George W. Bush saw himself far more as the political and ideological heir of Ronald Reagan than as his father's son. Like Reagan, Bush would push the envelope in pursuit of ideological goals and, in the process, use a variety of weapons, tactics, and even a number of former Reagan administration troops to do so. With respect to the attack on regulation, Bush, like Reagan, would rely heavily on executive branch action and, like him, Bush would make use of techniques and initiatives launched by his Democratic predecessor. As with the Reagan administration, the George W. Bush White House would make effective, even dramatic use of counterstaffing, strategic resources, and antipersonnel attacks. In addition, Bush would enjoy, for much of his administration, a compliant Congress and the ability, when pressed, to use the war on terrorism and to invoke the 9/11 attacks to sweep away, or sometimes simply to dismiss, opposition. There was one additional irony that created more of a defense against the administration's battle against regulation than support for it. The fact was that the success of his predecessors in their fight against regulation, from Carter through Clinton, had contributed to a series of serious problems that compelled the George W. Bush administration to regulate more when it would have preferred to roll back some regulatory activity. Even so, when the immediate public outcry died down, the administration was ready to launch surprisingly effective counterattacks.

Bush in Direct Attack: Aggressive Advocate of the Market and Proud of It

Like Reagan, Bush had inherited an active and effective war against regulation fought by his Democratic predecessor. Indeed, between the work of the Carter and Clinton administrations and their cooperation with Congress, there was little legislative work left to be done with respect to deregulation. Moreover, many of the weapons of administrative attack had already been developed and effectively deployed by the Clinton administration, so that the new president was able to leave some of those devices, like the rulemaking review order, in place for a time. Rather, the focus for the new administration was, initially at least, primarily on other weapons and tactics, but, like the Reagan administration, Bush would use all of those and even invent a few new modes of combat. In the process, his actions were often more significant than his words and, except to those who watched closely, often not recognized for what they were—at least not until the later years of his administration. His direct attacks included administrative devices, counterstaffing, central control and clearance of agency policymaking, constraints on enforcement, and preemption.

The President's Management and Political Agendas

Some parts of the battle plan for the administration became clear in the early years of the administration in documents that received relatively little attention at the time and in Bush's selection of appointees, some of whom did engender public controversy. It must be said that after 9/11, the nation's attention was focused, both in fact and as a matter of deliberate Bush administration design, on global issues, and particularly on the question of international threats.

There were some direct and loudly announced antiregulatory activities, and particularly administrative efforts to block administrative rules issued under Clinton. Like its predecessors, the Bush administration put a moratorium on new rules until its people could get into place in their respective agencies. Immediately upon taking office, the administration, through White House Chief of Staff Andrew Card, issued a memorandum to the heads of executive branch agencies that instructed them as follows:

> 1. Subject to any exceptions the Director or Acting Director of the Office of Management and Budget (the "OMB Director") allows for emergency or other urgent situations relating to health and safety, *send no proposed or final regulation to the Office of the Federal Register (the "OFR") unless and until a department or agency head appointed by the President after noon on January 20, 2001, reviews and approves the regulatory action.* The department or agency head may delegate this power of review and approval to any other person so appointed by the President, consistent with applicable law.

> 2. *With respect to regulations that have been sent to the OFR but not published in the Federal Register, withdraw them from OFR* for review and approval as

described in paragraph 1, subject to exception as described in paragraph 1. This withdrawal must be conducted consistent with the OFR procedures.

3. *With respect to regulations that have been published in the OFR but have not taken effect, temporarily postpone the effective date of the regulations for 60 days,* subject to exception as described in paragraph 1. [Emphasis added.]

4. Exclude from the requested actions in paragraphs 1–3 any regulations promulgated pursuant to statutory or judicial deadlines and identify such exclusions to the OMB Director as soon as possible.

5. Notify the OMB Director promptly of any regulations that, in your view, impact critical health and safety functions of the agency and therefore should be also excluded from the directives in paragraphs 1–3. The Director will review any such notifications and determine whether exception is appropriate under the circumstances.

6. Continue in all instances to comply with Executive Order 12866, pending our review of that order, as well as any other applicable Executive Orders concerning regulatory management.[102]

In one highly publicized effort to communicate its intentions to battle regulation, the administration joined with Republicans in Congress to make the first use of the Congressional Review Act, adopted during the Clinton years, to strike down the long-delayed ergonomics rules[103] issued by OSHA as the Clinton administration departed.[104]

That said, the more direct statement of the Bush administration's intentions came when Bush issued what was known as "The President's Management Agenda." While phrased in standard business management terminology, there was more at issue than just an effort to enhance governmental performance, a goal sought by virtually all modern administrations of both political parties, including, of course, the reinventing government initiatives of Bush's predecessor. In fact, while the full document was not published by the OMB until later, the administration began implementing the agenda as soon as it took office. Within the administration, the announcement of the new agenda came in a memorandum issued by Andrew Card to agency heads imposing a freeze on government hiring. However, that was but one piece of what was to be the effort to implement the president's management agenda.

The President has asked me to communicate to each of you his plan for managing the Federal employment process at the outset of his Administration. As you know, during the campaign, the President expressed his desire to make

Government more responsive to the needs of citizens, more efficient, and more accountable. The President articulated his view of an effective Federal Government—one that is citizen-centered, results-oriented, and characterized by quality of service. . . .

In order to ensure that, from the start of this Administration, the President's appointees have the opportunity to make personnel decisions consistent with his goals for Government reform, he asks that you institute the hiring control procedures described below.

1. Effective immediately, no decision relating to hiring shall be made unless and until such decision is reviewed and approved by a department or agency head appointed by the President after noon on January 20, 2001. . . . These procedures are subject to such exceptions as the Director or Acting Director of the Office of Management and Budget (the "OMB") may grant as necessary. . . .

2. For the longer term, every agency head will be instructed to develop a plan to permit the agency to meet the President's goal of reducing management ranks. This plan will be developed in cooperation with the Director or Acting Director of OMB.[105]

The George W. Bush administration came to the White House with a private sector management approach that called for maximum executive control of the administration and a fervent, ideologically driven commitment to increase dramatically the powers of the president. These characteristics would lead the president and his key colleagues to seek to eliminate internal governmental regulations put in place for purposes of transparency and accountability. They also worked to exempt various kinds of activities from regulation by government or to outsource them so as to take them away from internal governmental controls, and did so when possible in a manner that also exempted the operations, to the extent possible, from regulations in place to control government contracting and ensure accountability of both contractors and government contracting organizations.

Thus, in 2002, the White House began an effort to remove agency operations from the constraints of the civil service system, starting with provisions in the Homeland Security Act that authorized the agency to create its own human resources management system apart from the standard civil service. The Homeland Security Act provided that "the Secretary of Homeland Security may, in regulations prescribed jointly with the Director of the Office of Personnel Management, establish, and from time to time adjust, a human resources management system for some or all of the organizational units of the Department of Homeland Security."[106] The Department of Homeland

Security (DHS) issued its policy creating its own system in 2005.[107] That was followed by provisions in defense authorization legislation that permitted the Department of Defense (DoD) to do the same thing.[108]

The administration made outsourcing one of the core elements of its approach to governance as explained in the President's Management Agenda.[109] The administration had a fortuitous partner in this effort. David Walker had been appointed Comptroller General in 1998 by President Clinton and he brought with him a background in private sector consulting and service with the Reagan administration. Before coming to what he later renamed as the Government Accountability Office, Walker had been a partner at Arthur Andersen, LLP; before that he served as an assistant secretary of labor in the Reagan administration, and before that he was with Price Waterhouse, Coopers & Lybrand, and Source Services Corporation.[110] Congress adopted a provision in the Floyd D. Spence National Defense Authorization Act for Fiscal Year 2001, a requirement that the comptroller general chair a commission known as the Competitive Activities Panel to study the way in which the federal government made decisions about what function should be offered for bid by private contractors, a process known as competitive sourcing.[111] The work was done during 2001 with a membership primarily made up of Bush administration officials and private sector business people.[112] Not surprisingly, the primary thrust of the commission's report, issued in April 2002, was to seek major changes in the Office of Management and Budget Circular A-76 that prescribed conditions under which work currently performed by federal government agencies should be let out to bid by private firms and the manner in which those bids would be evaluated to determine whether the function should be moved out of government to the bidder.

Over the years, the A-76 document had included efforts to delineate work that was inherently governmental, and therefore not appropriate for outsourcing, and to recognize that, for a variety of reasons having to deal with legal and other restrictions on the way government agencies can function, a direct head-to-head competition with private bidders was not as fair or reasonable as it would appear on the face of it. However, the commission recommended a much stronger move toward what would be essentially a direct competition under the Federal Acquisition Regulations of the sort in which private sector bidders compete with each other for government contracts. However, the members of the panel were sharply divided on that core recommendation, with Tobias, Harnage, Prior, and Kelley issuing strongly worded individual statements dissenting from that majority's demands.[113]

The administration moved to implement the recommendations of the panel, though the revised A-76, a document that would make far more governmental work available to bid on terms more likely to result in a decision to contract, did not go as far as the majority of the panel had suggested. In the initial years of the Bush administration, agencies were required to meet targets for work to be contracted out, though the White House was later forced to halt that practice under pressure from Congress. Additionally, the administration was able to use the post-9/11 political environment to obtain provisions in the Homeland Security Act and other legislation that exempted agencies from some standard contract regulations as well as disclosure requirements. The situation at the time of Hurricane Katrina also led to shortcuts through existing contract policy in an effort to make up for the initial failures to be ready for or adequately respond to the disaster. The effort to move action out of direct government control and into contractor responsibility, often in situations in which the agencies doing the contracting were inadequately staffed, trained, or supported to manage the contracts adequately, and in a number of situations, using exemptions from basic contract management policy, predictably led to major problems in the later years of the administration.[114] To the degree that the administration was moving to increase dramatically the amount of the government's operations going to contractors, the decision to avoid contracting regulations or to fail to provide essential resources in terms of both people and dollars to manage those contracts represented a major front in the battle against regulation, but one not generally seen for what it was even by otherwise knowledgeable observers.

The president, the vice president, and legal officials in the White House and at the Department of Justice (DOJ) also worked to eliminate regulations that Congress sought to impose legislatively on executive branch officials through the use of presidential signing statements. These statements, issued at the time the president signed bills into law, increasingly—and in terms that expanded over the first several years of the Bush administration—set out to nullify accountability and transparency provisions that had been relatively standard for years. In the signing statements, the Bush administration declared that a host of provisions in bills that he signed into law were nevertheless violations of his executive powers and other provisions of the

Constitution. He therefore instructed officials of the executive branch to implement the statute as he instructed them rather than as Congress had written the legislation.[115] That included declarations that the administration would not be held to disclosure and reporting requirements included in legislation that were essential for effective oversight. The president made a variety of claims to support these actions, but most commonly claimed the ability to do so by virtue of what the administration referred to as the unitary theory of the executive.[116]

Additionally, the administration moved to exempt its officials from other existing constraints by claims of executive privilege or by assertions of national security. It did so not only on the basis of the unitary executive theory but also on claims of commander in chief and foreign affairs powers under Article II in a manner that was nothing short of an assertion of a prerogative power in the presidency.[117]

The Central Rulemaking Controls Intensified:
Low Visibility, but Effective Attack

What was not as clear to many outside the administration was the fact that although they kept the Clinton regulatory review order in place, the Bush White House was moving to restructure the central regulatory control mechanisms to further discourage the issuance of regulations. The administration issued an amendment to the Clinton EO 12866, but, the major change, until later in the Bush years, was to remove the vice president from the rulemaking review process as compared to the pattern from the Reagan years through the Clinton era.[118] Instead, formal control over the process would be focused primarily in the OIRA of the OMB, though a variety of other administration troops were given particular responsibilities.

It soon because clear, however, that this change in formal processes did not indicate that Vice President Cheney would stay out of regulatory policy. Indeed, his leadership of the National Energy Policy Development Group (NEPDG), charged with developing a new energy policy as the Bush administration began its first term, engendered ongoing debate over what the White House intended to do with energy policy given the problems that had followed in the wake of deregulation in the energy sector and how it was going to go about it. Just as controversial was the administration's refusal to disclose information about members of the energy group and the people consulted by the group from the industry.[119] An important part of the controversy was the fact that, in addition to officials of the administration, private individuals were reportedly also made members of the group, including Ken Lay, CEO of Enron; Mark Racicot, then chair of the Republican National Committee and previously a lobbyist for Enron; Haley Barbour, who had formerly served as Republican National Committee chair and whose firm lobbied on behalf of electrical utilities; and Thomas Kuhn, then president of the Edison Electric Institute. Groups including the Sierra Club and Judicial Watch sued Cheney, the NEPDG, and the private individuals who were allegedly members of the group, charging violations of the Federal Advisory Committee Act[120] and calling for a full discovery process that would disclose who was involved in the NEPDG, how the group operated, and who else might have been members apart from those listed in the suit. The White House made a sweeping assertion of executive privilege in the cases and the U.S. Supreme Court ultimately ruled in the administration's favor, setting a new and broadly deferential standard in the process.[121]

However, interest groups were not the only ones seeking to understand the role of the vice president in this process and the influence of the energy sector lobbyists on the new administration. Comptroller General David Walker sued the vice president in the U.S. District Court for the District of Columbia. Representatives John Dingell (D-Mich.) and Henry Waxman (D-Calif.) had requested what was then known as the Government Accounting Office (GAO; since designated the Governmental Accountability Office) to investigate the composition and operation of the NEPDG. The comptroller general, who heads the GAO, engaged in an ongoing exchange of correspondence with the counsel for the vice president from May through July 2001. Cheney's counsel then informed both houses of Congress by letter that the requests intruded upon the constitutional separation of powers and that the vice president would not provide the requested information. In January 2002, following demands from a number of Senate committee chairs, Walker brought suit. The court dismissed the case, finding that the Comptroller General lacked standing to sue.[122] Ultimately, the report of the NEPDG became the Bush administration's policy proposal, major portions of which were ultimately enacted in the Energy Policy Act of 2005, legislation that was extremely favorable to the energy industry and about which more will be said later.[123]

Another group sued, seeking to learn whether there was a back-channel through the vice president into the administration's regulatory policy. This time, the Citizens for Responsibility and Ethics in Washington called for disclosure of records under the Freedom of Information Act (FOIA) and the Federal Records Act with respect to visits by the later disgraced lobbyist, Jack Abramoff, and his associates to the vice president's residence. Once again the administration refused to provide the information, and again the district court dismissed the case on standing grounds—though in a separate case issued at the same time, the court ruled that the kinds of records involved in this case were public records within the meaning of the FOIA.[124]

The use of sweeping claims of executive privilege to cover actions within the administration was matched by a range of other tactics to block access to information about the administration's antiregulatory operations, such as the guidance issued by Attorney General Ashcroft on the FOIA and the president's executive order on access to presidential records and files.

Even though the vice president under the Bush policy did not have a formally designated role in the rulemaking review process, central control over rulemaking in the form of regulatory review, clearance, and other modified and new control tactics in the battle against regulation would be an important feature of the Bush battle plan. In fact, the Bush OIRA would be aggressive in fighting the battle against regulation, as this office made increased use of devices known as OMB circulars, bulletins, and memoranda as effective policy tools through which to pursue its campaign. In the process, the administration could be secure in the knowledge that few members of the press and even fewer Americans—including many academics and the informed public with substantial knowledge of public affairs—had any idea what such policy tools were or how to find them, much less how they could be used.

In the fall of 2001 and again in 2003, the administration would use these devices to expand the requirements and agency compliance guidelines for regulatory cost/benefit analyses that were to be submitted to the OIRA under the rulemaking review order.[125] In 2004, the administration moved to require peer review of regulatory agency expert analyses, a significant departure from the standard deference to administrative expertise long recognized by reviewing courts.[126] Such peer reviews not only removed the standard presumptions of validity from regulatory agency action, but also raised serious questions about the potential political character of what purported to be neutral peer reviews.

The irony of the demand for peer reviews was that agencies were constructed to be repositories of expert opinion in their policy domains, but a number of them had been so weakened by strategic resource and antipersonnel attacks over the years that their capabilities could now be called into question by regulated groups and by the administration itself. Of course, peer review takes time, adds expenses, and is likely to engender controversy that will delay issuance of new rules.

In 2005, the OIRA issued a draft bulletin on proper practices for the issuance of guidance documents.[127] This was an attempt to block one of the key devices to which many regulatory agencies had resorted in their efforts to meet the requirements imposed by legislation for the issuance and implementation of rules (often within relatively limited time frames given the complexity of the subjects they were attempting to regulate) while dealing with the increasingly burdensome load of procedural and analytic requirements that had been piled onto these agencies with each administration from Carter through Bush II. Generally known as interpretive rules in administrative law, guidance documents are usually not intended to add new substantive—which is to say new legally binding—rules, but to provide regulated organizations with additional information about their existing policies so that these organizations, whether public or private, can more easily and fully comply with regulatory requirements. The administration clearly decided that these were in fact ways to evade attack through the central regulatory clearance process.

With little media attention, President Bush then issued in January 2007 Executive Order 13422 in the form of amendments to the existing regulatory review order, EO 12866, initially imposed by the Clinton administration. One of the key changes was to add the words "or guidance document" after the word "regulation" throughout the order, essentially requiring the same cumbersome and complex process for guidance documents as for substantive rules.[128] In addition, the order made changes that increased requirements to be met for rules that agencies hoped would pass through the preclearance process. Just to make certain that agencies were fully engaged and did not attempt to evade this additional burden-loading attack, the president ordered that "within 60 days of the date of this Executive order, each agency head shall designate one of the agency's Presidential Appointees to be its Regulatory Policy Officer, advise OMB of such designation, and annually update OMB on the status of this designation."[129] Under these conditions, agencies are discouraged from providing additional guidance on existing programs lest the OMB should decide that they represent significant guidance documents that are required to run the full gauntlet normally reserved for substantive rules.

The OIRA also went on in 2006 to issue a complex and controversial set of requirements for risk assessments,[130] which were so problematic that a

National Academy of Sciences study found the Bush policy to be unsupported by contemporary science and called for its withdrawal. The review of the proposal warned, "In several respects, the bulletin attempts to move standards for risk assessment into territory that is beyond what previous reports have recommended and beyond the current state of the science. Such departures from expert studies are of serious concern, because any attempt to advance the practice of risk assessment that does not reflect the state of the science is likely to produce the opposite effect."[131] The report only became more critical from that point on, concluding that "the OMB bulletin is fundamentally flawed and recommends that it be withdrawn."[132] While the report agreed that risk assessment is an important enterprise, it found that its use of concepts and approach to processes "conflicts with long-established concepts and practices";[133] "the committee found many of the standards to be unclear or flawed";[134] "the description of uncertainty and variability in the bulletin is oversimplified and does not recognize the complexities of different types of risk assessments or the need to tailor uncertainty analysis to a given agency's particular needs";[135] "the bulletin's treatment of adverse effects is too simplistic and restrictive and ignores important factors in determining appropriate effects to evaluate, the scientific information available, and an understanding of the underlying biochemical mechanisms for an effect of interest";[136] and the document's "incomplete and unbalanced approach to engineering risk assessment (as well as ecologic and other types of risk assessment) contradicts its stated objective of improving the quality of risk assessment throughout the federal government."[137] The OIRA risk assessment policy was clearly an unbalanced document with glaring omissions and, when judged against the state of existing science, unacceptable on many counts.

Besides, the National Academy report concluded, the review supported what should be a readily understood principle: that although it may be appropriate to state general goals for risk assessment, "OMB should limit its efforts to stating goals and general principles of risk assessment. The details should be left to the agencies or expert committees appointed by the agencies, wherein lies the depth of expertise to address the issues relevant to their specific types of risk assessments."[138] Instead, the report found that the OMB action was likely to undermine ongoing analytic efforts in regulatory agencies, since the new requirements would add substantial burdens to organizations that already lack the ability to meet those kinds of demands.[139] Nevertheless, the OMB issued a memorandum on "Updated Principles for Risk Assessment" in September 2007.[140]

Then there was the matter of agency guidance documents. The concern was that agencies had come to use guidance documents of various types to circumvent the procedures required for substantive or legislative rules. There was some evidence to support that claim, but it was also clear that in some instances the practice had developed as a coping strategy for agencies compelled to take regulatory action by Congress. These were agencies that had been stymied in their efforts to meet time lines and burdened by substantive workloads of new policies to be developed and by hosts of procedures piled onto the basic rulemaking process originally provided in Section 553 of the APA by Congress and the White House. The administration went to work to block the issuance of policy through guidance documents by requiring most of the same kinds of clearance processes for these documents as were required for substantive rules. Indeed, the White House amended EO 12866 in early 2007 precisely to capture guidance documents. Guidance documents had traditionally been employed to provide regulated groups with additional information on how to comply with regulations. This effort not only discouraged the attempt to escape and evade by agencies under siege by the administration's attack on rulemaking; it also discouraged the development of information that could be helpful to those most directly affected by regulation.

In this case, there was no question that the administration succeeded in its direct effort to constrain rulemaking and discourage future efforts. However, it also succeeded at several levels of indirect attack. Indeed, Thomas O. McGarity, Sidney Shapiro, and David Bollier declared the use and abuse of these regulatory analysis and clearance techniques during the Bush administration to be nothing less than "Sophisticated Sabotage."[141]

Counterstaffing: The Selection of His Officer Corps
for Action against Regulation

Like Reagan, Bush was more than ready to use his appointment powers to commission reliable leaders for the fight against regulation, fully aware that those appointments would communicate clear messages to the agencies that those appointees were to head, the regulated firms, and political opponents in Congress. The point was not lost on anyone when Bush, with a major energy problem already in progress that promised to become even more complex, chose Spencer Abraham, who had made the effort to eliminate the Department of Energy a mission while he was in the Senate, to be the secretary of energy. The appointment was eerily reminiscent of Reagan's appointments to the Energy and Education posts following his campaign pledge to eliminate both agencies.

As if he had not made his point forcefully enough, Bush underscored his intentions with the opportunity to appoint members to and then choose the chair of the Federal Energy Regulatory Commission (FERC). The FERC was front and center in the debate over electricity deregulation and would be even more highly visible as Californians melted down under the assault by Enron on the state's rate payers—an attack that, as would be made clear in months to come, was a very deliberate and malicious assault.[142] The administration's appointments were controversial, to be sure; all the more so because of the president's and vice president's backgrounds in the energy industry and because of the interactions between the White House and Enron during the period when it was clear that the firm would be at the center of controversy over its actions in the West Coast energy crisis and while the vice president was leading the National Energy Policy Group. In particular, it quickly became clear and public that Enron was engaged in a systematic campaign to constrain FERC regulatory actions, including through efforts to influence appointments to the commission. Congressional staff investigations of that set of activities yielded a report issued in November 2002 that laid out elements of the Enron effort.

> The company launched a major public relations and lobbying campaign in early 2001 apparently designed to indirectly influence the outcome of FERC's decision-making with regard to California. The Enron campaign consisted of an extensive multi-faceted effort to influence policy decisions not only in California, but throughout the Western U.S., in other key markets such as New York, where it was feared that other potentially damaging electricity shortages and price spikes would occur, and at the federal level.(138) The campaign was directed by Enron's corporate head of government affairs with the assistance of the Washington DC–based lobbying firm Quinn, Gillespie and Associates.(139)
>
> A February 5, 2001 briefing on the campaign identified six overall objectives— "Isolate California and communicate a market based message; Retain a market-based electricity structure in California; Minimize California impact and Governor Davis' message across the West; Facilitate federal action: FERC and Congress; Identify and manage potential energy crisis in other states—New York,

Florida, others?; Refine and increase public affairs effort among policy makers, the media, opinion makers, electricity consumers."(140)

As the campaign progressed, the goals and objectives were refined. A May 4, 2001 campaign briefing identified five federal goals relevant to FERC: to encourage FERC and the White House to promote competition in electric markets; to convince FERC to extend its jurisdiction over all aspects of electricity transmission, including over federal, state, and municipal power agencies that are not otherwise subject to FERC jurisdiction; to encourage the Administration to complete confirmation of its FERC nominees; to educate Members of Congress and the Administration about the West Coast energy crisis and encourage them to allow the market to work and to take efforts to increase supply and reduce demand; and to block price cap legislation and administrative orders.(141)

As reflected in the May 4 briefing, one of Enron's goals was to complete the confirmation of FERC nominees in hope of creating a more proactive FERC that would address the growing threat that the California crisis presented to deregulation. On January 8, 2001, Enron's Chairman and Chief Executive Officer Kenneth Lay wrote to Clay Johnson, Executive Director of the Bush-Cheney Transition team, and Vice President–elect Cheney, to offer Enron's recommendations on "the kind of individuals we think you should be looking for" when filling vacancies at FERC.(142) Attached to the letter was a list of seven potential candidates, with brief biographies of each candidate, including Pat Wood [whose full name is Patrick Henry Wood III] and Nora Brownell. Lay called Johnson twice to follow up on the January 8(th) letter.(143) A February 12, 2001 memo to Mr. Lay from Linda Robertson, head of Enron's Washington office, described Enron's priorities in preparation for a call by Mr. Lay to Mr. Johnson concerning " . . . Commissioner vacancies at FERC." The memo stated that "Enron has strongly supported Pat Wood, a Republican, as Commission Chairman." The memo continued, "(a) number of candidates are said to be under consideration for the second Republican seat at FERC. Enron has on several occasions discussed with transition and now Bush Administration officials the candidacy of Nora Brownell as our first pick for the second open seat." The memo noted that Ms. Brownell was under consideration "on the strength of Enron's interest," but faced competition from another candidate reportedly supported by Pennsylvania Governor Tom Ridge and that Enron was working to ". . . mitigate the Governor's alleged concerns with her candidacy."(144) In addition, Lay called Senior Advisor to the President Karl Rove to express his support for Nora Brownell's appointment to FERC.(145)

Even after Wood and Brownell were nominated, it appeared that Enron's government affairs office continued to push for a quick confirmation of their nominations. In a memo to Lay prior to his April 17, 2001 meeting with the Vice President, Linda Robertson and Tom Briggs, who oversaw federal regulatory affairs for Enron, urged him to ". . . take the opportunity to convey to the Vice President the imperative of an expedited confirmation of Pat Wood and Nora Brownell." The memo suggested that their appointments would " . . . mitigate one of the significant political problems confronting passage of the Administration's energy agenda, namely the call by Democrats and Western state members for price caps." It further suggested that these appointments would allow FERC to "release some of the political steam in the system" by adopting more visible pricing steps in Western markets, such as the bid cap measures in place in Texas and the Northeast ISO. Thus, more aggressive action by the FERC on both market power issues and pricing issues would give the Administration enormous political cover and would allow them to redefine the debate on their own terms.(146)

According to Ms. Robertson, the confirmations were not actually discussed during the meeting with the Vice President.

Beyond the matter of FERC nominees, Enron executives appeared to bring their message on the California power crisis directly to key Bush Administration officials. On April 5, 2001, Jeffrey Skilling met with Secretary of Treasury Paul O'Neill, and other Treasury Department officials, to discuss the West Coast energy crisis.(147) Ken Lay and Linda Robertson apparently raised the California issue during their 30 minute meeting with the Vice President on April 17, 2001.(148) The White House has indicated that Assistant to the President and Director of the National Economic Council Larry Lindsey had "a few communications" with Ken Lay, "most likely about the California electricity shortage."(149).[143]

The president ultimately appointed Nora Brownell as a member of the commission and then chose as chair of the FERC the man who had worked with him when he was governor in a failed effort to get Bush's plan for electricity deregulation adopted in Texas, Patrick Henry Wood III, former chair of the Public Utility Commission of Texas.

Another longtime friend of the energy industry and mining interests, and an equally ardent opponent of environmental regulation, Gale Norton, was appointed secretary of the interior. Secretary Norton had a long record as a zealous officer in the battle against regulation. She was a protegé of Reagan's arch deregulator at Interior, Secretary James Watt. Watt came to the Department of Interior from the Mountain States Legal Foundation, a group that has worked diligently for years to open public lands to drilling and mineral exploration and extraction. Norton worked for Watt there and later at Interior where she served as solicitor. When she was at the Mountain States Legal Foundation, Norton and her mentor filed a brief in support of the effort to strike down the strip mine legislation, the Surface Mining Act, on constitutional grounds. Norton had opposed the Endangered Species Act when she was attorney general of Colorado. In addition to her work at Mountain States, Norton has been a board member of other prominent organizations that have fought to eliminate or block regulation, including "Defenders of Property Rights (board member), the Washington Legal Foundation (board member), and the National Council of Republicans for Environmental Advocacy (CREA), which she founded."[144] Another Bush appointee who was with Norton at Interior as assistant secretary for water and science was Bennet William Raley, who had also worked with Mountain States as a board member and Defenders of Property Rights Attorney Network, which handled claims of regulatory takings.[145]

Norton was only one of a number of appointees from cabinet level through agency counsel and assistant secretary ranks appointed to agencies with health and safety regulation mandates who came from positions in the oil, mining, chemical, and other organizations that had for many years fought against rigorous regulatory policy. The OMB Watch organization detailed the backgrounds of a variety of these appointees. For example, Secretary of Commerce Donald Evans had been CEO of an oil and gas firm in Denver and sat on the board of an affiliated firm. The report notes that "Evans was campaign manager and chief fundraiser for President Bush's last three campaigns, raising more money from the oil and gas industry for the 2000 presidential race than the ten-year total of any other federal candidate in history."[146] Samuel Bodman III, who was deputy secretary of commerce and later moved to the Department of the Treasury, was the CEO of a chemical firm. Carl Michael Smith, who was named assistant secretary of energy in the fossil fuels energy area, was a former oil and gas producer and an attorney representing firms in that industry. David D. Lauriski, who took over the Mine Safety and Health Administration, an agency that would later take considerable criticism for its lack of regulatory action following deadly coal mining events, had spent a career in the mining industry.[147] Also in mining, Michael F. Duffy was named a member and later chair of the Federal Mine Safety and Health Review Commission. He was formerly with the National Mining Association and the American Mining Council as well as holding key administrative positions with Massey Energy.[148]

Another of the high-visibility counterstaffing appointments was Michael Powell (son of Secretary of State Colin Powell) as chair of the FCC. Powell was to the FCC what Antonin Scalia was to the U.S. Supreme Court. He told reporters in his first press conference after he was appointed that "I do not believe deregulation is like the dessert you serve after people have fed on their vegetables. . . . It's a critical ingredient to facilitating competition."[149] Ironically, he was such an outspoken advocate for deregulation that he engendered opposition to his own initiatives within the FCC. He was even publicly embarrassed by his inability to bring a majority of his colleagues with him on some issues.

When Powell stepped down in 2005, President Bush replaced him with another young and equally ardent officer in the deregulation forces, though one whose style and manner were different from those of his predecessor. Kevin Martin, while described by those at the FCC and others who know him as ideological, hermetic, and secretive, was willing to fight very public battles in his single-handed effort to push through deregulation of multiple media outlet ownership restrictions—a battle that Powell had not been able to win. Even so ardent a deregulation warrior as Mark Fowler, Reagan's appointee to head the fight against regulation as FCC chair, had to admit that Martin's tactics were sometimes extreme both within and outside the commission, though he also expressed to the media a grudging admiration for his effectiveness.[150]

It is true that the George W. Bush White House used a few appointments as political nods to opponents such as those Republicans as well as Democrats who were increasingly concerned with environmental issues. However, it became clear that these appointees would not be taken seriously unless they demonstrated a loyal commitment to the administration's priorities, including enlistment in the war on regulation. The president made a point of highlighting the appointment of Christine Todd Whitman to head the EPA. While a Republican governor of New Jersey, Whitman had established a reputation as a political leader who saw environmental protection as a key policy domain. What she did not know at the time, however, was that she would often be paired with Secretary of Energy Abraham in administration policymaking that had virtually anything to do with energy or Clean Air Act issues; and it was very clear who would prevail in those contests. Whitman ultimately resigned, having been publicly embarrassed and rendered essentially meaningless in administration decisionmaking.[151]

Another appointee who found himself used to make a point, but sidelined when he did not meet expectations to fight regulation, was SEC Chair William H. Donaldson, whose plight is discussed later in this chapter.

The naming of Mary Sheila Gall to chair the CPSC brought immediate criticism because she had previously established, during her tenure on the commission, a record supportive of regulated industries and critical of the advocates of safety regulation. Gall had been nominated as a member of the commission by George H. W. Bush and reappointed by Clinton. However, over her years on the commission, she made clear a strong commitment to voluntary as compared to mandatory standards, and she displayed a tendency to blame consumers for what she termed the misuse and abuse of products in situations in which others clearly saw manufacturers' demonstrably defective merchandise.

Criticisms arose with regard to her tendency to favor industry over consumers and her accusation that those who pressed for mandatory standards and enforcement in a variety of areas were advocating a "federal nanny state."[152] In particular, the criticism grew with Gall's votes against mandatory standards to address problems with baby walkers, bunk beds, flame-retardant children's sleepwear, and crib slats.[153] The Senate eventually refused to confirm her for the position.

Gall was followed by two other appointees for the CPSC chair. There was outrage when the acting CPSC chair, Nancy A. Nord, resisted calls during congressional hearings for major increases in authority and resources and regulatory authority for the commission in the wake of massive toy recalls after dangerous levels of lead were found in the products. There was anger from members of Congress who were hearing loud complaints from their constituents about the failure of the CPSC to do its job and bipartisan congressional demands for new legislation, more resources, and serious regulatory action by the commission.

Not all appointments were as visible to the average American as the controversies at CPSC. One of those less discussed but very important fields was highway safety regulation of trucking—what little remained of it following the last round of deregulation during the Clinton years. Among the strong supporters of the Bush candidacy were officials of the trucking industry, a group that had long fought regulatory efforts. When President Bush came to the White House, the officers of these organizations were attractive recruits for the administration's fight against regulation. The president and chair of the American Trucking Association, Duane W. Ackie and Walter B. McCormick, Jr., respectively, were appointed to the administration's transition team to address transportation issues. Another trucking association officer,

Michael P. Jackson, was appointed as deputy secretary of Transportation. Joseph M. Clapp, who had formerly been the chair of Roadway trucking, was named to chair the Federal Motor Carrier Safety Administration (FMCSA). Although the administration denied that Vice President Cheney's counsel, David Addington, was involved in regulatory changes in trucking, he had previously been in the trucking sector and had opposed regulation.[154] The FMCSA would be an important unit in the battle against trucking regulation during the administration.

Appointments to other key positions put in place a cadre of deregulators who could be counted on to accept their mission and lead the attack. Indeed, learning from the Reagan administration, the George W. Bush administration paid attention not only to counterstaffing the top positions in various agencies and commissions, but also to taking the counterstaffing effort down into other appointed positions within the agencies.[155] It was clear to those inside the administration and out that those who did not fulfill their mission would deal with the White House for their dereliction of duty.

President Bush continued his use of the counterstaffing weapon in his second term, naming Indiana businessman Allan Hubbard, who headed a chemical conglomerate, E & A Industries, to be his Chief Economic Advisor. Hubbard, who had been a student in the MBA program at Harvard Business School along with George W. Bush, had been one of Bush's major financial contributors. This appointment was not, however, Hubbard's first tour in Washington. Neither was he new to the fight against regulation. Indeed, he had been the executive director of the Quayle Council (discussed in Chapter 2) during the George H. W. Bush administration, one of the leaders of what might easily be considered that administration's special forces unit in the fight.

The appointments noted above are but some of the many counterstaffing efforts by the Bush White House. Indeed, this is one of the factors that compelled the administration to make repeated use of recess appointments to bring to office a number of appointees who clearly faced serious confirmation difficulties because of their records and views supporting the administration's fight against regulation.

Strategic and Tactical Control of Information: Intervention in
Regulatory Agency Research, Reporting, and Standard-Setting
Once in office, Bush appointees could expect to operate under a command and control system that remained engaged and that was ready to intervene to

ensure that administration policies and overall doctrine remained front and center. One of the most controversial tendencies of the George W. Bush White House in the field of regulation was its willingness to step into the preparation of analyses, reports, and testimony to ensure that agency employees behaved as foot soldiers for the administration even when agency scientists and other agency subject matter experts reached findings that contradicted administration ideological or policy positions. At a more general level, that also meant withholding information from Congress or the public, claiming what amounted to a domestic version of the presidential prerogative, better known as the unitary theory of the executive. On the same doctrinal foundation, the administration asserted that the executive and no one else had authority to control what employees of the executive branch could say or do.

There have been occasional controversies in the past when an administration was accused of attempting to shape the presentation of expert analyses in a more favorable or perhaps less damaging manner. One that received considerable attention was the intervention by the George H. W. Bush administration into planned testimony by what was then known as the Abortion Surveillance Unit of the Centers for Disease Control on the increase in morbidity and mortality from illegal abortions following restrictions on federally funded programs that provided information on or services related to abortion. However, the George W. Bush administration had a record of frequent and persistent intervention by political appointees and others in the shaping and presentation of important reports and findings that would affect regulatory policy in important respects. In some instances, as the use of counterstaffing indicates, there was no need for White House intervention, since appointees were selected to bring a private sector approach to command and control and a regulated industry perspective to their positions. They were also chosen with care to ensure ideological orthodoxy.

The types of analyses and reports that were reshaped in service of the battle against regulation ranged from key environmental analyses to be used in shaping Clean Air Act rules to such mild documents as a Surgeon General's "Call to Action" on global health that really carried no regulatory authority or sanctions at all, but environmental regulation was a frequent target of attack. There was, over time, increasing frustration by state governments, both those headed by Republican governors and those led by Democrats, over the failure of the Bush EPA to develop and enforce effective rules in a range of environmental policy domains and particularly in areas covered by the Clean Air Act.

These disputes ranged from control over chemical emissions from power plants to refusal to issue rules governing greenhouse gas emissions from vehicles that contribute to global warming.

One that drew particular response when it surfaced in 2005 was the administration's treatment of the evidence supporting the standards governing mercury pollution. It was so controversial in large part because of the way the administration controlled the analysis and reporting of the data that drove the policy. In February of that year, the EPA inspector general (IG) issued a scathing report, which stated flatly that "EPA's development of the Maximum Achievable Control Technology (MACT) floor was compromised."[156] "Evidence indicates that EPA senior management instructed EPA staff to develop a Maximum Achievable Control Technology (MACT) standard for mercury that would result in national emissions of 34 tons annually, instead of basing the standard on an unbiased determination of what the top performing units were achieving in practice."[157]

The policymaking process on mercury pollution reached back into the 1990s. Although the EPA issued a report in 1998,[158] the IG noted, the agency deferred a decision on whether it was necessary to issue regulations to cover power plants.[159] However, Congress was alarmed by the EPA study and commissioned a further analysis by the National Academy of Sciences.[160] After the National Academy of Sciences issued a report in July 2000, indicating that "60,000 newborns a year could experience neurological damage due to mercury," the EPA instituted the process for determining that regulation of mercury from power plants was "appropriate and necessary" under the terms of the Clean Air Act. In line with that administration's efforts to avoid standard forms of regulation, the Clinton-era EPA discussed an emissions trading approach to the problem but did not issue a policy before George W. Bush came to office in 2001.[161]

The Bush administration plainly saw the growth of the energy industry as a priority and just as clearly saw environmental regulation as an impediment to that goal. The White House made it clear that the United States would not join the Kyoto agreement, intended to lead to reduced emissions of greenhouse gases, and would not pursue environmental controls that would hamper the growth of the energy sector or economic growth in general. Not only was the administration not prepared to increase air pollution controls, but it was in the process of developing a new proposal, known as the Clear Skies

Plan, that was intended to replace much of the existing regulatory regime with one that, despite claims to the contrary, would have dramatically reduced regulatory controls. The fact that this departure from past air pollution control policy was driven in no small part by support for and from the energy sector and that it would not address serious pollution issues was one of the factors that ultimately led to the resignation of EPA Administrator Christine Todd Whitman.

In the summer of 2001, the EPA MACT working group met to begin work on a standard to address mercury pollution. The term "MACT" comes from the Clean Air Act law, which requires reduction of such pollution by the maximum achievable reduction means. By this point, it was clear that:

> In the United States, the largest source of airborne mercury emissions is the coal-burning electric utilities industry, representing an estimated 40 percent of total U.S. man-made airborne mercury emissions. EPA has estimated that one-third of all U.S. emissions of mercury are deposited within the contiguous United States, while the remaining two-thirds enter the global cycle.[162]

The pollution occurs when the mercury falls from the air to the water and enters the food chain through fish and, by 2003, as many as forty-five states would issue safety advisories on the consumption of fish with particular concern for children and pregnant women because of mercury pollution.[163]

While the Clinton and later the Bush administration were deciding what to do with the question of mercury pollution, environmental groups led by the Natural Resources Defense Council sued the EPA to force the issuance of regulations. That suit was settled in 1998, with an EPA promise to issue proposed rules by the end of 2003 and final regulations by the end of 2004. Under a settlement agreement reached in 1998 with the Natural Resources Defense Council, EPA agreed to issue a proposed rule for regulating mercury from power plants by December 15, 2003, and a final rule by December 2004.[164] The EPA published a proposed rule for mercury from power plants at the end of January 2003.

The EPA IG, like the Congress, found it difficult to obtain needed information and access to administration officials for interviews during its investigation.

> The OIG [Office of the Inspector General] was not provided with several important documents it requested from the Agency; therefore, that information

was not available for consideration in this report. . . . Consideration of the inter-agency review process was limited to information from EPA staff and information available in the docket only. We were not able to discuss the inter-agency review process with Office of Management and Budget (OMB) staff who were responsible for coordinating the inter-agency review process.[165]

Nevertheless, the IG was able to determine that supervisors at EPA had intervened in the normal process for standard setting to obtain the result that the agency ultimately took. In fact, agency professional staff who were interviewed by the IG explained that "they would have expected greater adherence to the guidance for mercury rule development due to the significance of this particular regulatory action, but this did not happen."[166] That is to say that the administration's tactics were particularly heavy-handed in a situation in which it was clear that a great many people, including the litigants in the NRDC suit, would be watching. Departures from normal procedures are often used by those challenging a regulatory process as evidence that the decision makers behaved in a manner that was arbitrary and capricious, and therefore a violation of the APA.

The IG found that the analysts were told by their superiors that they were to support the 34-tons-per-year standard, even though the models they had been using produced a lower emissions level for a MACT standard. The e-mails obtained by the IG and interviews with staff indicated that there was an ongoing effort to modify the models to produce the desired result, with at least three different runs at the Integrated Planning Model to make the 34 ton figure work.[167] The results of analyses were rejected by management until the 34 ton figure was reached, though the IG points out that the information about alternative calculations was not included in the rulemaking docket. Moreover, interviews with staff indicated that an unbiased analysis would have produced a level "as low as 8 to 10 tons per year up to the mid-20s" but not higher, and certainly nothing like the 34-ton level that was demanded.[168] Here again, the administration's willingness to bend the science so far to support its political predisposition was not only wrong, but reckless in a situation where so many groups with their own experts would be watching the decision making and the analyses that supported it closely.

Far more public concern was raised by the overt battle by the Bush administration against demands by a variety of parties, including state governments headed by governors of both parties, that the administration in general, and EPA in particular, needed to adopt regulatory programs and standards to address global climate change issues. Again, the administration made clear from the start that it did not accept the mounting international evidence and findings with regard to global warming and that its priorities were on growth in the energy sector and in the economy as a whole. In the process, the administration was perfectly prepared to intervene in the development and presentation of analyses by the EPA and other analysts to make its case. It is a case that the administration ultimately lost in the U.S. Supreme Court.

A variety of parties had submitted a petition to the EPA in 1999, calling upon the agency to issue emissions standards that would address greenhouse gas emissions from motor vehicles that contribute to global warming. The EPA began a notice and comment period on the petition, but ultimately issued a decision not to grant the petition in the fall of 2003.[169] What was immediately surprising to those watching the decision process was that the administration did not rest its refusal to act on scientific analysis, but on what the Court of Appeals ultimately termed "policy considerations" and a claim that there was too much scientific uncertainty to act. Moreover, the administration asserted that EPA did not have the authority to regulate these emissions under the Clear Air Act and, if it did, then it had the discretion to refuse to act. Some sixteen states, a number of local governments, and a variety of environmental groups appealed the EPA decision, which ultimately found its way to the U.S. Supreme Court.

It was clear from the start that the administration had simply taken a position that it did not intend to alter. The Clean Air Act definitions stated that the agency was to regulate any emission that "endangers human health or welfare" or may reasonably be expected to do so. Section 302(h) of the statute goes on to explain that welfare "includes, but is not limited to, effects on soils, water, crops, vegetation, manmade materials, animals, wildlife, weather, visibility, and climate, . . . as well as effects on economic values and on personal comfort and well-being, whether caused by transformation, conversion, or combination with other air pollutants."[170] While it is the case that the specific pollutants presented by the petition were not listed in the statute, the language was broad and open-textured and had been interpreted that way by the EPA, the Congress, and the courts in past cases over both Republican and Democratic administrations.[171] Thus, whatever else it was, the administration's argument in the case was not really about statutory authority or a serious "endangerment analysis" under the Clean Air Act.[172]

Not surprisingly, the case attracted a great many parties who came in as intervenors or amici curiae (friends of the court). Of all these filings, perhaps the most interesting was the brief filed by four previous EPA administrators from both Republican and Democratic administrations, including Carol M. Browner (Clinton), William K. Reilly (George H. W. Bush), Douglas M. Costle (Carter), and Russell E. Train (Nixon and Ford). They opposed the administration's position and rejected its interpretation of the Clean Air Act. They provided examples from each of their administrations in which the EPA used the provisions of the statute in question to regulate substances that were not specifically listed in the act and about which one could argue that there was a degree of scientific uncertainty with respect to the precise levels of pollution that would be dangerous. However, in each instance, they relied on the agency's scientific analyses to adopt standards, and on each occasion the Congress indicated its approval by later amending the statutory language to support a broader interpretation and the courts upheld their decisions in such areas as "neurotoxic lead additives in gasoline, carcinogenic emissions of airborne benzene, ozone-depleting chlorofluorocarbons, and lung function–altering fine particulate matter."[173] In this case, according to these political appointees, the refusal to act was more than an erroneous reading of the legislation or incorrect science.

> EPA's decision not to regulate greenhouse gases based on non–science related policy considerations and residual scientific uncertainty undermines the bedrock principles that have guided the Agency's implementation of the Clean Air Act for more than three decades. Congress has already made the policy decision to regulate dangerous pollutants and has charged EPA with the role of applying its considerable technical expertise to the scientific question of whether a particular pollutant may endanger public health or welfare. The Agency is not empowered to subordinate science-based regulatory decisionmaking to non-statutory policy considerations and thereby avoid entirely the necessary regulatory decision.[174]

When the Supreme Court ruled against the administration in 2007, there was an expectation that the matter had been resolved and that the agency would move forward expeditiously to respond to the Court's ruling. After all, the Court had rejected the EPA and the administration's position completely, concluding that: "EPA has refused to comply with this clear statutory command. Instead, it has offered a laundry list of reasons not to regulate."[175] It was clear to the Court that, whatever the basis for the policy decisions that the administration made, "it is evident they have nothing to do with whether greenhouse gas emissions contribute to climate change. Still less do they amount to a reasoned justification for declining to form a scientific judgment."[176] However, President Bush made it just as clear that no standards would be issued by the EPA that would inhibit economic growth. The EPA did not act, and states once again resorted to litigation to force action. That litigation was in progress as the Obama administration came in.

At the heart of the dispute was the conclusion that the administration's decision about regulation was ideological and perhaps even driven by conflicts of interest, but that it was certainly not driven by science or professional regulatory decision making. One of the difficulties was that the administration had been emboldened by the fact that Congress simply was not seriously conducting oversight while the president's party was in control. Once control shifted at the beginning of 2007, several committees launched investigations into the administration's intervention into regulatory decision making.

That said, as the 2006 elections approached, some committees began to consider charges of Bush administration intervention into scientific decisions in such areas as global climate change. By the end of 2007, the House Committee on Oversight and Government Reform published a major study entitled *Political Interference with Climate Change Science under the Bush Administration,* involving some 27,000 documents (also published by the committee) that provided more than enough evidence to show the battle within the administration against its own regulatory professionals.[177] The report found systematic efforts to control which scientists were interviewed and by whom, to edit and constrain congressional testimony, and to control the contents of reports on climate change.[178] The report also concluded that the "White House played a major role in crafting the August 2003 EPA legal opinion disavowing authority to regulate greenhouse gases."[179]

Counterattack: Battling Back from Demands for Regulation
The administration's internal fight to defeat what were clearly seen as guerilla movements to support regulation with respect to climate change was one of a number of actions to block efforts to regulate in the face of events or problems that captured widespread attention. In some cases, such as global warming and the fossil fuel industry more generally, the approach was simply to beat back the calls for action. In others, the response involved counterattacks in which the administration had to execute a tactical retreat, but with a clear intention later to mount an offense to take down temporary regulatory advances.

In addition to the EPA examples, the administration also resisted demands for action with respect to regulatory failures in the FDA, the FAA, and the CPSC. Political appointees were quick to assert that they were fulfilling the regulatory role when it was clear that the FAA was not performing adequately and effectively. The FDA was unable and seemingly unwilling to address serious dangers from domestic and imported drugs and food. The CPSC sought to fend off calls for action and offers of more regulatory authority and resources in the face of massive toy recalls because of high lead levels in imported toys.

There were some places where action was required and even the regulated industries demanded it. That said, the reason for action was to deal with temporary emergencies, actions that could be quietly rolled back when the short-term issues of the emergency had been addressed. Two obvious examples during the Bush years were the corporate management and financial services scandals and the mad cow disease problem.

In the wake of the revelations of the manipulations of the markets by a variety of corporate bad actors, ranging from Enron to Arthur Andersen to WorldCom to Global Crossing and a collection of investment banks and brokerages, both Democrats and Republicans in Congress (well before the information broke about the misdeeds of banks and mortgage firms that played a key role in the mortgage meltdown of 2007–2008) moved to develop new regulatory policies and challenge existing regulators, particularly the SEC, to do its job more effectively and to enforce existing regulations more vigorously. Corporate officials and stock market players also called for action, fearing that the loss of confidence in the marketplace and in corporate America more generally was leading to a tendency of investors to pull out of the standard market institutions and processes and could produce even more dramatic governmental intervention in the future if steps were not taken in the near term. There were several different types of problems that surfaced during the period, running the gamut from corporate mismanagement and abuse to major conflict-of-interest issues involving investment banking firms and affiliated securities brokers, to a range of accounting abuses that ultimately forced firms to admit that their financial reports had been deliberately manipulated to misrepresent the company's success. As Stiglitz explained in his critique of the Clinton administration's fight against regulation, the deregulation of the 1990s and a range of incentives for executive performance at any cost, backed by outrageous levels of incentive pay to CEOs, produced exactly the kinds of abuses that anyone who had thought the policies through in advance would have foreseen.[180]

There were two general sets of action that policymakers pursued. The first was to pass the Sarbanes-Oxley legislation in 2002 that imposed a range of protections for investors and punishments for executives and firms engaged in accounting and corporate financial reporting abuses.[181] Second, there were demands for new and more committed leadership and action at the SEC. Harvey Pitt, then chair of the SEC, ultimately resigned from office in November 2002 as demands for aggressive action mounted.

However, as soon as the markets began to stabilize, and public attention had shifted to other matters, the business community and the Bush administration closed ranks and moved to relax and even roll back regulation developed or enhanced just a brief time earlier. William H. Donaldson, who had been appointed SEC chair to replace Pitt and who, it was thought, would be a caretaker, came under attack from the administration, his Republican colleagues at SEC, and the business community for taking an aggressive regulatory position. Donaldson resigned in mid-2005 to be replaced by conservative southern California Republican Representative Christopher Cox, well known as a friend of business who would, as newspapers quickly observed, back off from the active regulatory effort of his predecessor.[182]

At about the same time, a less visible offensive was being launched by the administration and antiregulation warriors outside government in business firms and think-tanks to roll back the actions taken in the previous period by the SEC. The administration and its allies worked through a unit established to lead the battle known as the Committee on Capital Markets Regulation. While the group was led by Professor Hal Scott of Harvard, it was clear that this was an effort in common cause with the administration to launch a major counteroffensive. Scott had two co-chairs; one had been a chair of the Council of Economic Advisers under Bush, and the other had formerly been president of Goldman Sachs, where, as press reports noted, "he reported to Mr. Paulson," who was by that point secretary of the treasury. Paulson, in turn, praised the initiative to reporters and announced that the group's intention to enhance the competitiveness of American business (language often used to avoid more direct statements about elimination of regulation) "is important to the future of the American economy and a priority for me."[183]

The group would be studying the effects of Sarbanes-Oxley and the new SEC regulations on American competitiveness. Its membership consisted of corporate executives and academic and think-tank writers well known for their attacks on regulation, but "no former agency chairmen or commissioners, or people who held major S.E.C. staff positions." In fact, Scott told reporters, "We generally tried not to include regulators. . . . We would not want to put people in the position who had formulated these rules in the past. They may have a lack of objectivity."[184] Given the makeup of the group, such a statement could hardly be taken seriously. It was, of course, no accident that the group timed the release of its report for after the November 2006 elections.

Soon after the elections the administration and its appointees at the SEC began to roll back regulations. On December 13, 2006, the SEC announced a series of decisions relaxing regulatory constraints in a variety of areas. Just a day before that, the DOJ announced new guidelines for federal prosecutors for charging and prosecuting white-collar crimes, guidance that placed more restrictions on those prosecutors. That was important not only for the obvious reasons, but also because many had seen the possibility of criminal prosecutions for extreme cases of corporate abuse as an alternative to strong regulatory programs administered by federal agencies. From the other side, it reduced some of the fear by corporate management of the most stringent sanctions under the Sarbanes-Oxley legislation.

The 2006 assault was only the first wave in the counterattack. The second wave began when the Bush administration launched a series of meetings with corporate officials in the spring of 2007. The opening dinner for a conference of those involved in the counteroffensive was held in March and was sponsored by the Department of the Treasury, with opening remarks from Vice President Cheney. The meeting also included members of Congress. Secretary Paulson and SEC Chair Cox led the closed-door sessions the following day. In addition to a cast of CEOs, other participants included Robert Rubin, who, as Clinton's treasury secretary, had been a leader of the economic deregulation forces in the 1990s, as well as Alan Greenspan, former Federal Reserve chair. Interestingly, the extensive story detailing these meetings and their participants was reported in Section C of the *New York Times*.[185] Only four weeks later, the SEC once again took up suggested relaxations of regulations.

Another of those situations that forced the administration to regulate, even as it was waging war against regulation, was the mad cow disease problem that arose in late 2003. On December 23, the U.S. Department of Agriculture (USDA) held a news conference to announce: "Today we received word from USDA's National Veterinary Services Laboratories in Iowa that a single

Holstein cow from Washington State has tested as presumptive positive for BSE or what is widely known as mad cow disease."[186] This was the first time that the animal disease bovine spongiform encephalopathy (BSE) had been identified in the United States, though it had previously created fear in the populace and a crisis in the livestock industry in Britain and later in Canada. The concern arose from the fact that BSE was linked to the fatal Creutzfeldt-Jakob disease in humans and also from the fact that, in an effort to avoid the spread of BSE among animals and to protect the human food supply, other countries had refused to import animal products from countries that had experienced the disease.

The USDA assured Americans that U.S. beef was safe and that no part of the diseased cow had reached the human food chain. Additional assurances were given that this was only one cow and that there was no reason to fear the spread of BSE. However, it was soon learned that there was no effective way to track either the animals or the distribution of the parts of the slaughtered livestock. Additionally, it turned out that the cow was what is known as a "downer animal," one not really physically healthy when it was sent to slaughter such that it was not necessarily able even to walk into the slaughterhouse. In the weeks that followed, it emerged that the cattle industry had beaten back efforts in previous years for tighter regulation and tracking as well as to prevent some kinds of animals from being taken to slaughter and that there really was not anything like an effective regulatory program in place to address the situation.

In less than a month, the USDA generated several sets of interim final rules, including the "Prohibition of the Use of Specified Risk Materials for Human Food and Requirements for the Disposition of Non-Ambulatory Disabled Cattle,"[187] "Meat Produced by Advanced Meat/Bone Separation Machinery and Meat Recovery (AMR) Systems,"[188] and "Prohibition of the Use of Certain Stunning Devices Used to Immobilize Cattle during Slaughter."[189] Those actions were followed by rulemaking by the FDA to address the "Use of Materials Derived from Cattle in Human Food and Cosmetics."[190] Consumers were assured that all of the necessary steps were being taken to protect the food supply and to bar the use of animal products that might be tainted with BSE. Among other things, consumers were pleased to learn that the practice of slaughtering downer animals would end.

However, early in 2008, there was a jolt to the public confidence when it was learned downer animals were indeed still being slaughtered for the human food supply. A group recorded the process used in one California slaughterhouse to abuse animals into moving into the line for slaughter. To make matters worse, a good portion of meat from that plant had found its way into school lunch programs. The outcry forced the nation's largest voluntary recall of meat ever.[191] The regulators claimed that the firm had violated agency rules regarding "nonambulatory animals," since each such animal was to be examined by an inspector to ensure that it was healthy enough to go to slaughter. However, what the public wanted to know was what had happened to what had apparently been a set of regulations banning the use of downer animals in any case.

What had happened was that between the time that the interim final rules were issued in January 2004 and the issuance of final regulations in July 2007, public attention was drawn away from the demand for regulation, but the attention of the administration and the industries it regulated remained focused on changes in those regulations so as to back away from some of the immediate demands for more stringent regulatory controls.[192] Whereas the interim final rule had "prohibit[ed] the slaughter for human food of non-ambulatory disabled cattle that are offered for slaughter,"[193] the final rules provided that "FSIS inspection personnel will determine on a case-by-case basis the disposition of cattle that become nonambulatory after they have passed antemortem inspection."[194] It was a quiet counterattack, but a successful one.

A third example arose midway through the administration, with a number of mining disasters, with the Sago mine collapse drawing particular attention in the media and in Congress. Here again, there was immediate action, but it was clear, particularly given its effective use of counterstaffing, that the administration was unlikely to maintain the aggressive regulatory approach demanded by those speaking with grieving families and in media interviews thereafter.

There have been a host of other targeted administrative counteroffensives, ranging from battles to limit Endangered Species Act protection, to further relaxation on what limited regulatory constraints remain on truck driving safety regulations, though some of those efforts pushed so far that federal courts repelled the attack.[195] Not surprisingly, while it was working to roll back regulatory policy, the administration also significantly relaxed enforcement in a variety of areas. Eric V. Schaeffer, director of the EPA Office of Regulatory Enforcement, resigned in protest over the administration's efforts to undermine even ongoing enforcement actions, let alone new ones. In his letter to EPA Administrator Christine Todd Whitman, Schaeffer wrote in part:

> I cannot leave without sharing my frustration about the fate of our enforcement actions against power companies that have violated the Clean Air Act. . . .
>
> We are in the 9th month of a "90 day review" to reexamine the law, and fighting a White House that seems determined to weaken the rules we are trying to enforce. It is hard to know which is worse, the endless delay or the repeated leaks by energy industry lobbyists of draft rule changes that would undermine lawsuits already filed. . . .
>
> It is no longer possible to pretend that the ongoing debate with the White House and Department of Energy is not effecting [*sic*] our ability to negotiate settlements. Cinergy and Vepco have refused to sign the consent decrees they agreed to 15 months ago, hedging their bets while waiting for the Administration's Clean Air Act reform proposals. Other companies with whom we were close to settlement have walked away from the table. The momentum we obtained with agreements announced earlier has stopped, and we have filed no new lawsuits against utility companies since this Administration took office. . . .
>
> The relative costs and benefits? EPA's regulatory impact analyses, reviewed by OMB, quantify health and environmental benefits of $7,300 per ton of SO_2 reduced at a cost of less than $1,000 per ton. These cases should be supported by anyone who thinks cost-benefit analysis is a serious tool for decision-making, not a political game.
>
> I believe you share the concerns I have expressed, and wish you well in your efforts to persuade the Administration to put our enforcement actions back on course. Teddy Roosevelt, a Republican and our greatest environmental President, said, "Compliance with the law is demanded as a right, not asked as a favor." By showing that powerful utility interests are not exempt from that principle, you will prove to EPA's staff that their faith in the Agency's mission is not in vain.[196]

Of course, Whitman would soon be gone as well, without having accomplished Schaeffer's hope.

The Preemption Attack: The Federal Government Would Not Regulate
Effectively, and the States Were Barred from Doing It Themselves
The Bush administration was also more than ready to employ preemption tactics not only to ensure that the federal government would remove regulations, but to prevent states from stepping into the breach. The most glaring

example of the use of this weapon was the Energy Policy Act of 2005, but there were others as well.

The energy problems that existed at the beginning of the administration provided what John Kingdon called a "policy window," a receptivity to new policy.[197] But there was one more push to open the window even wider when, in August 2003, there was a massive power blackout that started in Ohio and spread throughout much of the northeast. The administration, working with Representative W. J. Tauzin (R-La.), successfully moved the Energy Policy Act through Congress. The act provided a range of incentives for energy sector firms and relaxed a variety of restrictions on their development and operation, but it also preempted states from stepping in to address abuses by those companies, such as the Enron debacle and other problems. One of the goals of industry had been to escape the burdens of state control over siting decisions for power lines and other power facilities. Indeed, barriers to development of more high-power transmission lines was blamed by industry and Energy Act proponents for the 2003 blackout. The window was open, and the Energy Policy Act was pushed through.

Almost immediately after passage of the legislation, Mr. Tauzin left the Congress to become the CEO of the chief lobbying organization for the pharmaceutical industry, the Pharmaceutical Research and Manufacturers of America. The following September he was made a member of the board of directors for Entergy Corporation, a major energy company that operates mainly in the area of electrical energy. At the time of this writing, the state of Oregon is attempting to deal with efforts to locate new Liquified Natural Gas terminals and pipelines in the state that will provide energy not to Oregon, but to California and other states, but its prospects to halt the project are clearly limited by the 2005 Act and the FERC refusal to take action in response to state requests.[198]

Another area of preemption in the Bush years was the refusal to grant waivers to states that wished to adopt more stringent regulations than federal agencies require. California and a host of other states went to court in an effort to overturn an EPA refusal to allow those states to impose more stringent vehicle emissions standards than the federal government mandates. Initial decisions in lower federal courts challenging the Vermont and California regulatory efforts saw the states prevail against suits by automotive dealers and manufacturers who claimed that the state regulation was preempted by the

Clean Air Act, the Energy Policy and Conservation Act, and federal government foreign policy. The first decision came in federal district court in Vermont, rejecting the claims of preemption in *Green Mountain Chrysler v. Crombie.*[199] After that, the U.S. Supreme Court rendered its decision in the *Massachusetts v. EPA* case, discussed earlier. Then the U.S. District Court for the Eastern District of California announced its ruling in *Central Valley Chrysler-Jeep v. Goldstone,* also rejecting the preemption claims, including the claim of foreign policy preemption.[200] The courts were saying that action by the states in this area was not preempted by federal law, but the administration would have none of it.

California had previously been granted the waivers, which had long been recognized. When the Bush administration refused to take action to address global warming, California and other states decided that they would choose to undertake policies in their states that went beyond the federal requirements to increase fuel economy and decrease emission of greenhouse gases. The EPA administrator denied the waiver in December 2007, but internal EPA documents released by Congress demonstrated that the administrator had been informed by his staff that a denial of the state waiver request was not justified either by law or by policy analytic findings.[201]

Then there was the case of the FDA and the effort to assist drug companies by seeking to preempt state failure-to-warn litigation. Until 2002, the FDA under both Republican and Democratic administrations had viewed state law failure-to-warn suits as a useful complement to FDA drug labeling requirements.[202] The drug companies were fiercely opposed to such state court suits and took one decided by the Vermont Supreme Court in 2006 to the U.S. Supreme Court, which rejected the preemption claim.[203] The Vermont Supreme Court rejected the claims by Wyeth that FDA legislation and rules preempted such state suits.

However, investigators from the House Committee on Oversight and Federal Reform produced a report in the fall of 2008 detailing efforts by the Bush administration to change the rules to provide protection for the firms, using the preemption weapon.[204] The report concluded that this was done over the objections of FDA career staff whose arguments were similar to those advanced publicly later by two former FDA commissioners, Drs. Donald Kennedy, who served during the Carter years, and David A. Kessler, who was appointed by George H. W. Bush and reappointed by Clinton, serving from 1990 to 1997.

Kennedy and Kessler presented their rejection of the preemption argument in an amici curiae brief filed in the fall of 2008 in the Vermont case.[205]

Different Kinds of Wars and Different Kinds of Tactics: Indirect Attacks

The Bush administration employed the full range of indirect attacks as well. In particular, it employed a variation on the antipersonnel attack as well as strategic resources attacks to weaken regulatory agencies.

The antipersonnel effort came in a slightly different form from that employed in previous administrations and was used along with the strategic resources attack. This chapter explained the Bush administration's efforts early on to change the OMB A-76 circular in a way that would support demands by private sector organizations under the so-called FAIR Act that agencies offer more of the work they were then doing within the agency for bid by outside organizations and that would then make the external bidders more successful in bids to take that work outside the government agencies.[206] This chapter also explained that this effort was related to the president's commitment in his management agenda to contract out more of government's activities. There was pressure from the administration in the early years for agencies to move significant portions of their work out by contract. All of this then made some administrative agency human resources positions surplus and available for cut. Of course, the administration did not take action to dramatically increase the trained and fully staffed contract management capacity within those agencies, which led to major contracting problems across agencies, and particularly in agencies such as the DoD.[207] Additionally, this chapter also explained the effort to move agencies out of the traditional civil service system, such as the DHS and the DoD, in a manner that provided greater flexibility for the administration to make its own human resource rules and administer them as it saw fit.

The dramatic effort to outsource government work, coupled with significant funding cuts in domestic programs, and the overtly political and conflict-oriented appointments to top levels in the agencies, provided disincentives for many young professionals who were entering public service from public administration and other professional programs. Those dynamics when taken together also were effective in the break-the-system-and-blame-it-for-being-broken tactic reminiscent of the Reagan era.

There was no question to those in the regulatory arena that the Bush White House was very deliberately pursuing aggressive strategic resource attacks on domestic programs, and regulatory programs took particularly serious hits at a time when demands for action by those agencies was increasing dramatically. The administration's initial strategy came directly from the battle plans of the Reagan era. When the administration took office in 2001, it immediately moved to obtain passage of a major tax cut. It also had plans for significant increases in military and other security expenditures. As Reagan's OMB Director David Stockman had argued in the 1980s, the pressure brought on by increased spending and decreased tax revenues would make possible cuts in otherwise untouchable domestic programs, and the Bush administration moved to do precisely that. Bush had his OMB notify domestic agencies during the summer of 2001 that they were to prepare for a 5 percent cut in their next budgets. These steps were taken before the September 11, 2001, terrorist attacks. After the attacks, all controls were off and the administration made it clear that it would make massive calls for increased military and national security spending, but that increased deficits would require significant cuts in domestic programs.

On occasion, the political superiors in some agencies sought to use their lack of resources as a defense for failure to take the regulatory actions required by statute. In two cases involving failures to comply with the requirements of the Endangered Species Act, for example, lawyers for Secretary of the Interior Norton and, later, Secretary Kempthorne argued that the agency could not meet its obligations because of inadequate funding. This is a strategy first made famous (or infamous) by Governor George Wallace of Alabama, known as financial interposition. Wallace had argued that civil rights protests and requirements of civil rights could not be supported because the appropriate state agencies lacked the resources to ensure safety and execute the law. That strategy did not work for Wallace, and it has not been acceptable in the recent regulatory cases. The courts rejected both of the interior secretaries' arguments, warning that their issues with resources needed to be dealt with by the appropriate institutions, but the requirements of the regulatory statutes they were to administer were obligatory.[208]

Quite apart from tactical uses of the problem, the fact was that regulatory agencies would not do well even in terms of the cuts generally applicable to domestic programs in this environment. The EPA, for example, faced a cut of almost $300 million in the president's request with respect to the agency's discretionary funds in FY2003, and the FY2005 request once again called for a cut in spending. However, the administration proudly announced that defense spending had increased by some 48 percent from the time Bush had taken office to his FY2007 budget request, and that did not count the costs of the wars in Iraq or Afghanistan, which were handled primarily off-budget through supplemental appropriations requests.[209] Then there were dramatic expenditures and annual increases for the DHS created by statute in 2002. While these expenditures were shooting upward, domestic spending was being cut, both in real dollars and by virtue of inflation. President Bush claimed in his FY2007 request that "again, I am proposing to hold overall discretionary spending below the rate of inflation and to cut spending in non-security discretionary programs below 2006 levels."[210] He used similar language in several of his budget proposals.

Thus, in his resignation letter to Christine Todd Whitman, EPA enforcement chief, Eric Schaeffer wrote in part:

> Our negotiating position is weakened further by the Administration's budget proposal to cut the civil enforcement program by more than 200 staff positions below the 2001 level. Already, we are unable to fill key staff positions, not only in air enforcement, but in other critical programs, and the proposed budget cuts would leave us desperately short of the resources needed to deal with the large, sophisticated corporate defendants we face. And it is completely unrealistic to expect underfunded state environmental programs, facing their own budget cuts, to take up the slack.[211]

The FDA is another agency that has been dramatically weakened over time, with an actual decline in numbers of people in key areas, such as food inspection, over a period when the amount of complex food issues and food imports have grown dramatically. Thus, even former Bush Health and Human Services Secretary Tommy Thompson, who joined a group called the Coalition for a Stronger F.D.A., warned reporters that "you can't do it on the cheap. . . . You are going to have to put more dollars in the F.D.A."[212] The situation continued to be dire even when *E. coli* contamination and other national food and drug safety issues drew headlines around the nation.

In an effort to drive home the fact that the situation at FDA had gone past the point of being serious, the Subcommittee on Science and Technology of the FDA Science Board issued a report in November 2007 entitled *FDA Science and Mission at Risk*.[213] The group, made up of experts from outside the agency, announced that while its focus was to identify issues with respect to the scientific expertise of the agency, what it found itself forced to deal with was the fact that the lack of resources was at the heart of virtually all of the problem areas that it investigated.[214] The subcommittee found that the agency had not grown significantly in almost two decades in the critical areas, while its tasks were expanding dramatically.

Specifically, the report explained that in the twenty years leading up to the report, there were 123 additional statutes adopted that required FDA action. However, "during the same 20-year period from 1988 to 2007, while faced with 123 new statutes, FDA gained through appropriation only 646 employees—an increase of 9 percent—and lost more than $300 million to inflation."[215] The stresses had produced a turnover rate "twice that of other government agencies."[216] In sum, the subcommittee said:

> We found that FDA's resource shortfalls have resulted in a plethora of inadequacies that threaten our society—including, but not limited to, inadequate inspections of manufacturers, a dearth of scientists who understand emerging new technologies, inability to speed the development of new therapies, an import system that is badly broken, a food supply that grows riskier each year, and an information infrastructure that was identified as a source of risk in every Center and program reviewed by the Subcommittee. We conclude that FDA can no longer fulfill its mission without substantial and sustained additional appropriations. Numerous reports by the National Academies of Science . . . , the Government Accountability Office (GAO), the Health and Human Services (HHS) Inspector General, Congressional committees, and other expert groups have come to the same conclusion. The opinion of these studies is unanimous— current gaps are due to chronic underfunding of the Agency, and if these gaps are not addressed immediately, FDA is in jeopardy of losing its remaining dedicated staff. The extraordinary efforts of these committed FDA staff members are the very reason further catastrophic food and drug events have been averted.[217]

Other agencies are facing similarly bleak financial pictures and also confront increasingly complex and challenging obligations. Given the leadership of a number of these agencies stationed there through the counterstaffing offensives, the situation for those in the agencies and those members of the public seeking regulatory action from those institutions have been made more difficult by actions both outside and inside the agencies.

The strategic resources and antipersonnel attacks were successful in weakening the regulatory bodies and, in the process, have also been extremely successful psychological warfare tactics. The intentional lack of regulatory action, the rollbacks of previous protections, and the simple inability to respond, even by those dedicated individuals of whom the FDA subcommittee and former EPA enforcement chief Schaeffer wrote, because the agencies have been hollowed out and loaded with procedural and substantive barriers to action, have contributed to the picture of government as incapable of functioning effectively. The picture of government as "the problem" sounded in Ronald Reagan's inaugural address and continued by the repeated pronouncements of lack of performance during the George W. Bush administration only supported continued attacks on regulatory programs and the agencies responsible for their implementation.

End Game: Midnight Rulemaking and Deregulation amid Demands for Regulation

As the Bush administration entered its last year in office, it dealt with two important dynamics in American society. The first was the phenomenon known as midnight rulemaking, according to which administrations preparing to leave office seek to push a torrent of rulemaking through the procedural pipeline in order to complete their agendas before leaving office. The second was the need to address the disastrous downturn in the economy, a crisis that was in large part the result of deregulation in a variety of areas over time. Even in this context, the Bush administration pressed the battle against regulation, even as some of its officials promised new and improved regulation to address the economic disaster.

Midnight Rulemaking: A Final Offensive in the Fight against Regulation

Most recent administrations have moved dramatically in their last months in office to push new regulations through the policy process in order to accomplish unresolved items on their agendas. And the George W. Bush administration was among the most aggressive in modern history in pressing its policy priorities. So, it came as somewhat of a surprise when the Bush administration announced to the media that it would do all that it could to assist the incoming president, whoever that would be, and that it would not use midnight rulemaking to push new policies out the door as its term came to a close. To underscore the point, the administration announced that White House Chief of Staff Joshua Bolten had issued a memorandum on late-term rulemaking to the heads of executive branch departments and agencies on May 9, 2008. This

appeared to be part of a charm offensive at the end of the Bush term to improve the president's image as he left office.

It turned out, however, that the administration had no intention of rejecting midnight rulemaking and indeed embraced the practice in order to adopt
regulations to accomplish controversial policy objectives. In the process, Bush
and his appointees clearly intended to use this process more effectively than
their predecessors in order to make it much more difficult for a successor administration to undo their actions. Second, many of the initiatives they chose
to press were part of the continuing war against regulation. Third, they did so
even at a time when the country was entering an economic crisis of historic
proportions and even as the administration proclaimed that it was going to
ensure effective regulation in the face of evidence that the crisis had been
brought on by the past deregulation.

It is true that Bolten issued the memorandum in early May. However, it
conveyed a message rather different from the one portrayed in the media. The
agencies were warned that they were not to start any rulemaking after July 1
and not to issue any final rules after November 1.[218] The subtext is that it is
much more difficult for an incoming administration to stop rules that have
already been formally issued when the thirty-day *Federal Register* public notice period required by the APA has elapsed and the sixty-day period for legislative consideration under the CRA has passed.[219] At that point, the agency
involved would have to undertake a new rulemaking proceeding to amend or
rescind the rule.[220]

The administration was fully aware of this transition dynamic because it
had moved quickly upon taking office to block end-of-administration rulemaking by the Clinton administration. Then Chief of Staff Andrew Card had
issued a memorandum to freeze rulemaking in progress and to pull back regulations that had not moved completely through the process and gone into effect. As Curtis W. Copeland, the Congressional Research Service (CRS) expert
in this field, put it in hearings before the House Subcommittee on Commercial and Administrative Law on "Midnight Rulemaking" held in February
2009:

> Viewed in this context, the May 2008 memorandum by White House Chief of
> Staff Bolten represents both a continuation of a trend of presidential involvement
> in rulemaking related to transitions, and an evolution in that involvement.
> Therefore, because the Bolten memorandum required that all final rules be
> published in the *Federal Register* by November 1, 2008, full compliance with this

requirement would result in all rules having taken effect before President Obama took office on January 20, 2009. Some observers have noted that this approach was quite effective, as many of the controversial final rules that were issued at the end of the Bush Administration had taken effect by the time President Obama took office. In contrast, many rules that were issued at the end of the Clinton Administration had not taken effect.[221]

It quickly became clear that the administration would accelerate its efforts to push through regulations that were, paradoxically, part of its ongoing war against regulation. Indeed Bolten wrote in his memorandum,

> We need to continue this principled approach to regulation as we sprint to the finish. . . . Every regulatory agency and department has a responsibility for continuing to ensure regulations issued in this final year are in the best interests of the American public. To ensure we continue to serve the American people through carefully-designed regulations, the Administrator of the Office of Information and Regulatory Affairs (OIRA) of the Office of Management and Budget (OMB) will coordinate an effort to complete administration priorities in this final year while providing for an appropriately open and transparent process and controlling regulatory costs. In this effort, OIRA will work closely with the heads of the President's policy councils, and rely on its centralized review authority under Executive Order 12866.[222]

The administration's actions in the months following the Bolten memorandum were monitored carefully not only by congressional staff, including the CRS, but also by interested nongovernmental organizations like OMB Watch. The CRS released a study in late November that showed clearly that the administration was indeed engaged in an energetic period of midnight rulemaking, with the intention of pressing its deregulation agenda.[223] The OMB Watch organization issued its own report in January 2009 that reached similar conclusions.[224]

Copeland continued his studies at the CRS in the final weeks before the Bush administration left office and President Obama was preparing to begin his term. At House subcommittee hearings on February 4, 2009, Copeland presented his findings.

> During the first six months of 2008, the agencies sent GAO a total of 32 major final rules, but in the second six months, the agencies sent GAO 53 rules—a 65% increase. The number of major rules in the second six months of 2008 was also higher than the number in the second six months of 2007 (53 major rules in 2008 compared with 41 major rules in 2007—a 29% increase). The biggest differences

between 2007 and 2008 were in the months of October and November. In 2007, federal agencies submitted 13 major rules to GAO in October and November, but in the same two months in 2008, the agencies submitted 30 major rules—a 131% increase.

The surge in rulemaking at the end of the Bush Administration is also apparent in the number of "significant" rules that OIRA reviewed pursuant to Executive Order 12866. According to the Regulatory Information Service Center, from September 1, 2008, through December 31, 2008, OIRA reviewed a total of 190 significant final rules—a 102% increase when compared to the same period in 2007 (94 rules).[225]

The CRS and OMB Watch reports provided detailed charts, showing the content and timing of rules developed and issued in the waning months of the Bush administration.

The irony in all this flurry of rulemaking activity was underscored by OMB Watch Executive Director Gary D. Bass at the February hearing. "Ironically, the Bush administration chose to use regulations at the end of its term to promote its anti-regulatory philosophy."[226] Among the actions taken were rules relaxing application of Clean Air Act rules with respect to so-called New Source Review; rules exempting factory farms from air emissions reporting requirements; rules relaxing limits on maximum driving hours and minimum rest periods for truck drivers; Department of Interior rules that would relax requirements for protecting streams from being polluted by mining wastes; rules that would have relaxed application of the Endangered Species Act in certain circumstances; DOJ rules that appeared likely to ease restrictions on the use of sensitive information by local police even in the absence of probable cause; rules easing the stringency of Americans with Disabilities Act standards and enforcement; EPA rules that intended to limit application of Resource Conservation and Recovery Act regulations in some circumstances involving so-called hazardous secondary waste; rules relaxing emissions standards on facilities near national parks; rules from the Park Service allowing local determinations as to whether concealed weapons could be carried in the parks; and rules that would change occupational health risk determinations, among others.[227]

Economic Crisis: A Promise of Action,
but a Continued Focus on Market Solutions

The other irony in the midnight rulemaking effort was that it continued the war on regulation at a time when the nation was in the throes of a dramatic economic downturn in which earlier deregulation was clearly a major factor. As the evidence of serious problems in the markets and in the economy grew through the spring and into the summer of 2008, it was becoming increasingly clear that major financial institutions appeared to be vulnerable. With the collapse of Lehman Brothers in early September, it was plain beyond any question that the nation was entering a critical period even worse than the recession in the preceding months. Mortgage markets collapsed, banks were in serious trouble because of bad loans, and unemployment was on the rise. It was also becoming painfully obvious that relaxation of banking regulations and regulations concerning derivatives and other complex financial instruments were taking their toll.

Loan originators and some bank employees had tolerated, and in some cases encouraged, the filing of false income information as well as the use of false property valuations to facilitate loans that should not have been granted. The questionable mortgages were bundled together into mortgage-backed securities that were themselves extremely problematic devices. It became clear that the use of high-risk financial instruments such as derivatives that were used to backstop the mortgage-backed securities was rampant, despite the fact that these were dangerous devices in many ways and given that the forms of these instruments had become so complex that even some of the most sophisticated financial professionals later admitted that they did not fully understand their operation.

The administration shifted into crisis mode and insisted that it would, with the cooperation of the Congress, ensure creation of substantial regulatory authority in the Treasury and the Federal Reserve. At the same time, the administration sought a bailout package from Congress for financial institutions of more than $700 billion, later known as the TARP, or Troubled Assets Relief Program. The Congress rapidly agreed to the measure after briefings from the Bush administration warned that a failure to act promptly would trigger a massive economic disaster comparable to the Great Depression.

Yet even as the Bush administration promised strong action to stabilize the economy and restore effective regulation, the administration was in fact moving in a very different direction. From the spring and as late as July the treasury secretary and the SEC chair were speaking of the need to shift U.S. market regulatory standards to those used internationally by countries like Great Britain because U.S. markets would lose business to the even less controlled international markets. Even as it sought a dramatic bailout bill from Congress, it was becoming clear that the administration was not likely to actually take strong regulatory action. The first version of the bailout bill sent to Congress was extremely brief, only a few pages in length. Rather than require a careful regulatory structure under which to implement the program and ensure accountability and transparency, the treasury secretary requested a bill that gave him virtually unlimited authority. Section 8 of the proposal also provided that "decisions by the Secretary pursuant to the authority of this Act are non-reviewable and committed to agency discretion, and may not be reviewed by any court of law or any administrative agency."[228]

While there were announcements of enhanced regulatory powers for the Federal Reserve and the Department of the Treasury, these agencies had not been adequately prepared for significant operations with respect to these regulatory challenges, and there was little evidence that Secretary Paulson, long a foe of regulation, intended to press for serious and sustained regulation. The SEC had been so under-resourced and weakened that it was incapable of dealing with the situation even assuming that its leadership had wanted to do so, and there was little evidence that the SEC chair had wanted to take an aggressive approach. Even as late as October 23, the SEC chair, who had earlier opposed regulation of derivatives, suggested during questioning by members of the House Oversight and Government Reform Committee during hearings on "The Financial Crisis and the Role of Federal Regulators," that no one had foreseen that derivatives would be so dangerous. The derivatives that were the subject of this discussion were specifically those known as credit-default swaps. To his comments and those of former Federal Reserve chair Alan Greenspan, Representative Eleanor Holmes Norton (D-D.C.) noted that while some of the contemporary forms of derivatives may be new and complex, the fundamental dangers of the use and abuse of derivatives as financial mechanisms had been known for many years.

As long ago as 1994, the GAO had emphasized the dangers of derivatives and the need to regulate their use carefully.[229] Indeed, later that year, in December 1994, Orange County, California, went into default because of the use and abuse of derivatives by its treasurer and the brokerage house advising him. Notwithstanding these problems, Congress adopted in 2000 the Commodity Futures Modernization Act, which was supported by the Clinton administration and which under the promise of modernizing the financial markets effectively exempted derivatives trading from regulation.

Throughout the fall of 2008, the House Oversight and Government

Reform Committee concluded a series of hearings "on the role of federal regulators in the economic crisis,"[230] the collapse of Lehman Brothers,[231] the AIG crisis and bailout,[232] and on "The Role of Fannie Mae and Freddie Mac in the Financial Crisis,"[233] which presented damage assessments from the war against regulation and the condition of the regulatory infrastructure that played a key role in the economic crisis facing the nation.

While this was in progress, the president had demanded, and the Congress had provided, massive bailout legislation known as the TARP.[234]

The legislation gave the secretary of the treasury broad authority to implement the more than $700 billion package. While Section 125 of the act created a body called the Congressional Oversight Panel (COP), that panel was only given authority to review data and produce reports. There was little serious accountability built into the program. In January 2009, as the Bush administration was preparing to leave office and after the first $350 billion had been committed, the COP issued a report on TARP accountability that indicated that the panel had not been able to obtain the data it needed from the treasury secretary. The panel complained that:

> The Panel still does not know what the banks are doing with taxpayer money. Treasury places substantial emphasis in its December 30 letter on the importance of restoring confidence in the marketplace. So long as investors and customers are uncertain about how taxpayer funds are being used, they question both the health and the sound management of all financial institutions. The recent refusal of certain private financial institutions to provide any accounting of how they are using taxpayer money undermines public confidence. For Treasury to advance funds to these institutions without requiring more transparency further erodes the very confidence Treasury seeks to restore.[235]

It was clear that the secretary of the treasury was not concerned about either transparency or accountability. Indeed, the panel found that the secretary was clearly concerned with assisting financial institutions and not with the several purposes of the legislation. The panel's frustration was clear.

> The Panel's initial concerns about the TARP have only grown, exacerbated by the shifting explanations of its purposes and the tools used by Treasury. It is not enough to say that the goal is the stabilization of the financial markets and the broader economy. That goal is widely accepted. The question is *how* the infusion of billions of dollars to an insurance conglomerate or a credit card company advances both the goal of financial stability and the well-being of taxpayers,

including homeowners threatened by foreclosure, people losing their jobs, and families unable to pay their credit cards.[236]

By the time the COP report on accountability was issued, there was serious concern that firms that had received the funds were not using that assistance to help the mortgage market or other specific concerns but were in some cases using the money to improve their cash positions so that they could, in turn, acquire other firms or pursue other corporate strategies that had nothing to do with the purposes members of Congress had in mind when they enacted the bailout bill.[237] Then there were headlines about lavish bonuses for some of the executives or firms receiving federal assistance and other behavior that members of Congress and many Americans who were in increasing financial distress saw as nothing short of scandalous. In hearings before the House Financial Services Committee in February 2009 that called corporate executives to testify, Representative Paul Kanjorski (D-Pa.), said:

> Mr. Chairman, today we will learn how some of the richest and most powerful men in America are spending billions of dollars of taxpayer money. Because some of my colleagues will probably ask our witnesses to explain their enormous bonuses being issued at a time of great national suffering, I will not do so. And because my colleagues will likely inquire as to their ownership of numerous vacation homes while millions of Americans face foreclosure on the only home they have, I will leave that subject alone. Because some Members will doubtlessly seek to understand how you can underwrite frivolous junkets when most Americans would do almost anything for a job—let alone a vacation—I will defer that question, too. Instead, I want to know where the money has gone and why it went there.[238]

And Then There Was Madoff: Years of Warnings to the SEC Ignored

While all of these matters were unfolding, another storm was about to break over Wall Street as once highly regarded fund manager Bernard Madoff turned himself in to authorities and admitted to operating a massive Ponzi scheme that resulted in the loss of more than $50 billion in assets. Madoff took down with him a wide range of investors from highly regarded institutions to large numbers of individual retirees. Unfortunately, the evidence indicated that the SEC had been repeatedly warned about the scheme and its massive size since at least 2000 and yet did not take action to stop it.

Madoff was a former chair of the NASDAQ stock market and head of Bernard L. Madoff Investment Security, LLC. As the U.S. Attorney for the

Southern District of New York explained in announcing Madoff's arrest and charges against him, "On December 10, 2008, MADOFF informed the Senior Employees, in substance, that his investment advisory business was a fraud. MADOFF stated that he was 'finished,' that he had 'absolutely nothing,' that 'it's all just one big lie,' and that it was 'basically, a giant Ponzi scheme.'"[239]

As the impact of the Madoff scheme became clearer, the Subcommittee on Capital Markets, Insurance, and Government Sponsored Enterprises of the House Financial Services Committee held hearings on the question of just how this scheme could have gone undetected for so long with such devastating consequences.[240] It turned out that there was abundant evidence that the SEC had known since 2000 that there was an urgent need to pursue a vigorous investigation of Madoff. The hearing took testimony from Harry Markopolos, who is a Chartered Financial Analyst and Certified Fraud Examiner.

Markopolos testified that he had first informed the SEC of the Madoff scandal and indicated that an investigation was needed in May 2000.[241] He repeatedly contacted the SEC and provided additional information until the time when Madoff turned himself in. The SEC rejected his efforts to bring the scheme to light and ensure prosecution. In order to demonstrate how his team and he had tried to force SEC action, Markopolos provided copies of his documentation and e-mail correspondence to the SEC as part of his voluminous testimony. He stressed that his team had been able to unearth the scheme quickly, easily, and with only materials readily available in the public domain.

In sum, the war against regulation during the George W. Bush era was extremely successful up to and including the final months of the administration and even as the nation fell into an economic morass. It will be years before a complete damage assessment can be concluded, but it is clear that the victims not only number in the millions throughout the United States, but may reach the billions as the U.S. economic disaster affected other countries around the globe.

CONCLUSION

Although they cannot claim total victory in the war against regulation, the aggressors have scored a variety of major victories and can claim several successful campaigns throughout the Carter, Reagan, George H. W. Bush, Clinton, and George W. Bush administrations. Using direct and indirect weapons, strategies, and tactics, these administrations have rolled back a variety of regulatory programs legislatively or by administrative means and have so burdened others and weakened their administration by resource and antipersonnel attacks that the regulatory protections that many Americans have assumed are in place are not truly available for their health, safety, and financial well-being.

Sadly, there have been casualties, not merely among public service professionals in the regulatory community, but also among those the regulatory agencies were originally created to defend. This language is not merely metaphorical. Real people, both adults and children, rich and poor, of all ethnicities and races, have suffered and some have even died as a result of these conflicts.

As in any war, the adversary—in this case regulation and those who administer it—has often been demonized to the greatest extent possible in order to rally support for the fight and to justify the costs in blood and treasure that have been paid and that likely will be spent in the future. Whether it is characterized as an attack on the "bloated puzzle palaces on the Potomac," as the Reagan administration depicted them, or as bad systems with good people trapped inside, as used by the Clinton administration, the idea has been to take the already unpopular aspects of regulation and expand them to the point of caricature.

The last two chapters have focused on the battle against regulation waged in Washington and largely from the White House. Chapter 4 considers a different arena, the conflict in the courts.

4. The Battle against Regulation in the Courts: The Fight against Regulation in the Burger and Rehnquist Eras

The previous chapters have focused on the war against regulation led by presidents of both political parties and by members of Congress on both sides of the aisle. However, there has been another front to which even less attention has been paid. It is the battle against regulation that has been waged in the courts. The same presidents who were leading the fight through direct and indirect tactics in the executive branch and in cooperation with members of Congress were also appointing federal judges whose records and inclinations, insofar as the White House was able to discern them, were in line with the presidents'. The hope and expectation was that these appointments would produce courts ready and willing to enter the lists in the war against regulation, and they did. The Burger and Rehnquist courts played major roles in the fight, rendering a variety of important rulings that constrained federal regulatory action and others that blocked action at the state and local levels as well. One of the products of these attacks has been to stimulate efforts at regulation by lawsuit, but that effort in turn produced a counteroffensive in the courts and among deregulation warriors in Congress and the White House as well.

This chapter examines the effort in the courts to constrain federal regulatory authority. It then turns to the constraints imposed on state and local governments. Finally, it addresses what happened when, frustrated by the ineffectiveness of regulation by legislatures and executives, attempts were made to regulate by lawsuit.

THE CONSTITUTION "DID NOT ENACT MR. HERBERT SPENCER'S SOCIAL STATICS": THE FIGHT AGAINST REGULATION IN THE BURGER AND REHNQUIST ERAS

In an earlier era, the Supreme Court was an active combatant in the war against regulation. Ironically, the Burger and Rehnquist courts have behaved in ways that are reminiscent of the Court's attacks of that time a century before. Frustrated by a continuing array of assaults on regulatory authority and practices, Justice Oliver Wendell Holmes protested at the turn of the twentieth century that the Constitution "did not enact Mr. Herbert Spencer's social statics."[1] His reference was, of course, to the writer considered the great social Darwinist of the period, whose works were holy writ in the Gospel of Wealth that shaped the so-called Gilded Age of the late nineteenth and early twentieth centuries. It was a time in which the fight to block government regulation was so effective that the period is still described as the "laissez-faire era." The set of rulings about which Holmes was complaining, along with a number of similar decisions that came after it, were roundly condemned and rejected by the Court years later in opinions that restored what had long been recognized as the constitutionally vested regulatory authority of government to address a variety of economic and social problems.[2]

However, decades after that, led by Associate and later Chief Justice William Rehnquist, the Court would once again fight to constrain regulatory authority in a manner that had not been witnessed since before 1937. A number of these decisions came in sharply divided courts, but, once rendered, they were used as if they represented long-held and consistently applied constitutional doctrine. The attack had several components. It began with an offensive probe in force and then escalated to a direct confrontation to the authority of the Congress and of administrative agencies to launch regulatory policy.

A Judicial Probe in Force: The Usery Attack
on the Commerce Power of Congress

Justice Rehnquist led the Court on an audacious sortie into uncharted waters which he clearly expected might create a barrier to federal regulatory authority. It was audacious because it not only lacked a firm basis in the language, history, or case law of the Constitution, but actually flew in the face of a host of the Court's precedents over the nation's history, including some directly on point that had been issued just prior to Rehnquist's opinion in the key case of *National League of Cities v. Usery.*[3] Although the antiregulatory forces on the Court succeeded for a time with what became known as the *Usery* doctrine, this particular attack was ultimately beaten back. Nevertheless the Court's ruling in *Usery* served as a probe that provided experience for and intelligence to be used in later and far more successful assaults on national regulatory authority.

At the outset, the *Usery* case did not seem likely to be a particularly exceptional case. It came about as a challenge to amendments to the Fair Labor Standards Act, a law adopted in 1938 that created a regulatory framework to ensure minimum wages and protections for overtime compensation, among other features designed to protect workers. Over time, the coverage and terms of the FLSA were extended, with amendments in 1961, 1966, and 1974. Of particular importance to the *Usery* case was the fact that the 1966 amendments had removed the exemption in the original law for state and local employees and specifically included public school employees, as well as those who worked in state institutions and health-care facilities. The original FLSA was upheld by a unanimous Supreme Court in 1941 as a valid exercise by Congress of its power to regulate interstate commerce under Article I, §8 of the Constitution, and the 1961 and 1966 amendments were also found to be supported by that same authority in a 1968 ruling.[4] The 1974 amendments extended the act to more employees, including state and local agencies. The National League of Cities and a collection of state and local governments challenged the amendments, but that attack was rejected in the lower courts on the basis of the previous FLSA precedents.

The parties agreed that the activity covered by the legislation did indeed fit within the commerce clause authority of the Congress. The question was not whether the commerce power reached these employers and their employees. Since the early years of Supreme Court interpretation of the power to regulate interstate commerce, it had been clear that the reach of the commerce power was extensive and that it constrained state and local action.[5] After all, Congress has not only the specific grant of authority to regulate commerce power, but also the additional support of the necessary and proper clause, which provides that Congress shall have the power "To make all Laws which shall be necessary and proper for carrying into Execution the foregoing Powers and all other Powers vested by this Constitution in the Government of the United States, or in any Department or Officer thereof."[6] And, insofar as the actions of states were in conflict with those federal regulatory actions, the Constitution made clear in the Supremacy Clause of Article VI that the federal government would prevail. "This Constitution, and the Laws of the United States which shall be made in Pursuance thereof; and all Treaties made, or which shall be made, under the Authority of the United States, shall be the supreme Law of the Land; and the Judges in every State shall be bound thereby, any Thing in the Constitution or Laws of any state to the Contrary notwithstanding."[7]

Since the early years of the nation's history, the Court had stressed that once it was determined that the subject of legislation fell within the commerce power, that congressional authority was plenary. It barred state policies that contradicted the federal action. The Court also made it clear that the commerce power extended not only to the regulation of businesses but also reached state and local governments. Thus, even Justice Rehnquist recognized that:

> It is established beyond peradventure that the Commerce Clause of Art. I of the Constitution is a grant of plenary authority to Congress. That authority is, in the words of Mr. Chief Justice Marshall in *Gibbons v. Ogden*, 9 Wheat. 1 (1824), "the power to regulate; that is, to prescribe the rule by which commerce is to be governed." Id. , at 196.
>
> When considering the validity of asserted applications of this power to wholly private activity, the Court has made it clear that: "[e]ven activity that is purely intrastate in character may be regulated by Congress, where the activity, combined with like conduct by others similarly situated, affects commerce among the States or with foreign nations." *Fry v. United States*, 421 U.S. 542, 547 (1975).
>
> Congressional power over areas of private endeavor, even when its exercise may pre-empt express state-law determinations contrary to the result which has commended itself to the collective wisdom of Congress, has been held to be limited only by the requirement that "the means chosen by [Congress] must be reasonably adapted to the end permitted by the Constitution." *Heart of Atlanta Motel v. United States*, 379 U.S. 241, 262 (1964).[8]

In addition to the line of commerce clause cases, the Court had also long since established that, in those areas in which it has authority to act, the federal government is superior to the states and can control the states or their political subdivisions. Thus, as Justice Brennan pointed out in his dissent in the *Usery* case,

> We said in *United States v. California*, 297 U.S. 175, 184 (1936), for example: "The sovereign power of the states is necessarily diminished to the extent of the grants of power to the federal government in the Constitution. . . . [T]he power of the state is subordinate to the constitutional exercise of the granted federal power." This but echoed another principle emphasized by Mr. Chief Justice Marshall:
>
> > "If any one proposition could command the universal assent of mankind, we might expect it would be this—that the government of the Union, though limited in its powers, is supreme within its sphere of action. This would seem to result necessarily from its nature. It is the government of all; its powers are delegated by all; it represents all, and acts for all. . . .

The government of the United States, then, though limited in its powers, is supreme; and its laws, when made in pursuance of the constitution, form the supreme law of the land, "any thing in the constitution or laws of any State to the contrary notwithstanding." *McCulloch v. Maryland,* 4 Wheat. 316, 405–406 (1819)."

"[It] is not a controversy between equals" when the Federal Government "is asserting its sovereign power to regulate commerce.... [The] interests of the nation are more important than those of any State." *Sanitary District v. United States,* 266 U.S. 405, 425–426 (1925). The commerce power "is an affirmative power commensurate with the national needs." *North American Co. v. SEC,* 327 U.S. 686, 705 (1946). The Constitution reserves to the States "only ... that authority which is consistent with and not opposed to the grant to Congress. There is no room in our scheme of government for the assertion of state power in hostility to the authorized exercise of Federal power." The *Minnesota Rate Cases,* 230 U.S. 352, 399 (1913). "The framers of the Constitution never intended that the legislative power of the nation should find itself incapable of disposing of a subject matter specifically committed to its charge." *In re Rahrer,* 140 U.S. 545, 562 (1891).[9]

What Rehnquist tried to do in the *Usery* case was to create a barrier to federal regulatory authority by claiming that, even if the regulation imposed by the FLSA was within the commerce power of the Congress, it was limited by the so-called reserve powers clause of the Tenth Amendment. The Tenth Amendment provides that "the powers not delegated to the United States by the Constitution, nor prohibited by it to the States, are reserved to the States respectively, or to the people."[10] Of course, the commerce power was plainly "delegated to the United States by the Constitution," and therefore the Tenth Amendment literally does not apply to federal regulatory authority. It is also why the Court had previously upheld regulation of state and local activity conducted by the state governments themselves.[11] Even so, Rehnquist rewrote the Constitution, finding that even if what state and local governments were doing was within the regulatory reach of the federal government, it could be blocked by the Tenth Amendment. He was, quite literally, making it up as he went along.

Rehnquist justified his audacious attack on the Constitution and more than a century and a half of Supreme Court precedent by choosing bits and pieces from a number of cases dealing with intergovernmental tax immunity to construct this barrier to congressional action. That body of case law itself was extremely problematic, and the decisions to which Rehnquist pointed have themselves been significantly limited by other rulings. Nevertheless,

Rehnquist fashioned his new version of federalism in such a way as to create what became known (though it was not clearly explained as such in the *Usery* opinion) as a three-part test by which to limit federal regulation that would affect state and local governments. Justice Marshall later summarized that standard more clearly than Rehnquist had: "First, there must be a showing that the challenged statute regulates the 'States as States.' . . . Second, the federal regulation must address matters that are indisputably '[attributes] of state sovereignty.' . . . And third, it must be apparent that the States' compliance with the federal law would directly impair their ability 'to structure integral operations in areas of traditional governmental functions.'"[12]

Rehnquist found that the Fair Labor Standards Act application to state and local employees met this test and therefore violated the Tenth Amendment. In order to reach that conclusion, Rehnquist not only had to acknowledge and then ignore a great deal of case law on the commerce power, but he had also to deal with the 1968 *Maryland v. Wirtz* opinion that had upheld the extension of the FLSA. So, he simply overruled it.

This dramatic effort to create a barrier to federal regulatory authority only succeeded, even temporarily, because of a strange and undeveloped concurring opinion offered by Justice Harry Blackmun. The only thing that was clear from the ruling was that Blackmun was sympathetic to the policy arguments offered by the state and local governments against the FLSA. Just as clearly, he underestimated the nature and import of Rehnquist's opinion, which would reach far beyond this particular statute, as well as the fact that it was obviously intended to do so.

> The Court's opinion and the dissents indicate the importance and significance of this litigation as it bears upon the relationship between the Federal Government and our States. Although I am not untroubled by certain possible implications of the Court's opinion—some of them suggested by the dissents—I do not read the opinion so despairingly as does my Brother BRENNAN. In my view, the result with respect to the statute under challenge here is necessarily correct. I may misinterpret the Court's opinion, but it seems to me that it adopts a balancing approach, and does not outlaw federal power in areas such as environmental protection, where the federal interest is demonstrably greater and where state facility compliance with imposed federal standards would be essential. . . . With this understanding on my part of the Court's opinion, I join it.[13]

Others saw what Blackmun plainly did not comprehend. That included the four dissenters in the case, led by Justice William Brennan. Still others who understood the much broader implications of the *Usery* ruling were those outside the Court who were waiting for an opportunity to challenge federal policy. They promptly launched a variety of attacks on federal regulatory authority, using this new *Usery* standard that offered unprecedented ammunition.

Brennan began the *Usery* dissent with the recognition that Rehnquist's opinion rejected more than 150 years of judicial opinions, including the critically important explanation of the commerce power and necessary and proper clause provided by leading Marshall Court precedents such as *Gibbons v. Ogden*[14] and *McCulloch v. Maryland*.[15] It was not that the Court reversed all these rulings, but rather that it reversed the most recent precedent and simply ignored the law provided by all the rest.

Brennan also correctly explained that the Court's reasoning was moving the judiciary right back to the laissez-faire era in which the Court's majority of that day had manipulated the Constitution to serve its ideology in its efforts to block congressional regulatory authority to such a point that it precipitated a crisis during the 1930s, leading to the Court-packing plan. Following the Court's rejection of that extremist and unwarranted constraint on the commerce power, the Court's opinions had consistently rejected challenges not only by private firms but also by state and local governments.

Brennan not only recognized the dramatic reach of the *Usery* opinion in its constraint on the commerce clause, but also warned of the ominous effort by members of the majority to rewrite the entire structure of Constitutional powers. "My Brethren do more than turn aside long-standing constitutional jurisprudence that emphatically rejects today's conclusion. More alarming is the startling restructuring of our federal system."[16] He recognized, moreover, that the majority was only just beginning a modern assault on the commerce clause, the likes of which had not been seen for decades. "We are left then with a catastrophic judicial body blow at Congress' power under the Commerce Clause. . . . [T]here is an ominous portent of disruption of our constitutional structure implicit in today's mischievous decision."[17]

Justice Stevens also wrote a dissenting opinion in the *Usery* case. Although he expressed considerable sympathy for the criticism of the FLSA as a matter of policy, he absolutely rejected the Court's attempt to rewrite the commerce power. He wrote:

> The Federal Government may, I believe, require the State to act impartially when it hires or fires the janitor, to withhold taxes from his paycheck, to observe safety

regulations when he is performing his job, to forbid him from burning too much soft coal in the capitol furnace, from dumping untreated refuse in an adjacent waterway, from overloading a state-owned garbage truck, or from driving either the truck or the Governor's limousine over 55 miles an hour. Even though these and many other activities of the capitol janitor are activities of the State qua State, I have no doubt that they are subject to federal regulation.[18]

Given those realities, he could find no basis for the state's argument that "the Federal Government may not interfere with a sovereign State's inherent right to pay a substandard wage to the janitor at the state capitol."[19]

Justice Brennan had understood that there would be any number of parties who would see the *Usery* ruling as a clear signal from the Court's emerging majority that it was open season on commerce clause–based federal regulation and that those attacks would not be limited in the manner suggested by Justice Blackmun. Indeed, the next major *Usery* challenge to reach the Court was to exactly the kind of environmental protection policy that Blackmun's concurrence had warned would not justify a limit on congressional commerce power. It turned out to be the first in a series of cases in which Blackmun would end up fighting a rear-guard action in defense of federal authority against his colleagues who supported the *Usery* opinion that he had joined.

That next case was a challenge by mining interests and state and local governments to the newly enacted strip mine bill, formally known as the Surface Mining Control and Reclamation Act. The legislation regulated strip mining and required restoration of the lands on which it was conducted. The devastation wrought by strip mines was dramatic, not only in terms of the local effects from the mining, but also given the downstream pollution that flowed from it. Moreover, mining issues were the focus of attention of environmental policymaking across the nation. However, the mine industry had many allies, including a host of antiregulatory warriors, some of whom later were (as Chapters 3 and 4 explained) offered commissions in the antiregulatory armies of presidential administrations.

Two of the sets of challenges to the strip mine bill made it to the Supreme Court.[20] The lower courts accepted the argument made by challengers that the *Usery* ruling interfered with the state and local government authority to regulate land use. However, the Supreme Court concluded that the strip mine bill did not violate the three-part test from *Usery* and particularly that it did not regulate "states as states." The strip mine legislation set up what the Court termed a "cooperative federalism" system in which the states could do their own implementation of the law if they met federal standards. The challengers had argued that the law really coerced the state and local governments into acting because of a fear of more intrusion by the federal government if they did not. The Court rejected that claim and cited a litany of cases in which, once federal regulatory authority had been found, Congress had the recognized authority not only to regulate but to preempt state action altogether. The Court also rejected arguments that the regulation represented a taking of property without just compensation in violation of the Fifth Amendment to the Constitution.

Even Justice Rehnquist could not support the sweeping assertions made by the challengers and concurred in the judgments in the cases. However, he used his separate opinion as an opportunity to lecture the Court on the fact that its description of the commerce power was far too broad and unconstrained. He left open the opportunity to reengage in the fight in a more favorable case at some future date.

The strip mine cases were decided in 1981, but the Court would once again have before it *Usery*-based challenges to congressional regulatory authority in 1982 and 1983. The first case came when lower courts struck down provisions of the Public Utility Regulatory Policy Act of 1978. The lower courts found those parts of the federal statute unconstitutional under the *Usery* doctrine even though they only required state public utility commissions to "consider" certain factors in rate setting, though other portions of the statute did give the Federal Energy Regulatory Commission authority to issue direct federal regulations in some areas. Justice Blackmun wrote for the majority, rejecting the application of *Usery*.[21] This time, unlike the strip mine rulings, the other four member supporters of the *Usery* ruling disagreed with the majority, and it was clear that they intended to press the *Usery* barrier to federal regulation in the future.

In *EEOC v. Wyoming*,[22] the Court got another *Usery*-based case in which the federal government had lost in the lower courts in 1982. The state had challenged the validity of the Age Discrimination in Employment Act (ADEA) as applied to state and local employees. The majority opinion by Justice Brennan found that the state had met the first two parts of the three-part *Usery* standard, but found that the ADEA did not "directly impair their ability to structure integral operations in areas of traditional functions."[23]

Justice Stevens, by this point, had had enough and insisted in his concurring opinion that it was time that *Usery* be rejected outright.

The only basis for questioning the federal statute at issue here is the pure judicial fiat found in this Court's opinion in *National League of Cities* v. *Usery*. Neither the Tenth Amendment, nor any other provision of the Constitution, affords any support for that judicially constructed limitation on the scope of the federal power granted to Congress by the Commerce Clause. In my opinion, that decision must be placed in the same category as *United States* v. *E.C. Knight Co.,* 156 U.S. 1 (1895), *Hammer* v. *Dagenhart,* 247 U.S. 251 (1918), and *Carter* v. *Carter Coal Co.,* 298 U.S. 238 (1936)—cases whose subsequent rejection is now universally regarded as proper. I think it so plain that *National League of Cities* not only was incorrectly decided, but also is inconsistent with the central purpose of the Constitution itself, that it is not entitled to the deference that the doctrine of *stare decisis* ordinarily commands for this Court's precedents. Notwithstanding my respect for that doctrine, I believe that the law would be well served by a prompt rejection of *National League of Cities'* modern embodiment of the spirit of the Articles of Confederation.[24]

Four members of the Court, including Burger, Powell, Rehnquist, and O'Connor, however, dissented, claiming that *Usery* properly provided limits on the commerce power and that the lower courts had correctly applied it in the present case to strike down the application of the ADEA to state and local government employees.

Even so, Stevens's call for an end to the *Usery* campaign against federal regulatory authority was about to come to fruition in the 1985 case of *Garcia v. San Antonio Metropolitan Transit Authority*.[25] Justice Blackmun wrote for the Court: "Our examination of this 'function' standard applied in these and other cases over the last eight years now persuades us that the attempt to draw the boundaries of state regulatory immunity in terms of 'traditional governmental function' is not only unworkable but is also inconsistent with established principles of federalism and, indeed, with those very federalism principles on which National League of Cities purported to rest. That case, accordingly, is overruled."[26]

Once again four members of the Court dissented, with opinions offered by each of them. While Rehnquist recognized defeat in this campaign, he let it be known that the battle was not over. Concluding a dissent that was but a paragraph long, Rehnquist said: "I do not think it incumbent on those of us in dissent to spell out further the fine points of a principle that will, I am confident, in time again command the support of a majority of this Court."[27]

While this particular assault had been beaten back for the time being, Rehnquist not only promised future campaigns, but clearly saw the *Usery* campaign as an effective intelligence-gathering experience. He had learned a great deal about the way in which the defenders of federal regulatory authority would respond and when they would not. Perhaps more importantly, he saw that he had gained an important new ally with the appointment to the Court of Justice Sandra Day O'Connor. He was to gain others in the years to come.

The Direct Assault on Regulation: Rolling Back the Limits of Authority under the Commerce Power

Rehnquist's next attack on federal regulatory authority was a frontal assault on the limits on the commerce power, and this fight would be far more successful than his first effort. Ironically, he and his allies were aided by past failures by the Court and a lack of awareness by other policymakers that their authority was vulnerable to attack. By 2000, Rehnquist would redefine the standard by which congressional actions under the commerce clause were to be evaluated.

In order to understand the battle space as Rehnquist prepared his assault, it is necessary to look back in time to two important sets of developments. First, there was a vulnerability to attack created by the Court's failure in previous years to address bad precedent. Second, Congress and the White House failed to see the coming attack on the commerce power.

As indicated earlier, there was a time from the late nineteenth century until the 1930s when the Court had battled against regulatory authority, whether it was exercised by the federal government or by the states. The Thirteenth, Fourteenth, and Fifteenth Amendments adopted after the Civil War were specifically designed to place constraints on the states and, by extension, their political subdivisions. The Fourteenth Amendment was also designed to address failures by the prewar Court in *Dred Scott v. Sanford,* a ruling that sought to restrict the authority of the national government to govern and to protect the rights of citizens.[28] The Congress was specifically given authority to enforce each of these amendments. However, the Court quickly moved to read the "privileges and immunities" clause out of existence and then to block efforts by the Congress to enforce the equal protection of the law and to combat discrimination.[29] The Court told those seeking the protections of the "privileges and immunities" clause of the Amendment to look to the states for their assistance. It constrained the enforcement power of the Congress by imposing what became known as the requirement that only state action was subject to regulation. Specifically, the Court ruled in the *Civil Rights Cases* that Congress could only take action against the states and not against private discrimination.[30] These opinions were left on the books even as the law moved a great distance away from these clearly erroneous decisions. The Court never overruled the *Civil Rights Cases* or the related cases, and that later posed serious difficulties.

The Court, during the laissez-faire era, had also placed limits on the commerce power and the taxing and spending powers of the federal government. In asserting, with no basis in the Constitution, that the commerce power did not reach mining, manufacturing, or agriculture, the Court carved out a huge swath of national life as a regulation-free zone.[31] That apparent no-man's land resulted because, after the Court concluded that these areas of commerce were not interstate commerce but matters reserved to the states, it promptly ruled that the states could not regulate much of this activity either, because doing so would violate freedom of contract, which the Court claimed was protected by the due process clause of the Fourteenth Amendment or other aspects of substantive due process.[32] The Court also moved to block the use of federal taxing and spending powers for regulatory purposes.[33]

The Court's actions were clearly ideology masquerading as constitutional law, and they were roundly condemned by legal scholars and policymakers. Many of these rulings came long before the Great Depression and the New Deal administration of Franklin Delano Roosevelt, but it was the series of decisions that struck down efforts to address the problems of that time that brought the criticism of the Court to a high point. Although the president's court-packing plan was not enacted, the Court's majority was clearly changing.

Starting in 1937, the Court began in a series of decisions to reverse the laissez-faire era cases, denouncing them for what they were and returning the interpretations of federal regulatory powers to what they had been before.[34] The Court made clear, as had the Marshall Court many years earlier, that it was not the business of the Court to second-guess the judgment of the Congress as to whether a particular type of activity was commerce covered by the interstate commerce clause. That included activity that was local, but that could impact interstate commerce. The Court explained that even seemingly very limited activity could be reached by Congress if the cumulative effects of that kind of activity by many people around the nation would have an impact on interstate commerce.[35]

In the decades to follow, the Court underscored the fact that the standard for the commerce power of Congress under Article I was broad and deferential, following the opinions dating back to *Gibbons v. Odgen* in 1824. According to the Court, "The only questions are: (1) whether Congress had a rational basis for finding that racial discrimination by motels affected commerce, and (2) if it had such a basis, whether the means it selected to eliminate that evil are reasonable and appropriate."[36]

That summary of the law of the commerce power was presented in cases that had challenged the validity of the Civil Rights Act of 1964.[37] The question for many, though, was why there was a discussion of the commerce power in a civil rights case at all. When Congress adopted the Civil Rights Act in 1964, its members and staff were mindful of the fact that the *Civil Rights Cases* had never been reversed. They made it a point to provide a legislative record that supported the passage of the legislation both in terms of enforcement of civil rights amendments and also as an exercise of commerce power. Thus, the Court rejected claims by the Heart of Atlanta Motel and Ollie's Barbecue in Birmingham, Alabama, that the commerce power did not reach their discriminatory business activities. The Court explained that Congress had demonstrated the many significant impacts of discrimination in travel and accommodations in the South on the national economy and the ability of many to travel freely for business in the region. Even a local business, like Ollie's Barbecue, would buy less meat in interstate commerce if it discriminated in its service to patrons and, under the cumulative effects doctrine, the Congress could certainly reach such business practices.

Justice William O. Douglas, concurring, had no difficulty finding that Congress could regulate these kinds of business practices under the commerce clause, but he argued that the real basis for congressional action in civil rights should be the enforcement clauses of the Civil War amendments. The Court, he said, should stop dancing around the *Civil Rights Cases* and simply strike them down as bad precedent—which that opinion plainly was. The Court did not take that path and the *Civil Rights Cases* remained available to constrain congressional regulatory action in the future. That meant that Congress would continue to rely not primarily on its power to enforce civil rights, but on the commerce clause and the taxing and spending powers.

These factors were in the background, but, in the contemporary setting, Rehnquist was finding himself with reinforcements on the Court and ready for another assault on the commerce power. He was joined not only by Justice O'Connor, but also by Justices Kennedy, Scalia, and Thomas. He had his five votes. Rehnquist's new offensive on the commerce power would come in two parts. The first began in 1995, in a case challenging the Gun Free School-Zone Act of 1990, and the second in an attack on the Violence Against Women Act of 1994.

Rehnquist was ready when the *United States v. Lopez* gun-free schools case reached the Court.[38] He led his colleagues in a move to block congressional commerce clause power in a manner that had not been employed for decades. In this case, the majority concluded that "the Act neither regulates a commercial activity nor contains a requirement that the possession be connected in any way to interstate commerce. We hold that the Act exceeds the authority of Congress 'to regulate Commerce . . . among the several States. . . .'"[39] What Rehnquist was doing was to reverse the presumption in favor of congressional action unless it failed the very low-level rational basis test. Taking the Court back in time to the days when the Court had decided for itself what was and was not sufficiently "in commerce" to permit regulation, Rehnquist found that the Congress could only act in one of three circumstances, and only if and when the record supporting the legislation was sufficient to convince the Court that congressional action under the commerce clause was justified. Congress had not taken sufficient care in the passage of the gun-free schools act to make the commerce clause case, according to Rehnquist, and the statute must therefore fall.

Rehnquist had shifted the burden of proof in the matter from the challenger to the Congress and laid the foundation for the development of a test that would make it difficult in many circumstances for Congress to meet the Court's requirements for the exercise of its Article I powers. The very fact that Rehnquist had shifted the situation from a presumption of validity in the actions of the Congress, unless it failed a minimalist rational basis test, to one in which Congress must persuade the court of the validity of a commerce clause–based action represented a major victory in itself for the antiregulation forces.

Justice Souter issued a strong dissent, warning that the Court was obviously attempting to return to the long-discredited commerce clause jurisprudence of sixty years earlier. Yet it seemed as if perhaps this case was just an exception in an otherwise clear path of judicial deference to congressional action under the commerce power. However, Souter warned that "today's decision may be seen as only a misstep, its reasoning and its suggestions not quite in gear with the prevailing standard, but hardly an epochal case. I would not argue otherwise, but I would raise a caveat. Not every epochal case has come in epochal trappings."[40] In truth, he recognized that the majority was engaged in a major assault on regulatory authority and not simply a response to the particular statute under challenge. The majority had established a solid beachhead from which to launch future attacks.

That future action came in a case challenging the validity of the Violence Against Women Act.[41] Congress had enacted legislation aimed at those who committed violence against women and then escaped the jurisdiction of the state to avoid accountability. States were then left to deal with the costs and consequences of the violence faced by the women with little opportunity to ensure that the perpetrator could be made to pay for the damage done. The purpose was to ensure that there would be legal recourse available in federal court. But, for Rehnquist, the more important point was that this case provided an opportunity to renew the attack on when and under what circumstances the Congress could exercise its commerce power as well as its enforcement authority under the Fourteenth Amendment. Citing his *Lopez* opinion and the *Civil Rights Cases,* Rehnquist announced for the majority that:

> In these cases we consider the constitutionality of 42 U.S.C. § 13981, which provides a federal civil remedy for the victims of gender-motivated violence. The United States Court of Appeals for the Fourth Circuit, sitting en banc, struck down § 13981 because it concluded that Congress lacked constitutional authority to enact the section's civil remedy. Believing that these cases are controlled by our decisions in *United States v. Lopez,* . . . *United States v. Harris,* 106 U.S. 629 (1883), and the *Civil Rights Cases,* 109 U.S. 3 (1883), we affirm.[42]

Driving forward from the beachhead established in the *Lopez* case, Rehnquist reinterpreted his opinion in the gun-free schools case so as to create a four-part test that Congress would have to meet to justify use of the commerce power. First, he said, to be a commerce clause regulation, the subject must have "to do with commerce or any sort of economic enterprise, however broadly one might define those terms."[43] Second, there must be an "express jurisdictional element" that has "an explicit connection with or effect on interstate commerce."[44] Third, the court will look for "express congressional findings regarding the effects upon interstate commerce."[45] Fourth, "the link between [the action taken] and a substantial effect on interstate commerce" cannot be "attenuated."[46]

In the pending case, Rehnquist found violence against women was not an economic matter subject to commerce clause regulation despite the fact that Congress had offered a great deal of evidence on the economic impacts of violence against women. "We accordingly reject the argument that Congress may regulate noneconomic, violent criminal conduct based solely on that conduct's aggregate effect on interstate commerce."[47] Of course, the Court had for decades supported the use of the doctrine of aggregate or cumulative effects, and certainly that doctrine was very much a part of the Court's rulings in *Heart of Atlanta* and *Katzenbach* dealing with the Civil Rights Act of 1964. Nevertheless, Rehnquist simply waved off all of that case law and asserted his own definition of the significant burden Congress would have to meet to interfere in matters Rehnquist considered "truly local."[48]

Justice Souter, who had seen something like this coming at the time of *Lopez,* led the four dissenters. He found that, unlike the *Lopez* case, the Congress in passing the Violence Against Women Act has amassed a veritable "mountain of data" on the effects of violence against women on interstate commerce.[49] "The Act," Souter wrote, "would have passed muster at any time between *Wickard* in 1942 and *Lopez* in 1995, a period in which the law enjoyed a stable understanding that congressional power under the Commerce Clause, complemented by the authority of the Necessary and Proper Clause, Art. I. § 8 cl. 18, extended to all activity that, when aggregated, has a substantial effect on interstate commerce."[50] However, it was clear that the Court had simply determined that it would decide what was adequate, and the burden was placed on the Congress to satisfy the Court in order to obtain a vote in favor of new legislation very much in the style of the earlier laissez-faire era Court.

What was clear at the end of the *Morrison* decision was that Rehnquist had this time launched an effective offensive on the constitutional standard that had existed until then and created a new one that would define the limits of the commerce clause in a manner that had not been attempted since before 1937. It was not, however, the only offensive that he would lead against federal authority. For, even as he fought to limit the reach of the commerce power, he also sought to blunt the powers of Congress to enact legislation under the enforcement provisions of the Civil War amendments using the Eleventh Amendment.

Surprise Attack: The Eleventh Amendment Campaign
Further Limits Congressional Authority

Even as it fought to constrain commerce clause powers, the majority, once again led by Rehnquist, launched a new campaign in its war against federal regulatory authority. It began with a surprise attack that both constrained the use of the commerce power and other authority under the commerce clause and employed a new weapon against congressional action. Although he had failed in his earlier bid with the *Usery* case and afterward to use the Tenth Amendment to impose a barrier to regulatory action by Congress—even where the subject matter plainly fit within the sweep of the commerce clause—Rehnquist found another weapon to block federal action in the Eleventh Amendment. It would turn out to be a very effective weapon indeed. And once again, just a year after his tour de force in *Lopez*, Rehnquist found a case with which to launch this attack that was far more important than it seemed, not just because it presented a significant legal problem in its own right, but because, like other cases before it, this opinion could be employed as the vehicle that would carry the new attack forward.

The case was *Seminole Tribe of Florida v. Florida,* and it concerned the policy governing the way in which Native American tribes and nations would interact with state governments to regulate gambling establishments.[51] Under the provisions of the Indian Gaming Regulatory Act, a tribal government was to enter into negotiations with the state government on how gaming was to be regulated, but the legislation also included options for the tribal government in the event that the state refused to negotiate in good faith. Among those options was the ability to sue the state in federal court.

Florida contested that provision of the statute as a violation of its sovereign immunity. Of course, the Congress had long exercised its powers under various provisions of the Constitution to abrogate (nullify) that immunity and make states subject to damage suits for violations of federal law. Indeed, the Supreme Court had ruled as recently as 1989 that the Congress had that authority under its Article I commerce clause powers.[52] This time, however, there was a majority ready to carve out a new body of state immunity from federal controls and a Chief Justice more than ready to disregard or overrule contrary precedents and to use an obscure and long since outdated case—and one with entirely different facts—to claim that he was not forging new action but keeping faith with precedent.

The Court created a new test and within it a solid barrier to congressional action. Rehnquist wrote that the Congress could only abrogate state immunity—that is, make the state subject to a damage suit—if it made clear its intent to do so and if it was acting pursuant to a legitimate grant of authority. The first point was not an issue because Congress had very specifically declared its intention to abrogate in the statute. As to the second element, Congress in the Indian gaming act was exercising its authority under the commerce clause to regulate commerce "among the states, and with the Indian Tribes." However, Rehnquist concluded that the only legitimate authority with which to abrogate immunity was the enforcement clause of the Fourteenth Amendment. To the degree that other cases, like the 1989 Pennsylvania ruling, said otherwise, they were overruled. Just why only that provision of the Constitution was a valid authority to abrogate and not any other part of the Constitution, including the Supremacy Clause of Article VI, was not explained. In fact, the Court also did not make clear why only the enforcement clause of the Fourteenth Amendment was valid authority when the Thirteenth and Fifteenth Amendments contained exactly the same language in their enforcement clauses.

Once again, Rehnquist was making it up as he went along, citing only one nineteenth-century case—and one with completely different kinds of facts—in support of his audacious new constitutional creation. But since he had O'Connor, Scalia, Thomas, and Kennedy behind him, Rehnquist carried the day. Once presented, the *Seminole* ruling, like the *Lopez* decision of the previous year, provided a launching pad for the future rounds of attack on a much wider scale.

Rehnquist's opinion in *Seminole* was so outrageous that it was difficult for the four dissenters to decide where to begin to attack it. Justice Stevens, citing a string of cases in which the Court had found that Congress had the power to take the kind of action it had in the present case, called the majority's action what it was, a bold attack on the constitutional powers of the Congress.

Nevertheless, in a sharp break with the past, today the Court holds that with the narrow and illogical exception of statutes enacted pursuant to the Enforcement Clause of the Fourteenth Amendment, Congress has no such power.

The importance of the majority's decision . . . cannot be overstated. The majority's opinion does not simply preclude Congress from establishing the rather curious statutory scheme under which Indian tribes may seek the aid of a federal court to secure a State's good-faith negotiations over gaming regulations. Rather, it prevents Congress from providing a federal forum for a broad range of actions against States, from those sounding in copyright and patent law, to those concerning bankruptcy, environmental law, and the regulation of our vast national economy."[53]

Justice Souter wrote the lead dissent joined by three other justices, including those who issued their own separate opinions. Souter began with a recognition of the dramatic and novel holding reached by Rehnquist and his allies. "The Court today holds for the first time since the founding of the Republic that Congress has no authority to subject a State to the jurisdiction of a federal court at the behest of an individual asserting a federal right."[54] Of course, Souter's exhaustive treatment of the history of congressional authority, the Eleventh Amendment, and the Court's precedents in these areas over the previous century and a half was quite beside the point. This was a war, and Rehnquist and his allies were going to use any weapons they thought useful—and the Eleventh Amendment re-created as the majority had done it in *Seminole* was, as Stevens had warned, clearly going to be extremely useful.

Almost immediately, Rehnquist and his colleagues moved to press their newfound advantage. In a different case the following year the Court added a requirement to the limitation that Congress could only subject the states to such damage suits under Section 5 of the Fourteenth Amendment. Congress could only act, the majority said, under limited conditions even if it was using that Fourteenth Amendment authority. "There must be a congruence and proportionality between the injury to be prevented or remedied and the means adopted to that end."[55] Justice Kennedy, who wrote the opinion, cited no direct precedent for that test, but only made reference to general language in a voting rights case for the proposition that there is some limit to the extent of remedial action. Ultimately, it would be the Court that would decide for itself whether legislation was indeed congruent and proportional to the problem to be remedied by the statute.

Once again, many observers saw the case as a dispute about the Religious Freedom Restoration Act and the free exercise and establishment clauses of the First Amendment, rather than carefully considering the actual basis of the Court's ruling. Like other attacks, just what the case would mean for the larger conflict was not widely understood at the time. Even the dissenters in the case focused on the religious arguments and prior rulings that had prompted the enactment of the legislation. However, Kennedy's additional requirement for exercise of Section 5 authority would soon become strong ammunition in future battles about legislative powers.

The Court was about to undertake a number of cases in which it would rule against Congress with respect to the Patent and Plant Variety Protection Remedy Clarification Act,[56] the Fair Labor Standards Act,[57] Age Discrimination in Employment Act (ADEA),[58] and the Americans with Disabilities Act (ADA),[59] using the *Seminole* doctrine and the added requirement for congruence and proportionality. In the ADEA case, Justice O'Connor wrote for the majority, finding that, although Congress has clearly stated its intention to abrogate state immunity, it had exceeded its authority under Section 5 of the Fourteenth Amendment in so doing.[60] Writing as if the *Seminole* and *Boerne* requirements were long-established precedents, she found: "Applying the same 'congruence and proportionality' test in these cases, we conclude that the ADEA is not 'appropriate legislation' under §5 of the Fourteenth Amendment. . . . [T]he substantive requirements the ADEA imposes on state and local governments are disproportionate to any unconstitutional conduct that conceivably could be targeted by the Act."[61] She concluded that, because the Court had previously refused to find that the Fourteenth Amendment barred discrimination on the basis of age, the Congress could not add protections by statute and make them enforceable by damage suits. Of course, the Congress had done precisely that in a host of other cases, including, for example, the pregnancy disability amendments to the Civil Rights Act of 1964.

Once again the Court had propounded a novel assertion as if it were a well-established doctrine. This time the new twist was the idea that Congress could not add protections against discrimination or other rights, enforceable by a suit for damages, unless the Court had already found that such discrimination was prohibited by the Constitution. Thus, the Congress had to be prepared, in effect, to litigate a case in which it could plead and prove a violation of a previously established constitutional right before it could legislate. That is a very long way from the test of simple rationality applied to the civil rights statutes before *Seminole* rewrote the Constitution.

Justice O'Connor sought to cushion what was clearly a set of extreme assertions by admitting that "we have never held that §5 precludes Congress from enacting reasonably prophylactic legislation." That was, however, exactly what the Court was doing in the ADEA case; and just to underscore the point, O'Connor then promptly pronounced that her reading "of the ADEA's legislative record confirms that Congress' 1974 extension of the Act to the States was an unwarranted response to a perhaps inconsequential problem. Congress never identified any pattern of age discrimination by the States, much less any discrimination whatsoever that rose to the level of constitutional violation."[62] In a nice bit of circular logic, she determined for herself that since the Congress had not adequately proven a constitutional case of age discrimination by the states that met her view of the burden of proof—which she had already made clear could not be done given prior decisions of the Court—the legislature could not take action to prevent such discrimination in the future by providing a deterrent in the form of possible damage suits by victims of age discrimination. Then, as if to indicate that potential victims should go back to the nineteenth-century approach, even before the Civil War amendments, she dismissed the obvious problems with her opinion by saying that victims should simply look to the states to protect them. That was precisely the argument that had been employed in the *Slaughterhouse Cases,* the *Civil Rights Cases,* and even before that in *Dred Scott.*

Justice Stevens led the dissenters, rejecting the idea that *Seminole* represented settled law, much less all that had been added to its requirements since that 1996 ruling.

> Congress' power to regulate the American economy includes the power to regulate both the public and the private sectors of the labor market. Federal rules outlawing discrimination in the workplace, like the regulation of wages and hours or health and safety standards, may be enforced against public as well as private employers. In my opinion, Congress' power to authorize federal remedies against state agencies that violate federal statutory obligations is coextensive with its power to impose those obligations on the States in the first place. Neither the Eleventh Amendment nor the doctrine of sovereign immunity places any limit on that power.[63]

Clearly, according to Stevens, the Court was in the process of fundamentally redesigning the Constitution and the powers it accorded to the three branches as well as the system of federalism that it established.

However, if Stevens thought the Court had pushed the matter as far as possible, he was mistaken, for the Rehnquist majority next rejected the ADA's application of damage suits to the states. This ruling came in a case from Alabama, where a nurse who was the director of Nursing, OB/Gyn/Neonatal Services at the University of Alabama, Birmingham Hospital, was removed from her supervisory position after she took leave to receive treatment for breast cancer. There was also a companion case involving an employee of the Alabama Department of Youth Services. Both sued the state under the ADA.

Again Rehnquist wrote for the five-member majority, rejecting the congressional action abrogating the state's immunity from suit for violations of the ADA. He applied *Seminole* and the congruence and proportionality language from the *Boerne* and *Kimel* decisions, concluding that Congress had not provided sufficient evidence that there was a problem of discrimination by states against employees with disabilities to justify the statutory provisions. In so doing, he used the kind of argument advanced by O'Connor in the earlier *Kimel* case that because there was no proven case of a constitutional violation, Congress was not justified in applying the ADA damages remedy to the states. Just as O'Connor had decided that there was really no basis for a constitutional discrimination claim with respect to age, Rehnquist made essentially the same argument with respect to persons with disabilities. He concluded that "states are not required by the Fourteenth Amendment to make special accommodations for the disabled, so long as their actions towards such individuals are rational. They could quite hard headedly—and perhaps hardheartedly—hold to job-qualification requirements which do not make allowance for the disabled."[64]

This time, the four dissenters made the point directly that the Court was simply deciding for itself what good law and policy were and not really addressing the constitutional powers set forth in the Constitution. Justice Breyer wrote: "Reviewing the congressional record as if it were an administrative agency record, the Court holds the statutory provision before us, 42 U.S.C. § 12202, unconstitutional." The Congress was actually being treated more like a litigant before a trial court, forced to carry the burden to convince a judge to rule in his or her favor, than as a coequal branch of government carrying out its constitutionally assigned task. Besides, he said, even if Congress had to meet such a standard, its record was more than adequate to the task.

> The Court says that its primary problem with this statutory provision is one of legislative evidence. It says that "Congress assembled only . . . minimal evidence of unconstitutional state discrimination in employment." . . . *In fact, Congress compiled a vast legislative record documenting "'massive, society-wide discrimination'" against persons with disabilities.* . . . In addition to the information presented at 13 congressional hearings . . . and its own prior experience gathered over 40 years during which it contemplated and enacted considerable similar legislation . . . , Congress created a special task force to assess

the need for comprehensive legislation. That task force held hearings in every State, attended by more than 30,000 people, including thousands who had experienced discrimination first hand. . . . The task force hearings, Congress' own hearings, and an analysis of "census data, national polls, and other studies" led Congress to conclude that "people with disabilities, as a group, occupy an inferior status in our society, and are severely disadvantaged socially, vocationally, economically, and educationally." 42 U.S.C. § 12101(a)(6). *As to employment, Congress found that "two-thirds of all disabled Americans between the age of 16 and 64 [were] not working at all," even though a large majority wanted to, and were able to, work productively. S. Rep. No. 101–116, at 9. And Congress found that this discrimination flowed in significant part from "stereotypic assumptions" as well as "purposeful unequal treatment." 42 U.S.C. § 12101(a)(7).*[65] [emphasis added]

In addition to all of this evidence, Breyer responded to the majority's argument that there was not sufficient evidence that the discrimination was committed by the state governments specifically. Breyer answered: "There are roughly 300 examples of discrimination by state governments themselves in the legislative record. See, e.g., Appendix C, infra. I fail to see how this evidence 'falls far short of even suggesting the pattern of unconstitutional discrimination on which § 5 legislation must be based.'"[66] To the dissent was appended page after page, arranged alphabetically by state, of evidence of discrimination. Indeed, the dissenters found it ironic that the Rehnquist majority was applying a far heavier burden of proof to a Congress attempting to carry out its task than to states that stood accused of discrimination against persons with disabilities.

The Court's harsh review of Congress' use of its § 5 power is reminiscent of the similar (now-discredited) limitation that it once imposed upon Congress' Commerce Clause power. . . . I could understand the legal basis for such review were we judging a statute that discriminated against those of a particular race or gender or a statute that threatened a basic constitutionally protected liberty such as free speech. . . . The legislation before us, however, does not discriminate against anyone, nor does it pose any threat to basic liberty. And it is difficult to understand why the Court, which applies "minimum 'rational-basis' review" to statutes that burden persons with disabilities . . . subjects to far stricter scrutiny a statute that seeks to help those same individuals.[67]

Rehnquist and his allies knew that there were broad policy implications to this line of cases. The civil rights policy model had become an important design for regulatory policy over the years because it relied on individual lawsuits for implementation rather than the creation of a major regulatory agency to carry out the policy. The ability to sue for damages was integral to that design because it both provided a deterrent to those who might be inclined to ignore the policy and also provided for recompense that would allow those who suffered from the outlawed behavior to bring an enforcement action and for their attorneys to bring the suits on behalf of clients who often lacked independent resources to mount an enforcement suit. Rehnquist clearly knew as well that these decisions would prompt states to challenge federal policymaking, and they did.

One of the interesting challenges following on this line of Supreme Court decisions came not in one of the civil rights–related situations, but in a classic regulatory agency enforcement setting. In South Carolina, the state ports authority challenged the resolution of a complaint brought against that agency before the Federal Maritime Commission (FMC). A company had sought berthing services for one of its cruise ships. The ports authority denied the request on grounds that it had a policy not to support vessels that offered gambling. When the company brought a complaint against the authority, the ports authority countered with a claim that the agency was immune from FMC complaints processes on the basis of the Eleventh Amendment as interpreted by the *Seminole* decision. The Supreme Court, in another five-to-four ruling, this time with an opinion by Justice Thomas, agreed that *Seminole* applied. "Given both this interest in protecting States' dignity and the strong similarities between FMC proceedings and civil litigation, we hold that state sovereign immunity bars the FMC from adjudicating complaints filed by a private party against a nonconsenting State."[68]

Once again the four dissenters responded with frustration at the growing list of recent rulings in which the antiregulatory majority had simply made up constitutional law wholesale and then acted as if these novel arguments had the effect of settled law, and therefore of unquestionable precedent. Justice Breyer wrote:

> Where does the Constitution contain the principle of law that the Court enunciates? I cannot find the answer to this question in any text, in any tradition, or in any relevant purpose. In saying this, I do not simply reiterate the dissenting views set forth in many of the Court's recent sovereign immunity decisions. See, e.g., *Kimel v. Florida Bd. of Regents,* ... (2000); *Alden v. Maine,* ... (1999); *College Savings Bank v. Florida Prepaid Postsecondary Ed. Expense Bd.,* ... (1999); *Seminole*

Tribe of Fla. v. Florida, ... (1996). For even were I to believe that those decisions properly stated the law—which I do not—I still could not accept the Court's conclusion here.[69]

These opinions, he wrote, create a new kind of principle that interferes with a wide range of regulatory relationships that have historically been repeatedly upheld and have been essential to the nation. "Just as this principle has no logical starting place, I fear that neither does it have any logical stopping point."[70]

Another Novel Federalism Barrier to Federal Regulation: The Bar against Mandating State Regulatory Action

In addition to these other lines of attack, Rehnquist and his colleagues had another offensive in progress against federal regulatory authority, creating an entirely different legal doctrine in the process. The rulings created a new bar against regulation based on the assertion that various forms of regulation from the federal government attempted to force states into taking regulatory action in violation of the Tenth Amendment. This attack was mounted in two important cases involving the Brady bill, the well-known national gun control policy, and a case from New York, involving a less well known, but very important policy concerning low-level nuclear waste.

Congress adopted legislation in 1980 and then amended it in 1985 at the request of the states which were attempting to deal with the complex problem of low-level nuclear waste disposal. Different from the kind of waste generated by nuclear power plants, the type of waste that was the focus of this policy discussion was the type generated by hospitals and industrial facilities on a regular basis, but still a type of waste that required careful handling and disposal. The states had been trying to find ways to agree on what might be done, with studies and discussions carried out by the National Governors' Association and other groups. The result was a request by the states to Congress for legislation that would give the states the opportunity to negotiate regional interstate compacts. If they were not able to reach such agreements, then the idea was that states would be responsible for developing their own waste disposal facilities. Congress obliged with the passage of the Low-Level Radioactive Waste Policy Act in 1980 and then amendments to that legislation in 1985.

New York was one of the states that was not able to reach agreement on a compact, but it balked at the requirement that it then was responsible under the legislation to take action to deal with its own low-level waste. It challenged the federal legislation as exceeding the powers of Congress and as a violation of state authority reserved under the Tenth Amendment. The Supreme Court, in an opinion by Justice O'Connor, agreed and struck down that provision of the legislation. In so doing, the majority created a new set of limitations on the regulatory power of Congress.

In her opinion for the Court, O'Connor acknowledged that Congress could choose to have the federal government regulate all nuclear waste and that it could use its preemption authority to bar states from doing so. However, in this case, she said, the problem was that "rather than addressing the problem of waste disposal by directly regulating the generators and disposers of waste, petitioners argue, Congress has impermissibly directed the States to regulate in this field."[71] While she was unable to point to any case law that was a clear precedent for her conclusion, O'Connor found that the Congress could regulate directly but could not do what she saw as forcing the states to use their regulatory authority.

Justice White wrote a dissent in which he pointed out that the majority had approached the case as if its facts and central policy actions were entirely different from what was actually before the Court. "To read the Court's version of events, . . . one would think that Congress was the sole proponent of a solution to the Nation's low-level radioactive waste problem. Not so. The Low-Level Radioactive Waste Policy Act of 1980 . . . and its amendatory 1985 Act, resulted from the efforts of state leaders to achieve a state-based set of remedies to the waste problem."[72]

In fact, the states had worked for a long time to find a solution. When they did come to a proposal, it involved the use of interstate compacts, which required, under Article 1, Section 10 of the Constitution, the approval of Congress. The states had wanted a proposal that had both incentives and enforcement mechanisms for states that would not participate responsibly and reach agreements. Thus, Congress was in fact facilitating and assisting the creative policymaking efforts of the states and not intruding into their decisionmaking. Thus, White wrote, "the Court has mischaracterized the essential inquiry, misanalyzed the inquiry it has chosen to undertake, and undervalued the effect the seriousness of this public policy problem should have on the constitutionality of the take title provision."[73]

The 1985 amendments to the law provided additional time for the states to resolve the problem among themselves but also contained boundaries after which states would have to take responsibility for resolving their own situations if they would not or could not do so with other states. Indeed, White said, "The ultimate irony of the decision today is that in its formalistically rigid obeisance to 'federalism,' the Court gives Congress fewer incentives to defer to the wishes of state officials in achieving local solutions to local problems."[74]

Justice Stevens was even more direct.

> The notion that Congress does not have the power to issue "a simple command to state governments to implement legislation enacted by Congress," . . . is incorrect and unsound. There is no such limitation in the Constitution. The Tenth Amendment surely does not impose any limit on Congress' exercise of the powers delegated to it by Article I. Nor does the structure of the constitutional order or the values of federalism mandate such a formal rule. To the contrary, the Federal Government directs state governments in many realms.[75]

The *New York v. United States* opinion would be cited in a variety of contexts concerned with defining limits on congressional regulatory powers after it was issued in 1992. However, it became particularly important when the Court struck down requirements of the Brady bill, more formally known as the Brady Handgun Violence Prevention Act. The Brady bill focused heavily on a waiting period and a background check of purchasers of firearms. It required dealers to fill out the requisite forms for a purchase and required the chief law enforcement officer (known collectively as CLEOs) in the area to attempt to conduct a limited background check within the waiting period. Some law enforcement officials, particularly sheriffs, objected to the policy and challenged it on grounds similar to the *New York v. United States* case.

The opinion for the majority in *Printz v. United States* was provided by Justice Scalia.[76] At the end of the day, Scalia pointed to the *New York* case as a clear foundation on which to reject the Brady bill requirements.

> We held in *New York* that Congress cannot compel the States to enact or enforce a federal regulatory program. Today we hold that Congress cannot circumvent that prohibition by conscripting the State's officers directly. The Federal Government may neither issue directives requiring the States to address particular problems, nor command the States' officers, or those of their political subdivisions, to administer or enforce a federal regulatory program. It matters not whether policymaking is involved, and no case-by-case weighing of the burdens or benefits is necessary; such commands are fundamentally incompatible with our constitutional system of dual sovereignty.[77]

As the four dissenters pointed out, the majority was once again creating a doctrine for which there was no foundation in the Constitution. The Tenth Amendment speaks to powers "not delegated," but there was no argument that Congress has authority under its delegated power to regulate commerce that supports regulation of gun sales. Besides, Justice Stevens noted, the respect for the integrity of the states in our constitutional history "simply does not speak to the question whether individual state employees may be required to perform federal obligations, such as registering young adults for the draft, . . . creating state emergency response commissions designed to manage the release of hazardous substances, . . . collecting and reporting data on underground storage tanks that may pose an environmental hazard, . . . and reporting traffic fatalities . . . and missing children . . . to a federal agency."[78]

Notwithstanding the merits of the dissenters' criticisms, it is clear that the Court's majority under the leadership of Chief Justice Rehnquist waged a number of campaigns against federal regulatory authority that successfully— and quite dramatically—changed the law regarding the range of authority possessed by the Congress and the limitations on that authority imposed by the Tenth and Eleventh Amendments. But if state and local officials who applauded some of these victories thought that the Court's rulings meant greater deference to state and local regulatory action, they were about to find out that their authority, too, would be a target in the fight against regulation.

THE BATTLE IN THE STATES: LIMITATIONS
ON STATE REGULATORY ACTION

Just as the laissez-faire era Court had limited both federal authority and state regulatory action, so the contemporary Court's language that had seemingly been so solicitous of the states in cases challenging federal action did not prevent rulings by the same justices that placed constraints on what state and local governments had long successfully exercised as lawful regulatory authority. Where the court of a century earlier had fought the battle against state and local regulatory efforts on grounds of the right to contract and substantive due process, contemporary state and local governments have seen attacks in court on claims of regulatory takings, preemption, and the so-called dormant commerce clause, among other fronts. (The first two of these are discussed in detail below.)

It should be said that state and local governments have long been in the thick of regulatory action in everything from public utilities to transportation, at the state level, and, at the local level, from land use to taxicab regulation. In fact, some areas that could have been preempted by the federal government, such as insurance company regulation, have been handed over to the states by Congress.[79] In other areas, at least since the 1970s, the intergovernmental model of regulation in which federal legislation allows states to develop their own standards, if they meet or exceed federal requirements, and enforce those standards, if the federal agency responsible for that area of regulatory policy approves, has become extremely important in such areas as environmental regulation.[80] Indeed, one of the concerns about relying so much on state—and in some instances local—governments for regulation is that there are serious capacity challenges, not to mention the fact that so many fields of regulated activity simply move very quickly, even electronically, across state and local jurisdictional boundaries, making it very difficult for those governments to create regulatory policy or administer regulations. Business practices by mail order and Internet-based businesses are obvious examples of the challenge.

Notwithstanding those concerns, some state and local governments attempted, to some limited extent at least, to enhance or update their regulatory systems in areas of concern to their residents, even as the federal government has deregulated in some of those fields. At the same time, of course, state and local governments have also been battlegrounds for the same kinds of antiregulatory warriors who have been operating at the national level described in earlier chapters. In addition to the use of the various weapons, strategies, and tactics described in Chapters 1–3, the state and local governments have also faced a series of battles in the courts.

*Regulatory Takings Doctrine: An Effective Front
in the War against Regulation*

In the early twentieth century, one of the arguments often made by antiregulatory forces was that regulation was a kind of taking of property prohibited by the Constitution's Fifth Amendment unless the government provided "just compensation." While it was an argument made with considerable energy during the era of the Gospel of Wealth, when property was king and what was good for business was supposed to be good for everyone, it deliberately confused the difference between regulatory policy and specific condemnations of particular pieces of private property for public use such as roads or schools. It was an argument rejected repeatedly by the Supreme Court over time, but one that the more recent justices have reinvigorated and expanded as another front in the battle against regulation.

The Supreme Court had long upheld a wide variety of forms of regulation. In so doing, it rejected the idea that regulatory policy that affected all or a substantial range of people or enterprises was the same thing as what happens when government singles out a particular person or firm and condemns their property for public use. The argument that when government acts in such a way as to burden property rights, it is engaged in what critics term a "regulatory taking," was rejected, for example, when the Supreme Court issued its first rulings upholding the zoning powers exercised by local governments under state law.[81] The zoning ordinance was not a violation of property rights, the Court held, but a body of reasonable regulations issued under the police powers of the state pursuant to the Tenth Amendment to the Constitution to serve the public welfare.

> Regulations, the wisdom, necessity and validity of which, as applied to existing conditions, are so apparent that they are now uniformly sustained, a century ago, or even half a century ago, probably would have been rejected as arbitrary and oppressive. Such regulations are sustained, under the complex conditions of our day, for reasons analogous to those which justify traffic regulations, which, before the advent of automobiles and rapid transit street railways, would have been condemned as fatally arbitrary and unreasonable.[82]

Moreover, the Court said, such regulations are presumptively valid subject only to the most limited of constitutional standards: "If these reasons, thus summarized, do not demonstrate the wisdom or sound policy in all respects of those restrictions which we have indicated as pertinent to the inquiry, at least, the reasons are sufficiently cogent to preclude us from saying, as it must be said before the ordinance can be declared unconstitutional, that such provisions are clearly arbitrary and unreasonable, having no substantial relation to the public health, safety, morals, or general welfare."[83]

The Court later reiterated the fundamental point that regulation and taking of property are two different things, explaining that the costs of regulation are the price that we pay for civilization.[84] "Most regulations of business necessarily impose financial burdens on the enterprise for which no compensation is paid. Those are part of the costs of our civilization. . . . The public welfare is a broad and inclusive concept. The moral, social, economic, and physical well-being of the community is one part of it; the political well-being, another."[85] Such police power regulatory programs are presumptively valid and the burden is on the challenger to prove that they were clearly arbitrary and irrational.

In responding to complaints about the burdens of regulation on property, the Court warned that it was not going back to the bad old days when courts set themselves up as super legislatures to determine whether the policy produced was good policy according to the preferences of the justices.

> Our recent decisions make plain that we do not sit as a super legislature to weigh the wisdom of legislation nor to decide whether the policy which it expresses offends the public welfare. . . . [S]tate legislatures have constitutional authority to experiment with new techniques; they are entitled to their own standard of the public welfare; they may within extremely broad limits control practices in the business-labor field, so long as specific constitutional prohibitions are not violated and so long as conflicts with valid and controlling federal laws are avoided.[86]

In making this strong statement, the Court stressed that it was not going to go back to the era when the Court used what was termed the "freedom of contract" to block state and local regulation even in areas that same Court had previously ruled were the province of states rather than the federal government. To make the point, the Court cited both the cases in which an earlier Court had blocked regulation[87] and the later cases that rejected those earlier rulings and the antiregulatory approach that undergirded them.[88]

However, in later years, Justices Rehnquist and Scalia took a very different approach and were able to attract majorities in cases that permitted them to undermine that critical distinction between regulation and takings and to shift the presumption of validity and the burden of proof such that what would have been regarded as relatively common regulations could be successfully challenged. The justices understood full well that the new and increased burdens on government would not only provide ammunition with which individuals and groups could attack regulations but would also serve as a powerful deterrent against state and local governments that were considering whether and how to regulate in the future.

Scalia led this attack with two opinions that were clearly designed to render takings law an effective weapon against regulation. Rehnquist followed with another ruling that applied those Scalia creations and added additional inventions of his own. Then Justice Kennedy wrote for the Court in a case that added another novel weapon for use by antiregulatory foes, and, once again, it was both an active weapon and a deterrent.

In the first of these cases, Scalia used the *Nollan v. California Coastal Commission* case to reframe a dispute that began with a condition placed on a property development permit, transforming it into a taking of property without compensation. The case emerged from a requirement that in order to move forward with their plans to build a house on a California beach, the owners would be required to meet permit requirements issued by the California Coastal Commission. The commission was created for the purpose of ensuring that development in the coastal areas did not preclude public access or interfere with other public-interest values along the California coast. Since its creation, the commission had issued permits with various conditions attached to virtually all of those who wanted to build in the area; and the property owners were aware of the requirements before they purchased the property.[89] The commission acted on the well-established premise that a body with the authority to deny a permit completely could issue the permit subject to conditions. The burden for challenging the permit decisions had historically rested with the challenger, as the earlier precedents discussed above indicated.

While acknowledging the previous cases about the differences between regulation and taking of property, Scalia effectively set them aside in two important ways and created his own new requirements. First, he suggested that it was necessary to ask whether the government could have applied the controls over the property that it imposed in the absence of the permit process—which is to say in the absence of the regulatory framework. It was a way of setting aside the distinction between takings of property and regulation. Second, he required the government then to explain the "nexus" (the legal connection) that made it necessary to require the specific conditions on the permit that the Coastal Commission mandated, which was a way of reversing the burden of proof and placing the obligations on the government. He took these steps even as he conceded that the commission had regulatory authority and that the aims that the state sought to advance were clearly reasonable as a matter of the state's concern with the public welfare.

The second case, which the Court decided five years later, also concerned beachfront development, but this time in South Carolina.[90] Once again Scalia wrote for the Court. In this second case, he used the takings doctrine to push the boundaries of regulatory authority back even further, to a time when government had to demonstrate that the owner's intended use of the property was the equivalent of a nuisance at common law before government could impose regulatory constraints on the owner's plans.

The South Carolina case arose against a backdrop of legislation by Congress and by the state aimed at preserving and protecting the coastal zones against development that was contributing to damage to beach areas and related ecosystems and construction that was also dangerous and burdensome in its own right. Governments had been repeatedly called upon to deal with the destruction of houses and infrastructure in situations where homes and businesses were located in areas known to be subject to tidal action and periodic storms. A developer who was well aware of the problems, having previously developed property in the area, purchased two lots within a volatile beachfront area. The state of South Carolina adopted legislation that effectively precluded landowners from building residences on the property on such property.

Scalia, writing for the majority, rejected any obligation for deference to the police power regulatory authority of the state and insisted that "as it would be required to do if it sought to restrain Lucas in a common-law action for public nuisance, South Carolina must identify background principles of nuisance and property law that prohibit the uses he now intends in the circumstances in which the property is presently found. Only on this showing can the State fairly claim that, in proscribing all such beneficial uses, the Beachfront Management Act is taking nothing."[91] Scalia claimed that the state had deprived the owners of any ability to garner an economic gain from the property and therefore the matter was clearly a taking unless the state could carry the heavy burden of demonstrating something equivalent to a common-law nuisance.

Scalia's decision further eroded the distinction between regulation and takings and shifted even more dramatically the burden of proof in cases where the state or local government took regulatory action. The requirement that states demonstrate that a proposed use of property was the equivalent of a nuisance at common law added a very substantial set of burdens to state and local land-use planning. His actions were ironic, since regulatory systems had been developed in part at least to replace an unworkable system of numerous and inconsistent common-law suits brought on grounds of nuisance with something more rational and consistent as well as protective of the public welfare.[92] It was also interesting that Scalia, who was so often ready to reject cases on procedural grounds, was perfectly prepared to overlook the fact that the property owner in this case had not exhausted the remedies available to him before bringing the matter all the way to the Supreme Court.

Justice Blackmun, in dissent, saw the opinion for what it was—a far from subtle attack on the distinction between regulations and takings and an effort to dramatically undermine the police power regulatory authority of the state. It was a sweeping ruling supposedly penned to address what could and should have been a far more limited issue, and Blackmun said so in uncharacteristically blunt terms.

> Today the Court launches a missile to kill a mouse.... [T]he Court ... ignores its jurisdictional limits, remakes its traditional rules of review, and creates simultaneously a new categorical rule and an exception (neither of which is rooted in our prior case law, common law, or common sense). I protest not only the Court's decision, but each step taken to reach it. More fundamentally, I question the Court's wisdom in issuing sweeping new rules to decide such a narrow case.... My fear is that the Court's new policies will spread beyond the narrow confines of the present case. For that reason, I, like the Court, will give far greater attention to this case than its narrow scope suggests—not because I can intercept the Court's missile, or save the targeted mouse, but because I hope perhaps to limit the collateral damage.[93]

Blackmun recognized that Scalia was using the case to eliminate the normal presumptions in favor of the validity of state police power regulation and placing the burden squarely on the government. "Rather than invoking these traditional rules, the Court decides the State has the burden to convince the courts that its legislative judgments are correct.... [T]he State now has the burden of showing the regulation is not a taking. The Court offers no justification for its sudden hostility toward state legislators, and I doubt that it could."[94]

Blackmun also wanted to sound the alarm that the Court, without saying so plainly, was attempting to reach back to a time long before it had made clear that the police power regulatory authority of the state was broad and its actions presumptively valid. This was a new attempt to impose common-law requirements that the Court had specifically rejected in earlier rulings. "Until today, the Court explicitly had rejected the contention that the government's power to act without paying compensation turns on whether the prohibited activity is a common-law nuisance."[95] In fact, Blackmun saw that Scalia was engaged in what is often termed "law-office history" to support his attack on regulatory authority. "In short, I find no clear and accepted 'historical compact' or 'understanding of our citizens' justifying the Court's new takings doctrine. Instead, the Court seems to treat history as a grab bag of principles, to be adopted where they support the Court's theory, and ignored where they do not."[96] In the process, he warned: "The Court makes sweeping and, in my view, misguided and unsupported changes in our takings doctrine."[97] It was clear that Blackmun saw the ruling in the case as far wider than the narrow facts of the present case, and instead as an ominous portent of things to come.[98]

What was next was a major ruling authored by Justice William Rehnquist that used Scalia's beachhead developed in the *Nollan v. California Coastal Commission* opinion to launch an attack in a case involving the standard application of well-established and understood zoning powers. The decision was for that reason nothing short of shocking to many local government officials and elected officials. With the Court's ruling in *Dolan v. Tigard*, it was becoming clear, though, that regulatory authority and discretion at the state and local level was far from what it had been for decades and far more vulnerable to challenge.[99] The case arose in a Portland, Oregon, suburb and concerned what would generally be regarded as a routine dispute over whether a business owner would be granted a zoning variance to expand her store. However, before it was over, Rehnquist would recast the case as a dramatic constitutional issue of a regulatory taking.

The owner of a hardware store had sought to significantly increase the size of the business on the property and to increase the size and pave the surface of the parking lot, resulting in a larger impervious surface for purposes of drainage in a climate that sees a considerable amount of rain and storm water runoff. That situation was made more complicated by the fact that a portion of her property was in an existing flood plain. There was also a problem because the expansion of the store and its parking lot were expected to increase traffic on a road that already had a significant traffic burden. For these and other reasons, the expansion violated a valid existing zoning plan. The community could simply have refused the variance request, but instead offered to approve the business owner's plans subject to a number of conditions, including the development of a greenway area in part of the property in the flood plain, with an area for a bicycle path that would connect with existing paths to mitigate some of the traffic. (It should be noted that the Portland area sees the widest use of bicycle transportation in the nation, so that paths are by no means insignificant byways.)

In his opinion in the *Dolan* case, Rehnquist used the *Nollan* opinion as a base and extended its requirements even further. Then he added his own newly created requirements on top of that. By the end of the argument, it was clear that not only would the burden to justify restrictions on property use rest with the government, but that the local government's application of otherwise valid land-use regulations would be subject to a new standard that courts would apply without the traditional deference to regulators that the Court had ruled for years was due the police powers of the Constitution. Even if the regulator offered approval of a plan subject to mitigating conditions, that action would be treated as a violation of the doctrine of unconstitutional conditions—a requirement that the applicant trade away his or her constitutional rights in return for a government benefit—if the Court's new two-part standard was not satisfied.

> In evaluating petitioner's claim, we must first determine whether the "essential nexus" exists between the "legitimate state interest" and the permit condition exacted by the city. *Nollan*, 483 U.S. at 837. If we find that a nexus exists, we must then decide the required degree of connection between the exactions and the projected impact of the proposed development.[100]
>
> The second part of our analysis requires us to determine whether the degree of the exactions demanded by the city's permit conditions bears the required relationship to the projected impact of petitioner's proposed development. The question for us is whether these findings are constitutionally sufficient to justify the conditions imposed by the city on petitioner's building permit.[101]
>
> We think a term such as "rough proportionality" best encapsulates what we hold to be the requirement of the Fifth Amendment. No precise mathematical calculation is required, but the city must make some sort of individualized determination that the required dedication is related both in nature and extent to the impact of the proposed development.[102]

Although the Court remanded the case for further proceedings, the majority proceeded to determine for itself that the city's findings were not adequate and that it had not "met its burden" under the new standard.[103] Given the fact that the Court had just invented the standard, including the element of proportionality, and the requirement for the city to carry the burden, it is not surprising that the Court concluded the community had not in its earlier decision making satisfied a standard that did not exist at the time.

Justice Stevens, in dissent, made it clear that virtually everything about this ruling was newly created out of whole cloth. "The Court has made a serious error by abandoning the traditional presumption of constitutionality and imposing a novel burden of proof on a city implementing an admittedly valid comprehensive land use plan. Even more consequential than its incorrect disposition of this case, however, is the Court's resurrection of a species of substantive due process analysis that it firmly rejected decades ago."[104] The long-standing principle had been that the regulatory authorities should prevail unless the government's actions were irrational or arbitrary and the "strong presumption of validity" should be accorded to the government's claims. "The burden of demonstrating that those conditions have unreasonably impaired the economic value of the proposed improvement belongs squarely on the shoulders of the party challenging the state action's constitutionality. That allocation of burdens has served us well in the past. The Court has stumbled badly today by reversing it."[105]

There was one more ruling to come in this campaign against police power regulation, and it was one that attracted even less attention. It was a 1999 ruling in *City of Monterrey v. Del Monte Dunes,* authored for a plurality of the justices by Justice Kennedy.[106] This case involved a protracted dispute between the city and a developer that ultimately resulted in a claim that the city had engaged in a "regulatory taking" without compensation. The focus of the case as it reached the Supreme Court, however, was not on the merits of the case, but rather that the developer had demanded that the regulatory taking claim should be tried before a jury. The Court agreed. In the process, the plurality opinion suggested that a suit about whether there had been a regulatory taking was roughly akin to a tort liability suit in which a jury trial should be available under the Seventh Amendment. That marked a dramatic departure from a history of judicial review without juries in such matters, as the four dissenters pointed out.

Justice Souter explained that "respondents had no right to a jury trial either by statute or under the Constitution. . . . In holding to the contrary, that such a right does exist under the Seventh Amendment, the Court misconceives a taking claim . . . and draws a false analogy between such a claim and a tort action."[107] In submitting such inappropriate cases to a jury, the Court was undermining the regulatory authority of state and local government and opening a Pandora's Box.

Perhaps this is the reason that the Court apparently seeks to distance itself from the ramifications of today's determination. . . . It denies that today's holding would extend to "a broad challenge to the constitutionality of the city's general land-use ordinances or policies," in which case, "the determination whether the statutory purposes were legitimate, or whether the purposes, though legitimate, were furthered by the law or general policy, might well fall within the province of the judge." . . . But the Court's reticence is cold comfort simply because it rests upon distinctions that withstand analysis no better than the tort-law analogies on which the Court's conclusion purports to rest. The narrowness of the Court's intentions cannot, therefore, be accepted as an effective limit on the consequences of its reasoning.[108]

By the turn of the twenty-first century, the Court had dramatically altered the law governing the policy power regulatory authority of the state and local governments, but the regulatory takings doctrine was not the only area in which that transformation had taken place.

Federal Preemption: A Barrier to State Regulation Even When Congress Steps Out of the Arena

Another context in which state and local governments have found their regulatory efforts under attack has been in cases where challengers alleged that the regulatory authority had been preempted, either in express terms or implied by federal government action. Such assertions have been presented even where the federal government had been removing itself from the regulatory arena with deregulation legislation. And, as the antiregulatory forces have prevailed in the White House and in Congress over administrations and legislatures led by both political parties, states have placed been in increasingly difficult positions. Their efforts to protect the health and safety of state residents have been challenged not only by regulated firms, ideologically driven interest groups, and other national political interests, but also by other countries and business groups abroad. In a series of cases, the Supreme Court has repeatedly found state efforts to be preempted.

The concept of preemption is based on the supremacy clause of the Constitution, Article VI, Clause 2, which provides that "this Constitution, and the Laws of the United States which shall be made in Pursuance thereof; and all Treaties made, or which shall be made, under the Authority of the United States, shall be the supreme Law of the Land; and the Judges in every State shall be bound thereby, any Thing in the Constitution or Laws of any state to the Contrary notwithstanding." Congress may either specifically state an intention in legislation to block state policymaking or courts may find that such a ban on state action is implied by the language and general design of the national legislation. An implied preemption can occur where the national legislation occupies the whole field (field preemption), leaving no room for the states to act, or where there is a conflict between the federal law and the state requirements (conflict preemption), making it virtually impossible to comply with both.

In 1990, in an opinion by a self-professed champion of the states, Sandra Day O'Connor, the Court overturned a Pennsylvania law regulating what insurance plans could require with respect to damage awards as a result of civil suits from events outside the workplace received by workers in insured firms. The case was a quite complex matter in which the Court found that Congress had preempted the authority of the states to regulate certain aspects of insurance when it passed the Employee Retirement Income Security Act of 1974, better known as ERISA.[109]

The field of insurance regulation was particularly interesting not only because insurance was an area of regulation that was traditionally recognized as within the authority of the states, but because Congress had in fact adopted legislation that ceded regulatory authority in that area to the states; an action recognized early on by the Supreme Court.[110] The other important point to note, and one that was the focus of the dissent, was that the Court could very easily have found that the state's actions were consistent with ERISA and therefore it was unnecessary to overcome the traditional rule that the Court would not find preemption unless it was necessary to do so. Justice Stevens writing for the dissent reminded Justice O'Connor that the standard rule of interpretation is: "When there is ambiguity in a statutory provision preempting state law, we should apply a strong presumption against the invalidation of well-settled, generally applicable state rules."[111]

The states had long been in a difficult position on matters of insurance regulation, since few have the administrative capacity and in some cases the legal tools to regulate adequately the very large and sophisticated insurance corporations that do business with their citizens. At the same time, those same companies have been able to use their considerable resources and political support to obtain congressional action to protect them from some forms of state regulation.

In a case concerning airline deregulation decided in 1992, the Court once again chose to find preemption in a situation when it could have avoided it and allowed states to protect their citizens. After the Airline Deregulation Act had been in force for some time, state attorneys general found that their consumer protection units were receiving significant numbers of complaints from consumers who considered the manner in which fares were advertised and sold to be deceptive at best, and perhaps worse. The state attorneys general agreed to act. While they recognized that the federal government had withdrawn its regulation of routes and rates for the airline industry in the Airline Deregulation Act, they put the airlines on notice that the states would use their existing consumer protection laws to deal with deceptive practices.

Justice Scalia wrote for the majority. He began with the language of the act that "expressly pre-empts the States from 'enacting or enforcing any law, rule, regulation, standard, or other provision having the force and effect of law relating to rates, routes, or services of any air carrier.'"[112] Scalia seized on the "relating to" language to find that Congress had intended to preclude any regulation of any airline behavior by the states.

Justice Stevens wrote for three dissenters (Justice Souter did not participate), again arguing that the Court was ignoring its canon of interpretation that states should not be preempted unless it was clear that Congress intended that restriction. That is particularly true where the state is carrying out traditional state functions. In this case, Stevens wrote, "there is no indication that Congress intended to exempt airlines from state prohibitions of deceptive advertising. Instead, this history suggests that the scope of the prohibition of state regulation should be measured by the scope of the federal regulation that was being withdrawn."[113] The protection of consumers from deceptive advertising is a traditional state function and one that had nothing to do with setting routes, rates, or required service to particular locations, which had been the purposes of the federal airline regulatory authority that had been eliminated by Congress.

Again in 1992, a sharply divided Court, in another opinion by O'Connor, found a preemption of an Illinois regulatory process for worker safety.[114] This case arose at a time when there was considerable frustration in the states with the ongoing Reagan administration opposition to worker safety regulation by the Occupational Safety and Health Administration (OSHA). As the earlier discussion of the Reagan campaigns against regulation explained, OSHA and the Environmental Protection Agency (EPA) had been two agencies that were primary targets of the administration from the time of Reagan's first campaign throughout his presidency. States argued that they had traditional police power authority to regulate in the area of safety, health, and public welfare so long as their actions did not interfere with interstate commerce or other federal authority.

In 1989 the state of Illinois enacted two statutes, the Hazardous Waste Crane and Hoisting Equipment Operators Licensing Act and the Hazardous Waste Laborers Licensing Act. The state law required operators and their supervisors to receive significantly more training to obtain licenses as compared to the requirements imposed by the federal OSHA. Their purpose was to protect both the workers and the public from accidents that might pollute the environment.

Justice Souter wrote for the four dissenters who, once again, began from the rule that "Where, as here, the field which Congress is said to have pre-empted has been traditionally occupied by the States, . . . 'we start with the assumption that the historic police powers of the States were not to be superseded by the Federal Act unless that was the clear and manifest purpose of Congress.'"[115] Not only was there no express preemption in the statute, there was also a savings clause that permitted state law to survive. Therefore, Souter concluded, unless there was a clear conflict from the state regulations with the federal policy, there was no need or justification to strike the Illinois requirements.

Even so, O'Connor wrote for the plurality, finding not express, but implied preemption. Justice Kennedy concurred in the judgment, but rejected O'Connor's argument. In fact, he said, "I cannot agree that we should denominate this case as one of implied pre-emption. The contrary view of the plurality is based on an undue expansion of our implied pre-emption jurisprudence which, in my view, is neither wise nor necessary."[116]

It was becoming increasingly clear to officials at the state level that not only would the federal government not protect their citizens, but that the states would not be permitted to do so, either, even in fields that were traditionally subject to state regulation such as consumer protection or health and safety. To many of those officials who were increasingly frustrated by the unwillingness of the federal government to take protective action and still to preempt the states, insult was added to injury by the successful efforts of foreign countries and firms, with the cooperation of the U.S. federal government, to preempt efforts by the states to protect their environment, their safety, and even their fundamental community values.

Two of these important Supreme Court rulings came in 2000 and involved two very different state actions. The first grew out of frustrations by citizens of Washington state over the inability or unwillingness of the federal government to provide adequate protection from oil tanker leaks and accidents. There was serious concern in the state for the well-being of the beautiful but vulnerable Puget Sound ecosystem.[117]

The *Exxon Valdez* oil spill in Alaska intensified concerns in the state in March 1989, particularly since it was followed by a close call nearer to home only a month later. Another tanker, the *Exxon Philadelphia*, went adrift after it lost power just as it was about to enter the Straits of Juan de Fuca, the route taken to enter the Puget Sound from the Pacific. The Coast Guard was able to rescue the vessel and take it into harbor for repairs. Had this incident happened some time after the tanker had entered the sound, the vessel would have been without power or steering amidst dozens of islands with treacherous currents and frequently bad weather that limited visibility. A year earlier, Washington, California, Oregon, and British Columbia had created an oil spill task force following a major oil spill in December 1988 in waters near the Washington coast.

The Alaska Oil Spill Commission also reported, at about that same time, that states had better take steps to protect their waters, since the industry was responding to perverse incentives from the marketplace that meant increased risks and the Coast Guard was not adequately staffed to take the needed protective action. "There is a tendency in the industry to measure success as operating the biggest vessel with the thinnest hull and smallest crew at the highest speed with the quickest port turnaround consistent with meeting minimum government requirements. . . . In short, efficiency in a competitive world motivated by profit is the dominant factor. As a consequence, the system of carrying oil by sea is error-prone rather than risk-averse."[118]

In 1991, the state of Washington adopted the Oil Spill Prevention Act, which established an Office of Marine Safety and created new standards aimed not at cleanup but at adding to existing federal safeguards aimed at preventing spills and accidents in the first place and in a manner that the state could enforce. The state did not try to mandate changes in ship design, since an earlier Washington law of that type had been overturned in the U.S. Supreme Court.[119] This time the state relied upon long-standing Supreme Court precedent that allowed state and local governments to add operating requirements to shipping where unique local circumstances called for special

cautions.[120] The Court had affirmed that precedent even where the local actions were significant rules affecting the ability of vessels to enter local waters.[121] The state also indicated that the Congress had recognized an ability of
states to act in such cases when it provided in the Oil Pollution Act of 1990
that "nothing in this Act . . . shall in any way affect, or be construed to affect,
the authority of the United States or any State or political subdivision
thereof—(1) to impose additional liability or additional requirements; or
(2) to impose, or to determine the amount of, any fine or penalty (whether
criminal or civil in nature) for any violation of law; relating to the discharge,
or substantial threat of a discharge, of oil."[122] The rules imposed by the state
this time focused on crew training, steps to ensure adequate language capabilities among the crew to avoid serious communications breakdowns, navigation watch requirements, and reports from vessels on past incidents and
insurance coverage.

A challenge to the Washington law and the regulatory agency it created in
U.S. District Court by the International Association of Independent Tanker
Owners (INTERTANKO) failed,[123] and that ruling was upheld by the U.S.
Court of Appeals for the Ninth Circuit.[124] Before the district court ruling was
issued, some thirteen U.S. trading partners—Belgium, Denmark, Finland,
France, Germany, Greece, Italy, Japan, the Netherlands, Norway, Portugal,
Spain, and Sweden—and the Commission of the European Community (later
joined by Canada) filed a diplomatic protest with the U.S. government and
demanded that the Clinton administration take action to overturn the state
regulatory action.[125] The Clinton administration entered the case once it
moved forward on appeal, arguing that the state law was barred under standard preemption doctrine and that the state had violated the foreign affairs
powers of the federal government under the Constitution.

This time it was a unanimous Supreme Court that held the Washington
regulatory efforts to be preempted, in an opinion by Justice Kennedy.
Kennedy started by turning the *Cooley v. Bd. of Wardens* precedent about state
regulation in local waters on its head.[126] He quoted dictum (language in the
opinion not really central to the holding in the case) in the *Cooley* opinion
that indicated that of course general authority over shipping belonged to the
federal government and that authority might very well bar state action even if
there were no specific federal statute. But Kennedy added, almost as an after-
thought, that "in the case before it the Court found the challenged state regu-

lations were permitted in light of local needs and conditions."[127] That finding of state authority based on local needs and conditions was precisely the core holding of that long-standing precedent. In the end, Kennedy said: "We have determined that Washington's regulations regarding general navigation watch procedures, English language skills, training, and casualty reporting are preempted."[128]

The second case arose from the increasing recognition by states that they are not only market regulators, but also market participants that purchase a great deal of goods and services with public money every year—tax dollars that many taxpayers and state policymakers did not want to go to firms and governments that operated in ways contrary to the values of the state. When they are market participants, the Supreme Court had said in earlier rulings, they are not subject to restrictions like the interstate commerce clause.[129] In this case, it was the Commonwealth of Massachusetts that made a decision not to do business with firms that did business with the repressive government of Myanmar, which the United States government still refers to by its traditional name of Burma because it was an illegitimate government run by a brutal military junta.[130] However, once again, America's trading partners demanded action to block the state's policy and joined the business association that had brought suit against the Massachusetts rule. Once again the Clinton administration obliged, arguing against the state. The Supreme Court once again found that the state action was preempted by federal legislation and that it interfered with the foreign affairs powers of the national government. The provisions of the state law, it said, "threaten to complicate discussions; they compromise the very capacity of the President to speak for the Nation with one voice in dealing with other governments."[131] The state did not see what it had done as an interference with federal action, but a policy supportive of it.

Again in 2003, a sharply divided Court preempted state regulation on grounds of interference with the national government's foreign affairs powers. This time the case came from a state regulatory policy directed at insurance companies, a field that has, as noted earlier, been traditionally reserved to state control. It involved a challenge to California's Holocaust Victim Insurance Relief Act of 1999, which mandated that any insurer doing business in California disclose "information about all policies sold in Europe between 1920 and 1945 by the company itself or any one "related" to it."[132] The state undertook its study of the problem and policymaking to respond to it even as the Clinton administration was attempting to negotiate an agreement with Germany and Israel on related matters. The result was an executive agreement rather than a treaty. As such, the pact did not require Senate confirmation.

The agreement did not expressly preempt action by the states, but the administration promised to warn states that any actions they took would be counterproductive and present difficulties for the agreement and for the administration. However, California did not see its action as disruptive, but as regulation of insurance companies in the interest of its citizens.

Even so, five members of the court concluded that "the exercise of the federal executive authority means that state law must give way where, as here, there is evidence of clear conflict between the policies adopted by the two."[133] Moreover, the majority found that the fact that the implied preemption was in an executive agreement rather than legislation or a ratified treaty was of no consequence. In fact, the opinion used rather dramatic language to characterize the state regulatory action.

> The basic fact is that California seeks to use an iron fist where the President has consistently chosen kid gloves. We have heard powerful arguments that the iron fist would work better, and it may be that if the matter of compensation were considered in isolation from all other issues involving the European allies, the iron fist would be the preferable policy. But our thoughts on the efficacy of the one approach versus the other are beside the point.[134]

The dissenters recognized the significance and impact of executive agreements in general. However, they rejected the idea that an implied preemption from such an agreement alone, with neither legislation nor a treaty available to support it, should be used to displace state legislation in a field that is traditionally the subject of state regulation. "Despite the absence of express preemption, the Court holds that the HVIRA interferes with foreign policy objectives implicit in the executive agreements. . . . I would not venture down that path."[135]

The string of preemption rulings has served as encouragement for regulated industries to use every means at their disposal, including the use of political money, in their efforts to encourage members of Congress and presidential administrations to provide express or implied language that would preempt future state efforts to regulate. These preemption decisions have also encouraged regulated firms to launch legal assaults with considerable success on many significant efforts at regulation at the state level. Those challenges have succeeded not only in defeating the particular regulatory policies against which they are brought, but also in establishing precedents that constrain states more generally in their efforts to provide regulatory protections for their citizens in the face of a continuing failure of the federal government to provide those safeguards.

In a single week in 2008, the Supreme Court and U.S. Court of Appeals for the Second Circuit found three different kinds of actions at the state level preempted. One was a Maine law that required delivery companies that brought tobacco products to residences to check the identification and age of the recipient. The Court rejected that law on grounds that it violated the Airline Deregulation Act.[136] (Recall from Chapter 3 the fact that the Clinton administration had joined with Congress to support insertion of language in the airline act that sought to eliminate the last vestiges of state regulatory authority over trucking.) The purpose of the Maine policy was to block Internet purchases of tobacco products by minors. The Court found preemption notwithstanding the fact that the law dealt with protection of minors and regulation of tobacco products, two areas of traditionally recognized state police power regulatory authority.

Second, the Court ruled not only that states were prohibited by the Medical Device Amendments of 1976 from regulating medical devices directly—which they had done for many years before that legislation—but also that the same law implicitly banned suits brought in state courts by those who charged that they had been injured by medical devices, if the devices had been issued a premarket approval by the federal Food and Drug Administration (FDA).[137] Here again, before this legislation, the regulation of medical devices, as compared to drugs, had been done by the states on health and safety grounds. Also, this case did not involve an effort by the state to regulate, but merely a common-law claim by one who was allegedly injured by a device in a state court. There is no small amount of irony in the fact that the Court delivered this ruling concerning the importance of sweeping deference to the FDA at a time when virtually everyone had agreed that the federal regulatory agency was utterly incapable of fulfilling its regulatory obligations because of very successful and persistent strategic resources attacks.

Justice Ginsburg, dissenting, reminded her colleagues that the Court has repeatedly cautioned that the presumption should be against preemption in an area of traditionally recognized state regulation. That said, she asserted, this was not a close case since "state premarket regulation of medical devices, not any design to suppress tort suits, accounts for Congress' inclusion of a preemption clause in the MDA."[138]

The Court also held that the Federal Arbitration Act preempted state laws that required that disputes belonged in the first instance in state courts or administration agencies.[139] This was not a small matter, nor one as arcane as it may seem, since it is increasingly common for businesses to require customers or even employees to enter into agreements that require arbitration and bar standard lawsuits.

The U.S. Court of Appeals for the Second Circuit struck down New York's effort to provide health, safety, and consumer protection legislation aimed at mistreatment of airline passengers in aircraft parked on the ground for extended periods of time.[140] Citing the Supreme Court's recent ruling in the Maine tobacco products delivery case, the appeals court panel concluded that: "Although this Court has not yet defined "service" as it is used in the ADA, we have little difficulty concluding that requiring airlines to provide food, water, electricity, and restrooms to passengers during lengthy ground delays relates to the service of an air carrier."[141] The court found that the state's requirement that airlines "provide food, water, electricity, and restrooms to passengers during lengthy ground delays . . . substitutes New York's commands for competitive market forces."[142] The state policy was a reaction to the fact that conditions in the marketplace provided no effective requirement for even minimally adequate service. Just as clearly, the ongoing successful war against regulation in Washington had eliminated the existing requirements for even the most minimal consumer protections and blocked efforts to deal with a situation that no politician would dare to defend openly—much less on grounds that those stranded in airliners without food, water, or functioning restrooms for literally hours on end should wait for the marketplace to provide a resolution.

In sum, the federal courts, and the U.S. Supreme Court in particular, have become a very effective ally in the war against regulation in many important respects. Certainly, its rulings on preemption have fought a counterinsurgency action, protecting the president and Congress along with their allies outside government from efforts by the states to create some level of defenses for the health, safety, and honest consumer dealings of their citizens.

REGULATION LITERALLY GOES
"BACK TO THE FUTURE": THE FIGHT
AGAINST REGULATION BY LAWSUIT

There is no small irony in the fact that the effectiveness of the war on regulation has forced those who seek the protections long available through the regulatory process to try to obtain those protections by launching lawsuits, since it was, as explained earlier, the problems with regulation by lawsuit that were, in important respects, responsible for the efforts to create a modern collection of public policy, regulatory agencies, and a body of administrative law by which they should operate. However, since the policies, the agencies, and the law have been the subject of many successful campaigns against regulation, those injured have gone back to what had been done so many years before, which was to launch a host of individual legal actions brought either by private citizens to recover damages or by government lawyers seeking civil or criminal sanctions. Contemporary efforts to pursue what antiregulatory forces early on labeled "regulation by lawsuit" have included the effort to use the civil rights policy model, state attorney general suits as substitutes for regulation, criminal prosecutions in lieu of standard federal regulation by administrative agencies, and private tort suits for damages where no government agency or official would assist.

*The Civil Rights Policy Model: The Problematic Use
of Individual Lawsuits to Regulate in the Public Interest*

The civil rights policy model involves the passage of legislation by the Congress that identifies protections for individuals and then relies primarily on those people to implement and enforce the policy by bringing individual lawsuits. This concept evolved as an outgrowth of the effective efforts by the National Association for the Advancement of Colored People Legal Defense and Education Fund (NAACP LDF) to advance the civil rights cause.[143] For those effectively closed out of the political process, it seemed futile to wait for legislation or administrative action by the executive branch to address what were supposed to be fundamental rights under the Constitution. Not surprisingly, other groups who had historically suffered discrimination—including women, Native Americans, Latinos, and those with disabilities—learned from the successes of the NAACP LDF and launched their own efforts to shape policy and enforce existing rights. When the Congress and the president did come to support civil rights legislation, such as the Civil Rights Act of 1964, they advanced a model that announced the protected rights and made possible suits by those injured to enforce those protections. The legislation provided for an Equal Employment Opportunity Commission (EEOC) but gave it little meaningful authority and no significant resources. There was a Civil Rights Division of the U.S. Department of Justice (DOJ), but its task was largely to bring enforcement litigation in selected cases rather than to act as a regulatory agency. Though that has historically been an important role, the division has not had the capacity to do more.

Over time other legislation was developed using a similar model, with the expectation of implementation and enforcement largely by individual lawsuit rather than administrative regulation. It was an attractive model for politicians, since they could claim to resolve an important policy problem, but to do so, as politicians love to claim, without having created any new bureaucracy and without expending significant amounts of money. This was, for example, precisely the claim that George H. W. Bush made in signing the ADA.[144] The act did assign certain responsibilities to a number of federal agencies to ensure compliance with the legislation, and the DOJ received a mandate to provide some sorts of regulations under the act, but there really was no regulatory agency, new or existing, that was tasked with the primary obligation of implementation and enforcement of the act. That was left largely to individuals who considered that their rights under the act had been violated. The same kind of model applied to the ADEA[145] and the Family Medical Leave Act.[146]

While it is attractive for the reasons indicated, the civil rights policy model is a poor substitute for systematically constructed regulatory policy with an adequate and effective institutional foundation. First, because it relies on literally thousands of lawsuits brought in hundreds of courts across the country, there are serious issues of consistency, uniformity, and predictability. Different courts interpret different elements of the same law differently in many different jurisdictions. These difficulties can only be remedied if cases move all the way to the Supreme Court, and then the court will resolve only the particular issues presented and not related problems.

The DOJ is not a normal regulatory agency and is not designed for the kind of systematic and comprehensive rulemaking and monitoring normally expected from regulatory institutions. It cannot perform the same roles that they do. Clearly, though, these policies do not expect the DOJ to play that role, but rather to provide some minimal foundation with the primary regulatory work to be carried by individual lawsuits brought by those covered by the statute.

Second, and related to this expectation of self-implementing regulatory policy, is the fact that most people do not have the knowledge or the resources to perform effectively the role anticipated by the civil rights policy model. These policies require prompt action of the correct type if a claim is to be considered viable, much less to be resolved favorably to complainant. That also means, as a practical matter, that those involved must understand the need to act quickly to obtain legal representation and that they must know how to do that. Acquiring an attorney and developing a complaint requires resources that many do not have. In some cases those who are ultimately successful may be able to obtain attorneys fees under the Civil Rights Attorneys Fees Act. However, that is not uniformly the case. It was one thing for an organization like the NAACP LDF to use this approach to shape policy by bringing cases picked for the purpose and quite another to use civil rights suits as a substitute for large-scale regulatory operations.

Even more important than these problems is the creation by the Supreme Court, out of whole cloth, of a doctrine of Eleventh Amendment immunity, discussed earlier in this chapter, that has overturned the parts of these policies in which Congress abrogated state immunity from suits for damages. The lack of damages seriously undermines the effectiveness of the model and reduces the likelihood that attorneys will be enthusiastic about taking otherwise meritorious cases. Part of the effectiveness of the model is the fact that offenders will face significant monetary damages if they fail to comply with the law.

In theory, the complainant might still obtain an injunction against a state agency, requiring that it cease violations of the federal law and compelling it to comply. However, in reality, such a case is difficult for an individual to win and then to ensure that compliance will be forthcoming over time. Also, in theory, the individual might be able to persuade an attorney to carry the case with the hope of obtaining a Civil Rights Attorney Fees award, but states have been more than willing to fight the award phase with the knowledge that such burdens discourage attorneys from undertaking the risk and the trouble of these cases in the first instance. Advocacy groups may still be willing to carry such litigation, but most are small and have extremely limited capacity. While there are exceptions, the cost of law schools and general societal values are not supportive of the development of a large cadre of civil rights attorneys as compared with the lure of corporate law firm salaries.

State Attorneys General Suits as Substitutes
for Administrative Agency Regulation

In an attempt to protect some of the likely casualties of the war on regulation, state attorneys general have entered the lists in opposition. From Connecticut to California and from Texas to North Carolina, state attorneys general have sought either to force federal action or to use state law to fill the void left by deregulation. Thus, these state advocates have sued the EPA to force regulation of vehicle emissions of greenhouse gases that contribute to global warming.[147] The discussion earlier in the chapter of efforts by attorneys general to step into the consumer protection gap left by federal airline deregulation, though unsuccessful, is another example.[148]

In some instances, the state attorneys general sought to use existing federal or state statutes, but in other instances they have employed, either directly or indirectly—working with third parties—novel common-law approaches, like the application of common-law nuisance to gun cases, lead paint sales and marketing, vehicle manufacturers' contributions to global warming, and the manner of operation of a Tennessee Valley coal-fired generating plant.[149] One or more of these approaches lay behind the massive effort to rein in the abuses of tobacco companies, the attempt to force some kind of action against gun manufacturers and distributors who knew or reasonably should have known that they were providing weapons to gangs or others engaged in criminal activity, the project to address the long-standing problem and consequences of the marketing and sales of lead-based paint for residential uses, the campaign for responsible behavior by brokers and fund managers in the financial services industry, and the work to stop abusive practices in the student loan industry.

In a number of instances the attorneys general obtained victories without the need to win in the courtroom, since the costs of bad publicity and the promise of continuing high litigation costs prompted the targets of the legal action to settle. The success of the tobacco suit in obtaining a very large settlement was one example.[150]

That said, there have been distinct limitations to and problems with the effort by attorneys general to substitute legal actions from their offices for the lack of standard administrative regulation at the federal or state levels. The first and most obvious difficulty is that these kinds of actions can address only a very few cases in limited areas. While there have been a number of highly visible and potentially important cases, they cannot begin to address the range of issues and problems in the regulatory arena.

Second, and related to the first point, is the fact that state attorneys general lack the resources to be effective as drivers of the regulatory process. They often lead relatively modest state organizations that have many demands from across the state for their services. Most state attorneys general are political officials who do not expect to stay long in that office, though there are, to be sure, some exceptions. They are therefore often not able to build the capacity needed to be major players in the regulatory process beyond their normal obligations under state law. Indeed, the fact that states retained outside counsel in cases like the tobacco settlement and the lead paint case caused considerable criticism, though the officials involved were quick to point out that their state's share of the $246 billion tobacco settlement more than justified the contracting out of that litigation. That said, state attorneys general do not have the staff or other resources to be much more than a catalyst for change, mounting rear-guard actions against the war on regulation.

Part of the problem with the capacity issue is that effective regulation requires not merely rules and enforcement mechanisms, but also ongoing monitoring capabilities. These responsibilities demand skills and human resources that state attorneys general offices do not possess. And given that state regulatory agencies have been weakened in many states for political and fiscal reasons over the past few decades, they are rarely in a position to be of much help. In fact, in some states, attorneys general are lone political actors who may not be allies of the governor and may in fact be elected from the party that does not hold the statehouse, a situation that can and has generated conflict within state governments and outside them.

Even where state attorneys general are successful, the victories involve limited territory and populations, since state law is not binding elsewhere and may even have limited value as precedent. While judges in other states may look to decisions from elsewhere as trends or for the force of their arguments, they do not, of course, carry the full weight of precedent. And while state attorneys general suits brought in federal courts seek to overcome that limitation, they can do so only if they succeed at least at the level of the U.S. Court of Appeals and then win a binding precedent only within the circuit involved.

In part for this reason, state attorneys general have banded together in their effort to obtain favorable U.S. Supreme Court rulings in matters like the global warming case or to support or oppose other pending cases before the Court in amicus curiae briefs.

Criminal Prosecutions: A Blunt and Unsystematic Instrument and No Substitute for Regulation

Another way that state attorneys general or federal prosecutors can get the attention of what were once considered regulated communities is by bringing criminal prosecutions in an effort to send a signal to others to avoid similar misbehavior, even if there is not a strong regulatory agency with effective legislative authority, adequate resources, and clear political support to provide traditional regulation. During the years of the war against regulation, this has been a tool used in such areas as abuses in the marketplace for insider trading, bond market manipulations, or malfeasance by corporate officers. Examples are not all that common, but some, like the insider trading cases, the savings and loan debacle, or the prosecutions brought in the wake of the Enron and Worldcom scandals, provide well-publicized examples.

However, criminal prosecutions target a few individuals on an unsystematic basis for the most serious punishments, rather than seeking to set and maintain ongoing effective regulation, in a manner that both comprehends the nature of the regulated activity and the need for limits. There is little evidence that would indicate that such prosecutions have any significant regulatory effect over time or across industries. Curiously enough, criminal prosecutions may even engender sympathy for the defendant within industry or even among the public if the accused is a celebrity. For others, the targets are simply considered clumsy people who got caught by those who think themselves far smarter and quicker and therefore unlikely to suffer the same fate.

Once again, such prosecutions are ultimately reliant on prosecutors rather than regulators in most instances, though the Securities and Exchange Commission has some unique characteristics in terms of its role with regard to both civil and criminal matters. Other agencies, like the U.S. EPA also have some role in criminal matters in extreme cases. Even so, they remain principally regulatory bodies rather than prosecutors. Prosecutors lack the kind of ongoing engagement or resources to maintain a vigil over a regulated industry.

While criminal laws are regulatory in character, they are very different in operation from modern regulatory policies, and the law that governs them is unlike the administrative law that covers regulatory agencies. Hence, regulatory agencies do not face the kind of burden of proof encountered by prosecutors and enjoy, in law at least, a considerable level of judicial deference on review of their decisions.

Finally, prosecutions accuse and seek to punish rather than to correct problems and control business behavior. Most regulatory efforts are aimed not at prohibition or punishment, but at setting boundaries and shaping behavior within limits in a field of regulated activity.

Private Civil Actions: Lessons Not Learned from History and Added Judicial Roadblocks

Another approach to regulation by lawsuit, as the phrase is commonly used, is by private litigation or interest-group litigation. Certainly there has been a flood of critical literature concerning large-scale products liability and mass toxic tort suits and the class actions in which those suits are brought.[151] Indeed, the so-called civil justice reform moves by a number of recent administrations described in earlier chapters were aimed primarily at these kinds of suits. While civil suits have been instrumental in attracting attention to problems with products and corporate practices, they also have a variety of limitations that mean that while they may in some cases be catalysts for regulation, they cannot be effective substitutes. Indeed, it was noted earlier that administrative law was created in part to remedy some of the problems presented by regulation by lawsuit in the days when many efforts at what would today be considered regulation were done by private civil suits for nuisance, negligence, or other simple torts. Of course, one important form of litigation by individuals and interest groups in the contemporary environment is the effort to bring actions under administrative law to force regulatory responses by administrative agencies.

It is true that regulation by private civil lawsuit suffers from many of the difficulties discussed above with respect to attorney general suits with a variety of additional problems on top of that list. Like the attorney general suits, these actions are idiosyncratic and episodic. They represent plaintiffs who come forward to champion a cause, to collect damages, or both under circumstances that vary dramatically from one case to the next. They can draw attention to serious problems that government may then choose to target for regulatory action, but that is something apart from the individual cases themselves. In that respect, they can serve important functions, and indeed Congress has in some circumstances provided for citizen standing and in others has provided incentives like treble damage awards to encourage what are sometimes termed "private attorneys general" suits. Even so, they are clearly no substitute for effective traditional regulation.

Additionally, these cases, even if extremely meritorious, face a host of burdens if they are to succeed, particularly since the Supreme Court and legislatures engaged in the war against regulation have sought to constrain access to courts by all but the most traditional parties and have placed restrictions on the vehicles by which these types of suits are brought and sometimes settled. For example, there has been an ongoing effort since the Burger Court era to limit standing to sue and to impose other procedural barriers.[152]

In addition to other standard procedural limitations, the opportunity to obtain relief from violations of law has been constrained by the Supreme Court's efforts to limit what are termed "implied private rights of action"— cases that are brought by private parties because the government is either unwilling or unable to bring the case to enforce the law. In the past, the fact that a piece of legislation did not specifically state that such a private right of action was to be available did not stand as a bar to rulings by courts that this type of private attorney general action was available. In an era when antiregulation warriors in the executive branch—led by presidents, vice presidents, and administration political appointees—battled not only against issuing new or enhanced regulations but also either intervened outright or financially starved enforcement efforts, it mattered little what statutes required as written when the regulated industries had little to fear in terms of the willingness or capacity to enforce the law. Not surprisingly those who were injured by conduct that clearly violated regulatory laws have asked courts to bring the force of the law to bear to stop illegal conduct and provide relief to those injured. The Court not only issued rulings that made it more difficult to demonstrate an implied right of action,[153] but also rolled back previous rulings with respect to statutes where such a cause of action had been long and repeatedly recognized.[154]

The lack of ability to force action in court was all the more significant because the Court had ruled that administrative enforcement discretion was presumptively unreviewable, leaving those injured by illegal conduct by regulated individuals and firms with little or no meaningful recourse.[155]

The Court has also moved, ever since the early Burger Court years, to limit class-action suits—cases brought by a few parties in the name of a much larger class of injured persons—and to make it more difficult to reach settlements in large, complex cases that were brought as class actions.[156] The class-action device has been essential because suits to address the kinds of problems raised by the lack of regulatory action by the executive branch and independent agencies led by antiregulation warriors appointed by presidents who have led the fight require significant amounts of resources and affect so many people. While class-action suits can still be brought, the cost and level of effort required to have a class certified by a court and to receive judicial acceptance of a negotiated settlement by the parties in such a case have increased significantly.

If private parties are able to make their way through this minefield and maintain a successful legal action, there is still the question whether they can obtain relief adequate to make them whole again after they have paid their attorneys and also deter future similar conduct by the parties who caused the injury. One of the ways that problem was addressed for many years was by permitting those injured not only to collect compensatory damages for the injuries they suffered, but also to allow juries to award punitive damages in cases of particularly bad behavior. The purposes of punitive damages are to punish and deter harmful conduct.[157] A variety of cases that have been brought over the past several decades, as the war against regulation has raged, have sought to address harmful behavior by firms and individuals that should have been carefully and effectively regulated. However, the antiregulatory warriors on the Supreme Court, led by Chief Justice William Rehnquist, have fought to narrow the availability of punitive damages and to eliminate them if possible.[158]

One of the most visible of the punitive damages cases involved the decades-long effort by those injured by the *Exxon Valdez* oil spill to obtain adequate damages for the massive harm done from that spill. The Supreme Court upheld an award of punitive damages but limited those damages to an amount equal to the compensatory damages.[159] The jury in the civil suit, based on testimony regarding the behavior of company officials and the captain, awarded $5,000 in punitive damages against the captain and another $5 billion against the company.[160] The punitive damages against the company were reduced in the court of appeals to $2.5 billion. However, the Supreme Court ultimately concluded that the punitive damages could ultimately be no more than the amount of the compensatory damages, which, the Court indicated, were $507.5 million.[161] While that may appear to be a large amount of money, the firm involved had a net profit in the second quarter of 2008 of more than $11.68 billion, and, for the first six months of 2008, $22.57 billion.¹⁶² Damages of that amount are unlikely to deter executives concerned about short-term profit demands rather than the long-term possibility that there may be a punitive damage award that is a modest amount by comparison with the firm's size and resources. To all intents and purposes, then, civil suits that produce punitive damages cannot substitute for ongoing and properly supported regulatory policies and the institutions that are needed to implement them.

Some of those who proceed from a law and economics perspective, from traditional economic criticisms of regulatory policy, or others who simply operate from a plainly stated ideological perspective attack regulation by lawsuit as inefficient in economic terms and not truly responsive to clearly identified market failures.¹⁶³ Some, like W. Kip Viscusi, argue that there is no clear relationship between the damages sought in these cases and the costs actually incurred.¹⁶⁴ Of course, as the following chapter points out, one of the great fallacies of that discussion is that most modern regulatory policies were not designed in response to economists' views of market failures, but as political responses to problems on the public policy agenda. The criticisms are not so much wrong as not relevant to the reality of the most important policy choices. That said, there are many valid criticisms of efforts to regulate by lawsuit.

One of the important problems stems from the lack of accountability of those involved in the process of regulation by lawsuit. That is not to suggest that the causes they pursue are wrong or that they do so with any but positive motives, but that the way they do it is responsive only to their version of the public interest. Even if they succeed, the victory is limited to specific circumstances at issue in a particular case. Even advocacy groups that are well organized and supported cannot substitute for adequately resourced, professional regulatory agencies free from political interference. While there were relatively effective regulatory agencies, such suits provided a useful, if limited, adjunct to the normal regulatory process, but they are no substitute for it.

CONCLUSION

Clearly, the battle against regulation has been fought in the courts as well as in the executive and legislative branches of government. While they have not won every fight along the way, the antiregulatory forces have scored a series of important victories over a sustained period across a significant range of issues. The Supreme Court, staffed principally by presidents who were active leaders in the war against regulation and led by such regulatory foes as Chief Justice William Rehnquist and Antonin Scalia, has played an active role in the effort. In the process the Court has constrained federal authority with respect to the commerce power and in other important respects and then also limited state authority as well with particular emphasis on the application of the doctrines of preemption and regulatory takings.

These judicial constraints on government, and the efforts by those in the executive branch to limit regulatory action, have encouraged a return to the days of regulation by lawsuit, the practice of more than a hundred years ago, before the development of modern regulatory policy regimes and the administrative law under which they operate. There are a host of problems with the effort to use legal actions, either by state attorneys general or would-be private attorneys general, including the fact that courts have moved in a variety of ways to make such efforts more difficult. Even if those who sought assistance in the courts were more successful, their efforts could not substitute for a properly supported regulatory regime left free from political interference by antiregulation warriors.

It is past time, however, to move out of the morass that is the war against regulation to contemplate a different future, one that is both realistic and effective in providing responses to the devastation that has been wrought by the repeated attacks on regulation. That is the challenge of the next chapter.

5. "The Wrong War in the Wrong Place at the Wrong Time with the Wrong Enemy": Imagining a Different Future

The previous chapters have toured the battlefield, profiled the generals and other leading commanders, and examined the strategies, tactics, and weapons in the war against regulation. It has been a long war, waged by officers and foot soldiers of both Democratic and Republican administrations, as well as their allies and supporters outside government. The war has left many casualties, not only combatants, but, like much of modern warfare, there have also been many victims among noncombatants. They include children and senior citizens, women and men, injured by inadequate protection of their health, safety, and economic well-being. Casualties also include the environment and economic institutions and enterprises. It is time to take stock of the lessons of this war and the possibilities for a less destructive and more productive future.

It is an important time to take stock in part, of course, because the George W. Bush administration has ended, and a new administration led by President Barack Obama has taken office, promising major change. The time is right also because the nation is now experiencing terribly difficult economic circumstances in significant part because of damage done in the war against regulation. While the contemporary criticism of the lack of regulation in recent years and calls for improved regulatory policy might suggest that the war has ended, there is every reason to think it might very well resume in earnest in the not-too-distant future. It is well to remember, as Chapter 3 explained, that the Clinton administration came to office promising dramatic change, including a reaction against the regulatory policies of previous administrations. By the time Clinton took office, however, the focus had changed dramatically, with the overwhelming attention of the new president dedicated to economic matters. President Obama came to office facing an even more severe economic downturn and he appointed as advisors some of the very same people who led the fight against regulation during the Clinton years along with others who were their protégés. Finally, recent history shows that there has been a tendency, as soon as the crisis of the moment passes, forcing a cessation of hostilities, for the same factors that encouraged the war in the past to reassert themselves, and the war can easily and quickly resume in earnest.

What becomes clear to one who studies the matters carefully is that the criticisms leveled by General Omar Bradley of the actions by General Douglas MacArthur in Korea that brought the Chinese into that conflict are apt characterizations of the war against regulation. Bradley told Congress that it was "the wrong war, at the wrong place, at the wrong time and with the wrong enemy." With the explanation of the battle against regulation provided in the previous chapters in mind, this chapter addresses the fact that regulation is not the enemy, but merely one among a variety of available policy tools with which to approach public problems—sometimes appropriate, but inappropriate in other circumstances. Related to that simple reality is the fact that it is important to recognize what regulation really is and what it is not in comparison with other types of policy tools; since antiregulatory warriors have blurred the critical distinctions among these devices for their own purposes. Second, the reasons for pursuing regulatory options have in most important situations been primarily political rather than economic, demands by the public and pressure on their political leaders, in many cases by liberals but also in other instances by conservatives, to respond to a perceived public problem that demanded regulation rather than a discussion about economic efficiency. Third, there are lessons to be learned, as there are from all wars, from which the foundations of a different future can be built. What follows is not merely an introduction to regulation or the law related to it, but a discussion about those foundations that are essential for the development of a more constructive approach to the effective understanding and use of regulation as a critically important policy tool. These are foundations too often ignored in the heat of the battle against regulation.

BACK TO BASICS ON REGULATION: WHAT IS
REGULATION, AND WHAT IS IT NOT?

The discourse on regulation has displayed something of the qualities of the discourse about foreign affairs during a time of war. Professional diplomats may understand the subtleties and complexities of foreign policy and live with them on a day-to-day basis—even during a major conflict, but, for many political figures, some military officers, and even some professionals in public affairs, the discussion in times of war can be dramatically over-simplified, stereotyped, and laden with ideological and evocative rhetoric. Sadly, the same is true of much of the discourse on regulation through the years of the battle against regulation. Even for public affairs professionals, it is easy to get caught up in the group-think, political fashion, and hyperbole of the moment. Thus it is that many academic disciplines, whose participants ought to know better, move from one intellectual fad to another, though these trends are carefully justified by sophisticated rhetoric—the knowledge and facile use of which are taken to be verification of one's expertise and stature in the field.

In order to move forward, therefore, it is important to peel away some of the unhelpful baggage. One way to do that is to recall some regulatory basics. Consider first, a discussion of a simple question. Antiregulatory warriors assume the answer to this question is affirmative and therefore the fight against regulation is a just war. Is regulation bad? A second important question has not been so clearly addressed, and the failure to be clear about its answer has been part of the fog of battle in the war against regulation. What is regulation, and what is it not?

Neither Bad nor Good in Itself, but Merely One Type of Policy Tool

Consider the first question. Is regulation bad? Apart from a largely ideological reaction, the answer to that question clearly has a good deal to do with what we mean by regulation. For purposes of this discussion, assume a broad use of the term. In that sense, regulation is a setting of limits to certain targeted behaviors with a range of coercive sanctions to enforce the limits. There will be no hiding behind the idea that regulatory action is anything but that, even if it is called by some other name. Indeed, that specific issue—the centrality of the coercive nature of regulation—will come up later in the discussion.

So, once again, is regulation a bad idea? Consider the case of murder. Should homicide be prohibited? What an absurd question. Of course it should. If so, then the discussion starts with the basic premise that society should and indeed must, for its own protection, regulate certain kinds of behavior. If that is true, then the argument from this point forward is not about whether to regulate but concerns what to regulate, how to regulate, and who should regulate.

But, a critic might argue, regulation of conduct to prevent murder is about killing, and there is an obvious need to protect people from violence. It is true that society regards violent behavior, and particularly the killing of a person, to be a particularly heinous offense. On the other hand, there are some circumstances in which violent behavior, even the taking of a life, is not considered murder and may even be permitted. Hence, legitimate self-defense under some conditions, some forms of assisted suicide (in some countries even active euthanasia),[1] certain situations in which police officers are called upon to use deadly force, military combat, and the use of the death penalty by the state all involve the death of one or more people, but they are not considered crimes. Rather, society establishes regulations governing what circumstances justify that type of behavior, when and how it may be carried out, and who is authorized to do it.

It is also important to note that decisions about when and what violent behavior to punish are not controlled from the perspective of the victim. That is, regulation is not done only or even primarily to protect a particular potential victim, but for the larger good of the society. A felony charge, such as murder, is not brought by an individual or by the government on behalf of a particular individual, but by the state on behalf of the people. Thus, the styling of a criminal case is "People v. ___," "State v. ___," or U.S. v. ___." It is not up to the victim to determine whether a felony case will be brought, but it is left to the public prosecutor who decides what is in the interest of the whole community given the law and the facts. Obviously, decisions not to prosecute, to prosecute on a lesser charge than might otherwise be lodged, or to plea bargain the case, while often controversial, are judgments that are part of the system of regulation called criminal law. The individual victims, or their families, are provided with another avenue to redress their injuries in civil suits for damages, such as wrongful death.

Moreover, not all violent criminal behavior is treated in the same way. Societies create complex systems of regulation that establish what behavior is criminal and what penalties will be imposed for it. Indeed, from time to time, societies alter their priorities in order to convey strong messages, as in the case of efforts to increase penalties for child abuse, spousal abuse, or injuries caused by drunk drivers. These decisions are not necessarily based on the assertion that these crimes are more violent than others or cause more physical harm to an individual, but are addressed as a matter of political and social priority, established through the properly constituted process for making public policy in the public interest. In some cases, the decisions about what conduct is to be constrained or punished also are not based solely, or even primarily, on the motive of the person involved. There are some instances in which individuals are charged with criminally negligent homicide or manslaughter where the conduct that resulted in the death of another person was so reckless that society concludes that it should be treated as a crime even though there was no evidence of intent to harm anyone.

Of course, criminal law also deals with a wide range of behaviors that do not involve direct violence to anyone, but that are harmful nevertheless. Burglary, embezzlement, and fraud are all crimes, even though the harm they cause is economic or some other form of injury rather than physical assault. It is difficult to make the case that defrauding an elderly couple of their life savings or deliberately selling a family dangerous toys or food is less damaging than robbery at the point of a gun, or even in some instances a physical assault. The fact that the injury is often defined as economic does not make it less of a crime. Thus, the first regulation established by Governor Winthrop in Massachusetts Bay Colony was reportedly a prohibition on usury—the practice of charging of unconscionably high interest rates—issued because of its corrosive effect on the community.[2]

The argument may be challenged on grounds that criminal behavior is different because it is the most extreme type of behavior in the society, and the polity therefore regulates it. However, civil law also provides several vehicles for regulation of behavior, and intentionally so. That behavior ranges from the seemingly trivial dispute among neighbors to the wrongful taking of life. Civil law is also a vehicle through which emerging problems are identified for regulation.

It is important here to distinguish between public law cases and private civil law disputes. Civil cases are the traditional kinds of lawsuits brought by one citizen against another or perhaps against an organization to collect damages for a violation of legally established rights that causes injury. As a general matter, public law cases involve government as a party on either side of the case. The tendency of those who condemn regulation is to see public law cases as those in which the government seeks to intervene in the private lives or business dealings of citizens. And indeed, that is what most people tend to envision when the word "regulation" is used; but the process works the other way as well.

Public law disputes in which government is the party challenged are many and varied. Such suits are among the mechanisms used to constrain the power of government—to regulate those in positions of power and the organizations they head. Thus, when antiregulatory warriors from Jimmy Carter to the George W. Bush administration promised to reduce the number and scope of regulations, their victories meant not only a reduction of regulations by which government controls the governed, but also the law that allows citizens to challenge those who govern. As Madison made clear in his famous "if men were angels" warning in the *Federalist* 51, both kinds of controls are needed in an efficacious constitutional republic. Thus, one of the reasons for the increase in administrative rulemaking by regulatory agencies and requirements in legislation that mandated the issuance of more regulations was in response to long-standing criticism that government was making up the rules as it went along and failing to provide established policies so that businesses and private individuals could bring themselves into compliance.[3] Part of the criticism was also that government was not establishing agency rules that would bind the regulatory bodies as they went about their task.[4]

In general, these suits against government tend to be either status cases or policy cases. Status cases (also sometimes termed "compensatory cases") are disputes in which particular individuals or organizations (for-profit firms or nonprofit groups) seek compensation for an injury they allegedly suffered at the hands of officials or a correct determination of their qualification for a particular program or benefit. These range from the individual citizens seeking disability benefits, to businesses that want certain types of licenses, to nonprofit organizations that seek tax-exempt status. The challengers who seek to regulate government use the full range of regulatory laws from the Constitution, to statutes, and even the very regulations issued by the regulatory agencies of government themselves. Indeed, it is a classic challenge to government action to allege that an administrative agency is violating its own regulations.

In public law policy cases, those who challenge government seek not merely a narrow benefit or status for themselves, but attempt to force government to change the way it functions so as to bring itself within the boundaries of its substantive authority and procedural obligations. In these circumstances, the citizen or organization claims that government has: (1) exceeded its Constitutional authority or violated procedural requirements imposed by the basic framework document of government (at the federal or state level); (2) violated statutory constraints, either those that were adopted with specific reference to the agency involved or those, such as civil rights laws or the Administrative Procedure Act (APA), that were adopted to apply to all (or at least most) institutions of government; (3) acted in an arbitrary or capricious manner in developing or applying regulatory or social services rules; (4) failed to provide a reasoned decision supported by substantial evidence on the whole record; or (5) used its contracting powers in such a way as to seek through negotiated means to do that which it did not have the authority to mandate directly.[5]

In such efforts to regulate government, challengers may seek damages, which sometimes include punitive as well as compensatory awards, against the individual officials involved or, in some circumstances, the government unit itself. In some areas, special provisions are available that permit citizens to challenge state or local governments in federal courts to avoid the fear of biased judgments that might flow from parochialism. They may seek a straight judicial review of a government action in which the court is asked to find the government's actions to be illegal and overturn decisions made by the agency at issue. They may seek injunctive relief to stop illegal action or mandate government performance that is not provided but should be, according to law.

These requests for injunctive relief are often made in policy cases in which the payment of compensation to one or a number of individuals will not solve the problem of government misbehavior or make the victims whole again. Common examples include school desegregation or institutional reform as in the case of medical or mental health facilities.[6]

There is no small amount of irony in the tendency of political candidates of both major parties since the 1970s to promise that they will reduce the number of regulations and that therefore citizens will be free of bureaucracy. The fact is that eliminating rules and discouraging rulemaking can very often have the effect of removing existing constraints on government institutions and reducing the number of legal tools available to citizens to call public officials to account. One is reminded of British General Henry Clinton at Bunker Hill, who after receiving congratulations on the victory reportedly replied, "A few more such victories would have shortly put an end to British dominion in America." (He is sometimes thought to have replied in words reminiscent of King Pyrrhus of Epirus, "Another such victory and we are utterly undone.")[7]

Indeed, before modern administrative law developed with an emphasis on rulemaking and enforcement by administrative agencies, much of what we think of today as regulation was carried out through private civil lawsuits in such forms as nuisance or fraud.[8] It is more than a little ironic that it was the arbitrary, inconsistent, and problematic nature of that mode of action to stop harmful behavior that prompted efforts to develop a more systematic, fairer, and more effective form of regulation by administrative agencies governed by administrative law that is now so often the target of antiregulatory warriors. Another irony is the fact that the Supreme Court, during the 1980s and 1990s, moved the country back in that direction with its regulatory takings cases (see Chapter 4), suggesting that regulation was not a rational, policy-based activity but one that was more in the nature of an effort to abate a nuisance.[9]

Let us return to the key point here, which is that torts are civil delicts of law. That is, they are not defined as crimes, but are nevertheless behaviors that society, acting through legislatures and courts, has concluded should be blocked. In this case, they are often behaviors of which society disapproves, but the device used to address them is often private enforcement by a particular injured party in a civil case rather than enforcement by government. The invocation of a public court as a vehicle to obtain an authoritative ruling and then the use of public officials to execute the judgment that comes out of the suit is an involvement of government with some of the characteristics of regulation.[10] It is a form of regulation at the behest of private parties who act in their own interest, but the system of tort laws and courts to maintain them is still concerned with the enforcement of public norms created to advance the public interest. Hence, there is an ongoing debate over the nature and limits of tort suits; the mechanisms, like class actions, by which they may be brought; and the remedies that can be obtained where liability is proven.[11]

Although they may be private actions, at the root of tort law is a recognition that certain forms of behavior are unfair, injurious, and in violation of accepted norms of conduct. The appeal to the reasonable person standard is by implication a statement that there are behaviors that are regarded as reasonable and others that are not. There are rights possessed by people that imply duties for others to be observed for the enforcement of which the power of the state may be invoked, even if it is simply in the form of courts, rules, judges, and executing officials. Which rights shall be recognized and how they may be enforced are matters of public policy.

Even where a tort is not involved, and where the parties deal with each other primarily on the basis of negotiation, there is still regulation. Contracts create a set of regulations to govern a relationship. The parties may agree to a wide variety of enforceable rules and either side in the agreement can invoke those regulations when the need arises. Of course, while the parties have great latitude in most settings to develop the kind of regulatory regime they prefer for their relationship, contract law itself places boundaries. Hence, an agreement to violate the law is a conspiracy, not a contract, whether it is created by organized crime figures or by corporate officers. An agreement that is inherently and unfairly coercive is an unconscionable contract and therefore unenforceable. Some contracts, in the absence of legislation specifically allowing them, have simply been declared contrary to public policy and therefore void, as in the first cases of contract for surrogate parents.[12] Thus, when parties interact by contract they are very much operating in the realm of regulation. It is indeed a two-tiered approach to regulation, with one set of rules imposed by the parties on themselves, but within a broader set of public rules established by public policy to govern contracts and setting the terms by which violations of those agreements can be remedied.

One of the companion arguments of the deregulation era has been that rather than being more involved in many endeavors through regulation, government ought to move completely away from many fields by privatizing the activities. However, while the term "privatization" has often been used in such discussions, what is most often meant is not actual divestiture of governmental responsibilities, but the contracting out of those functions to for-profit or nonprofit organizations, which then perform the functions on behalf of the government for those who are to receive the services or benefits.[13]

When government contracts, it not only operates with the kind of two-tier regulatory system described above but actually has a third tier. That is true because of concern about corruption, to be sure, but this extra set of requirements governing public contracts responds to other demands as well.[14] For one thing, there are concerns that the parties at the table may not be as interested in the wider public interest as much as they are in serving their own priorities or those of their organizations. Hence, regulations, like the Federal Acquisition Regulations (FAR), are imposed to ensure transparency and accountability not just of the contractor to the government, but of all of the parties to various forms of oversight carried out by different political agencies. These oversight bodies include legislative committees and independent professional entities, such as the Government Accountability Office and inspectors general who are located in various operating agencies but whose independence, authority, and obligations are provided by law, in order to protect the public interest.[15]

Then there is the principle that government has certain special obligations not to enter into contracts that would make it a partner in unacceptable behavior, such as unfair labor practices or environmentally damaging production techniques.[16] Thus, a wide variety of statutes, executive orders, and regulations require contractors to provide a host of certifications guaranteeing that, on the negative side, they do not engage in prohibited business practices and, on the positive, that they will undertake steps such as use of recycled products or nondiscriminatory hiring to further policies declared to be in the public interest. In order to ensure that they live up to those commitments, contractors know that they will be subject to compliance audits in addition to performance audits and financial audits throughout the duration of the contract and various sanctions for violations of their commitments up to and including default on the contract and debarment from bidding on future contracting opportunities.

Then there is the fact that government contracts represent not only regulation of the contractor from which the government obtains goods or services, but also regulation of the government by the contractor. Unlike other forms of regulation in which government has discretion to enforce or not enforce that which is presumptively unreviewable in court, the contracting party has the legal ability to trigger enforcement.[17]

At the end of the day, of course, one of the important ideas behind contracting is the use of negotiated relationships rather than a one-size-fits-all set of regulations. (Of course, if regulations are more fully developed to make them more sensitive to a wide range of circumstances, they are promptly criticized for being excessively long and cumbersome.) The complaint about much of government contracting since World War II is that it has been turned into a set of government regulations in the form of the FAR or state-level equivalents. The point of contracting is to increase flexibility to make the best agreement to assure performance and price.[18] If that admonition is taken seriously, then there will be (and indeed there are) a wide variety of contract provisions in government contracts, each of which constitutes a set of regulations.

Of course, most regulation that is under attack by presidents, political appointees, and members of Congress was, ironically, created by legislation and administrative rulemaking over a long period of time for political reasons that will be discussed in more detail later in this chapter. It seems that it is regulation of this sort that has become the target of the antiregulatory warriors. When one reads much of the rhetoric that fires the troops for the fight against regulation, one almost has the idea that these programs and policies were the result of spontaneous generation—that no one in Congress or the White House wants to take responsibility for the fact that they exist. Some of the rhetoric seems to suggest that regulatory policy flies in the face of the Constitution and that contemporary regulatory policy would be appalling to those who wrote and adopted the Constitution. Of course, an examination of the document and the early experience under it demonstrates otherwise.

Most regulatory policy that comes from the federal government was adopted by the Congress under its constitutional authority "To regulate Commerce with foreign Nations, and among the several States, and with the Indian Tribes."[19] Congress may also create programs with a regulatory character indirectly through the use of the taxing and spending powers by providing grants to state and local governments, provided that the recipients of those grants agree to obey the federal rules that accompany the funds. These two powers are applied along with the Article I authority for Congress "To make all Laws which shall be necessary and proper for carrying into Execution the foregoing Powers and all other Powers vested by this Constitution in the Government of the United States, or in any Department or Officer thereof."[20]

Indeed, the concepts of regulation and rule are referred to in no less than fourteen provisions of the Constitution.[21] Of the eighty-five *Federalist Papers,* forty-eight refer to these concepts both in terms of problems that developed as a result of a lack of regulation and the importance of certain kinds of regulatory activities by the newly proposed federal government.[22] In most instances, the discussion concerns the power of the newly created national government to regulate, but in others the subject is the need to regulate government, national, state, or both. Indeed, Madison, on discussing the range of varied and conflicting interests in the evolving nation, insisted: "The regulation of these various and interfering interests forms the principal task of modern legislation."[23]

The early years of government under the Constitution saw regulation at the state and federal levels in a variety of areas from port operations to veterans' benefits.

In 1789, the first Congress established a complete administrative machinery for the collection of customs and duties, necessitating administrative adjudication of disputes; it provided for the payment of pensions to disabled soldiers "under such regulations as the President of the United States may direct"; granted power to the Secretary of State, the Secretary for the Department of War, and the Attorney General or any two of them to grant patents "if they shall deem the invention or discovery sufficiently useful and important"; and provided that persons trading with Indians must procure a license, and that such license shall be governed in all things touching upon said trade and intercourse by such rules and regulations as the President shall prescribe.[24]

As early as 1790 Congress enacted legislation "for protecting seamen against unseaworthy ships," with courts as the primary venue for enforcement until the middle of the nineteenth century when an administrative structure was created to do that work.[25] In 1797 and 1798 New York adopted regulatory legislation to address "noxious trades" that were thought even at that early date to be dangerous to health, to be enforced by the commissioner of health, the mayor, and a court.[26] In fact, Milton Carrow found that "of the fifty-one major federal agencies which the Attorney General's Committee on Administrative Procedure selected for its study of the administrative process in 1941, eleven traced their beginnings to statutes enacted prior to the close of the Civil War."[27]

On careful consideration, then, it is clear that regulation was not created by the New Deal or later administrations, was clearly understood and contemplated by the founders of the nation, and is not inherently bad or counterproductive, but a necessary tool for addressing important policy problems, appropriate in some circumstances and less useful or appropriate in others. Those who assume the contrary lie at points along a continuum, one end of which is a simple lack of understanding of the nature and role of regulation in society. Further down the continuum are those who oppose regulation or want only regulation that they think they can control because they profit from those states of affairs. Finally, there are those at the extreme end of the continuum who oppose regulation solely or primarily on ideological grounds.

That is not to say, however, that all regulation is good or that even necessary regulatory programs are designed or implemented well. On the other hand, the cynicism of those, discussed in previous chapters, who do everything possible to ensure the failure of a regulatory policy and then attack regulation because of the failed programs should not be rewarded by granting such behavior credence as legitimate conduct in a just war against regulation.

What Is Regulation, and What Is It Not?

Along with the recognition that regulation is simply one policy tool comes the importance of understanding what regulation is and what it is not. This clarification is significant because the term and its meaning have been distorted since the Carter years, by those inside and outside government. On the one hand, the effect of these distortions has been to confuse regulation with other policy tools. Another effect has been to devalue regulation by creating a label intended to carry opprobrium—"command and control."

Consider first regulation and its relationship to other policy tools. In one of the most thorough treatments of policy tools currently available, Lester Salamon and his contributors discuss the best-known tools for constructing policy responses to problems on the public policy agenda. They include such mechanisms as direct action by government; government corporations and government-sponsored enterprises; regulation; government insurance; public information policies; corrective taxes, charges, and tradeable permits; contracting; grants; loans and loan guarantees; tax expenditures; vouchers; and tort liability.[28] Each of these devices works differently, but all are designed either to address a set of troublesome conditions, a collection of problematic behaviors by groups or individuals, or both. They operate in a variety of ways, from simply calling on government agencies to fix a problem directly, to controlling or prohibiting targeted behaviors by people or firms with sanctions, to investment strategies, to the purchase of services to meet a need, to the development of incentives to encourage desired behaviors and discourage others.

Regulation is only one of these policy tools. It operates, as noted above, by setting limits to certain targeted behaviors with a range of coercive sanctions to enforce the limits. The limits may have to do with certain kinds of behavior, such as rules of professional practice for which the loss of one's license to practice may be the sanction. Other limits may address fares or fees, such as utilities rate-setting processes. Others establish systems of orderly interaction and operation, like the regulation of air traffic, operations on navigable waterways, or motor vehicle rules. Still others set rules for entry into certain types of business or professional activities and establish both obligations for and limits on behavior in that field, as in the case of banking regulations.

What all of these have in common, however, is that this policy tool sets limits and provides one or another type of sanction for failure to behave in accordance with those standards. Those subject to regulation are not simply encouraged to comply. They are mandated to do so. It is an inherently coercive policy tool.

Other policy tools work differently in that they are often designed to encourage positive behavior by providing incentives. Common examples include the use of tax expenditures by government in the form of tax deductions or even tax credits for people or firms that will use more energy-efficient or environmentally friendly products or make other choices that fit policy objectives. Still other tools, such as information policy, seek to shape individual behavior by providing information that policymakers hope and expect will alter individual or corporate choices. One of the most commonly known examples is nutritional labeling on food products.

Yet other policy mechanisms work through other means, but what is important is that, like any choice of tools, a lack of knowledge of how a tool works and which type is appropriate for a given task can lead to problematic results. The point is not that one tool is bad or another good, but that it is important to match the tool to the task.

Starting with the Carter administration's use of the so-called innovative techniques of regulation, discussed in Chapter 2, there was an effort to change the very meaning and application of regulation as a policy tool. The move to shift the understanding and discussion of regulation to make economics the primary lens for regulatory policy, and public policy more generally, was central to this effort. As Chapter 2 explained, the Carter and later the Clinton antiregulation warriors proposed a set of innovative techniques of regulation, a number of which were not regulation at all, but market-based and incentive-driven policy tools. The idea was precisely to move away from the establishment of clear standards and regular systems of enforcement backed by sanctions. Although it was mentioned in Chapter 2, it bears repeating here the administration's language as to the nature and purpose of its innovations program: "The Administration's reform program emphasizes the use of innovative regulatory techniques as an alternative to traditional command-and-control regulation; these techniques are generally less likely to interfere with competition. Many work by structuring incentives that will resolve regulatory problems through market mechanisms. These innovative regulatory techniques move away from centralized decisionmaking and allow industry and consumers more freedom of choice."[29] The Clinton administration's reinventing government efforts took the same approach, as explained in Chapter 3.

At the same time, what was in truth regulation was thenceforth referred to with the dreaded term of opprobrium, "command and control" regulation. Both Democrats and Republicans used that shorthand to refer to the enemy in the war on regulation, much as belligerents in other kinds of conflicts find terms of derision to devalue their opponents and make attacks on them more palatable and justifiable.

While it is true that certain of the innovative approaches, such as tiering (establishing different requirements for different types and sizes of regulated organizations) and the use of performance standards (setting regulatory standards and allowing the regulated organizations a choice in how to meet them) were potentially improvements in regulation properly so-called, most of the other techniques were not. Even those that were really about regulation as compared to some other kind of policy tool would work if and only if the regulatory agencies involved were provided with the requisite expert capacity and political and legal support to generate the standards and ensure adequate and effective monitoring and enforcement action. As Chapters 2 and 3 indicated, however, those essentials were not, in fact, forthcoming. Indeed, quite the contrary was the case. For the most part, however, the real effort was not on regulatory improvement, but alternatives to regulation. These were not alternative modes of regulation but other types of policy tools, ranging from market-based strategies that assumed some form of competition to tax expenditures.

Clearly, the use of the other tools to change (or at least to address) behavior that the public through government seeks to support or discourage is clearly appropriate. In fact, virtually all policy tools are expected to address behaviors and values that are in the public interest or are perceived to be contrary to it. However, each of the tools operates differently. Not every policy tool that is used for the purpose of changing behavior is regulation, nor should it be.

Ironically, some of the policy tools that are intended to be alternatives to traditional regulation can only work effectively if standard regulatory devices and the capability to implement them are present. For example, tradeable permits require that some authoritative agency set appropriate emissions standards both as to quantity and type for a given context in order to determine how many permits of what size are to be available in that region. Then a market needs to be established and regulated. However, in order to ensure the integrity of the process, some authoritative agency must monitor emissions to ensure that those holding permits operate within their limits and that those who do not have permits do not emit pollutants. In order to be meaningful, the system must be able to impose sanctions on those who violate the permit requirements or operate without any permit at all.

Another irony in the discussion of regulation is the effort by antiregulatory warriors, particularly those from the Carter years through Clinton, who came to be known as New Democrats, to justify an attack on one major portion of regulatory policy by attempting to classify it as somehow separate and different from regulatory policy more generally. Thus, the New Democrat antiregulatory forces launched a public diplomacy campaign to convince the public and reluctant policymakers that there was a difference between economic regulation, which they sometimes labeled cartel regulation, and what was termed "social regulation," designed to protect health, safety, and consumers in the marketplace. The argument ran that regulated industries, like airlines, telecommunications companies, and financial services firms, had captured their regulators and were using those agencies to support their own goals at the expense of everyone else. There was little appreciation for the fact that once they unleashed one type of activity from regulation to make it more responsive to the marketplace, the consequences would be widespread and would reach over into other types of activity not thought of as economic.

Thus, as Chapter 2 explained, one of the first major targets was airline regulation. The argument was that the airlines had captured the Civil Aeronautics Board and were using that relationship to keep ticket prices artificially high and controlling routes and rates so as to prevent competition that would drive those ticket prices down. What was not considered in the process was the fact that those ticket prices provided cross-subsidies that made it possible to ensure, and indeed to require, carriers to provide reasonable levels of service at reasonable costs. The fact that there was not a dramatic race to reduce costs to support the lowest possible ticket prices also meant that airlines could afford to spend more on maintenance facilities and people, to have available redundant aircraft to be used in the event of mechanical problems, and to make decisions about replacement parts or new aircraft acquisitions without the fear that the firm would be punished by the marketplace where competitors would make decisions more oriented toward cost than anything else. They certainly did not discuss the fact that such a cost-oriented focus would be a factor in a refusal by airlines to implement many important recommendations by the National Transportation Safety Board. Neither did they discuss the fact that the antiregulatory warriors would eliminate the capability, in terms of resources and political support, of the remaining agency responsible for some aspects of air operations, the Federal Aviation Administration, to ensure that start-up airlines and regional carriers were following proper safety practices, including maintenance operations and crew training and supervision. They certainly did not discuss the likelihood that firms would compete actively on the most profitable routes but leave many communities throughout the nation with little or no reliable and convenient service or that tickets from secondary markets could cost as much as a trip abroad, unless of course one could plan a month in advance and travel during certain, often inconvenient times and days. They did not discuss the fact that deregulation of fares and required routes would also mean fewer, more tightly packed aircraft with less service and fees or surcharges for everything from baggage to blankets. In fact, there was little knowledge on the part of the public, even the relatively informed public, of the fact that the deregulation legislation passed during the Carter and later amended during the Clinton administration not only would eliminate regulation of services as well as fares but also specifically preempt the states from taking actions to protect consumers.

The moral of the story is that once one begins to move critical decisions to the marketplace from a regulated context, the market dynamics will tend to drive a wide range of activities. The dynamics of the market are not sensitive to what is deemed economic and what is considered social activity. Indeed, for publicly traded companies in the modern global economy, the drive to reduce costs and increase profits are likely simply to displace most other considerations. In such settings, decisions are now too often made for short-term advantage without consideration of long-term implications for the firm or their customers. The idea that one can eliminate regulation on grounds that it is economic in character while claiming to support the environmental, health, safety, and consumer regulation that are termed "social regulation" is simply impractical and unreasonable in the contemporary world.

In the end, then, regulation is a certain type of policy tool among many others. It is useful or even necessary in some cases and not as appropriate in others. In many instances, regulation is one tool in what is termed a "policy mix," which combines a number of different tools to address different, but related, pieces of a policy problem. Thus, environmental agencies administer regulatory programs, but they may also provide grants or training programs as well in an effort to head off problems that might otherwise force regulatory action at a later time. If communities can, for example, be supported and encouraged to develop adequate waste water treatment and management problems at the outset, then the regulatory challenges at the other end of the pipeline are prevented or at least reduced in scope, cost, and complexity. These simple realities have not suited the politics or the tactics of antiregulation warriors and are too little understood.

IF REGULATION IS THE ENEMY, THEN WHY DO WE CONTINUE TO RE-CREATE IT? POLITICS, NOT ECONOMICS IS THE ANSWER

If regulation has been so bad for so long in so many ways that the war against it by both Democratic and Republican administrations is a just war, why is it that officials continue to adopt new regulatory programs? That question is particularly important if the same administrations that agree to support or even claim to lead the effort to develop regulatory programs demanded by the public then promptly turn around and work to undermine those programs as part of their general attack on regulation and regulations—attacks that have often been carried out indirectly and largely out of the public eye. The George W. Bush administration's response to the clamor, even from Wall Street, for effective regulation to restore confidence in the markets in the wake of the energy, corporate governance, and financial services scandals that it then promptly worked to undermine just a few years later (see Chapter 3) is an obvious example.

The answer is that most regulatory programs were created for political reasons to address problems for which the public demanded action and not because of some careful calculation of economic efficiency. The attempt by antiregulation warriors to recast the discussion of regulation in terms of economic efficiency or market failure has come with the move to reshape the discussion of regulation into a matter of economics in the years since the Carter administration (see Chapter 2). Most often regulatory policies were created to solve problems that the marketplace was never designed to address and may very well have encouraged. The effort to require justification of regulation by reference to the rules of the marketplace could be said at a minimum to miss the point, were it not for the fact that the effort here has been less neutral and far more a matter of public diplomacy in support of the war against regulation.

First, historically, particular regulatory efforts most often grew when political pressure mounted to address serious problems. Food and drug regulation and the agency created to administer it, the Food and Drug Administration (FDA), came as a reaction to the terrible conditions in the food and drug industries that produced adulterated food and impure, unsafe, and ineffective drugs.[30] There were also the false and deceptive sales practices that led to the infamous "snake oil" salesmen who peddled drugs that had no medicinal value or were in fact dangerous.[31] Securities regulation and the Securities and Exchange Commission emerged primarily because of the Great Depression and the revelations of fraud and manipulation that surfaced after the markets collapsed.[32] There are numerous other examples throughout modern history.

The National Labor Relations Board (NLRB) was created, and later strengthened, to address the need for effective regulation at a time when the country had experienced violent labor-management disputes. The Congress later enacted highway safety regulation statutes when it became clear that as many as 50,000 Americans died each year in traffic accidents, yet vehicle manufacturers would not voluntarily improve safety features on automobiles.[33] The Consumer Product Safety Commission was created because the legislature found that 20 million people were injured each year in product-related accidents, resulting in 110,000 suffering permanent disability and 30,000 deaths.[34] Similarly, Congress created the Occupational Safety and Health Administration when it became clear that more workers were killed in job-related accidents in the four years prior to the act than had died in Vietnam in the same period.[35] The Federal Elections Commission was a product of the Watergate debacle when evidence emerged of gross abuses of campaign financing at a time when the public had lost trust in government in any case.[36] Most regulatory legislative histories demonstrate similar foundations in serious problems that prompted political responses.[37]

Chapter 3 explained how, even as the war was being waged against regulation, there were demands for new or enhanced regulation in the food and drug, environmental, securities, energy, and financial services industries. Whether the cause was the revelation of abuses in the way in which drugs were tested and marketed, the disclosure of improper meat processing, the news of adulterated pharmaceutical products and pet food from abroad, the disclosure of dramatically high lead levels in toys sold by American companies that were manufactured in China, the realization that the weakening of environmental regulation was producing or contributing to serious problems such as global warming, or the *E. coli* outbreaks and the accompanying revelation of how little inspection and testing was actually being done in the nation's food supply, the demands for action and such response as did occur had everything to do with political pressure and virtually nothing to do with economics, except for the fact that some of these problems could be traced to the willingness to let the marketplace run unchecked.

It is true that many of the problems that produced a need for regulation had to do with allowing greed in the marketplace to function without effective limits. It is also the case that some of the problems emerged because the marketplace was not designed to protect against a variety of difficulties. In the mid-1970s, before the Carter antiregulation warriors took the field, Senator Abraham Ribicoff called for a major set of hearings on regulation for the purpose of improving its effectiveness. Those hearings produced a multivolume series entitled *The Study on Federal Regulation,* which pointed out that, among the other problems that called for regulation, there was a need to regulate natural monopolies such as public utilities; to encourage an appropriate use and conservation of natural resources; to deal with spillover effects of market activity that the market has no incentive to address; to ensure adequate and accurate information for consumers; to prevent destructive competition, sometimes known as a "race to the bottom" to achieve lowest cost and highest profit without regard to the dangers that result; to protect consumers from extreme prices and profits where the market provides no realistic check or effective limitation; to stop price discrimination and unfair trade practices; to promote or preserve important types of enterprise or infrastructure; a perceived need to provide service and support to groups identified as worthy through activities like cross-subsidy through regulation; to ensure adequate numbers of competing organizations through antitrust and related regulation; and to protect property rights.[38] Just because pieces of these motivations concerned the marketplace, does not reduce the policies that followed only to responses to market failures. That was a mode of analysis that came with the move to make regulation in many important respects a matter of economics as compared to the prior model, which emphasized political decisions first and law second.

James Q. Wilson has addressed the important differences between economic and political perspectives on regulatory policy, focusing on three key distinctions.[39]

> First, politics concerns preferences that do not always have a common market measuring rod. . . . In nonmarket relationships, such as in voluntary associations or in legislatures, we may also behave in a rationally self-interested manner— but we do so in a setting that does not usually permit monetary (or quantitative) values to be assigned to our competing preferences in any nonarbitrary way. . . .
>
> Second, political action requires assembling majority coalitions to make decisions that bind everyone whether or not he belongs to that coalition. When we make purchases in a market, we commit only ourselves. . . . When we participate in making decisions in the political arena, we are implicitly committing others as well as ourselves.
>
> The third and most important difference between economics and politics is that whereas economics is based on the assumption that preferences are given, politics must take into account the efforts made to change preferences.[40]

Wilson could have added a fourth distinction. The bias is often to focus discussion in economic assessments of policy on efficiency as a critical factor. The history of the development of regulatory policy demonstrates that efficiency, particularly short-term measures of efficiency, has not been a primary consideration and in many cases not a consideration at all. Meier, Garman, and Keiser went so far as to state that it is a myth that "the goal of regulation is efficiency" and to attack the tendency to pin criticism of regulatory policies to the claim of inefficiency.[41] Regulatory policies are primarily based in political decisions and not created because of their efficiency or inefficiency. "Arguing that efficiency is the goal of regulation is essentially a normative argument; it is an argument that efficiency should be the goal of regulation. To be sure, agencies can have more than one goal, and regulatory objectives should be accomplished in the most efficient way possible. But when efficiency conflicts with other goals, efficiency is often a second priority."[42]

In the end, decisions about whether to regulate and how to do so, including the actions of many of the antiregulatory warriors, have been overwhelming and predominantly political decisions, even if some were justified in the language of economics. Some of those political decisions, as is true of virtually all public policy, turned out to produce useful and effective public policy, while others did not. Arguments that regulatory programs are to be attacked because they are not efficient as that concept is used in economics or that they do not conform to the dictates of the marketplace supply justifications for the war against regulation, but they fly in the face of the purposes for which most such programs were created.

REALITY VERSUS MYTHOLOGY IN THE WAR AGAINST REGULATION

It is useful to summarize briefly some realities that should be clear from the discussion of this and previous chapters. Regulation is inevitable and essential in various forms. It is one type of policy mechanism that is useful in some circumstances and not others, but is not in itself either positive or negative. Regulation has not been primarily designed or justified on grounds of technical economic criteria but, like many policies, owes its existence and design to a range of factors from technical criteria on one end of the spectrum to simple political demands by the public for transparent and accountable programs of regulation to address perceived pressing problems. For a variety of reasons, it is and will be essential in modern American society to have a wide range of regulatory programs in place at the national level in addition to those traditionally operated by state and local governments. That said, state and local governments have important roles to play in regulation.

Many attacks on regulation, regulations, and regulatory agencies by political figures are disingenuous, often hypocritical, frequently deceptive, and sometimes harmful demagoguery that ought to be denounced for what they are and rejected. None of that means that all regulatory programs are good or should continue in existence, and a regular and continuing effort to improve their operation is necessary. However, efforts that are not designed to improve regulation but simply to eliminate or reduce it are not reform and ought not to be accorded the positive status of regulatory reform. Neither is it the case that so-called alternative approaches to regulation should properly be regarded as regulation when they are in fact simply other types of policy mechanisms. They may be effective or not for their intended purpose, but most are not regulation properly so-called.

The public needs better education at all levels of their formal schooling to arm them against the political gamesmanship that has been so commonly practiced in the name of deregulation and regulatory reform. At the end of the day, regulatory programs have too often been attacked by indirect strategies that have left them without the essential requirements for effective regulatory operations, whatever the legal shell of a policy may be that remains.

IMAGING A DIFFERENT FUTURE: POST-CONFLICT DEVELOPMENT OF ESSENTIAL REGULATION

Given these realities about regulation, it is useful to think carefully about the damage wrought by the war against regulation and to seek a more realistic and appropriate approach to the subject in the future that is not driven by ideology, or at least where ideology is not allowed to dominate the discussion and crowd out other considerations.

Where regulation is needed or appropriate or both, there are certain important conditions that are essential for its effective operation. Indirect attacks on regulation that purport to leave regulatory programs in place but remove or deny these essential elements are in many important respects as bad as direct attacks that draw more public attention.

First, regulators need an adequate and effective legal framework on which to operate. Even if the legislature enacts a statute with the necessary regulatory tools and authority to use them, there is not an adequate legal foundation if other bodies of law so burden the regulatory agency that it cannot effectively perform its job. That job includes the need to promulgate rules to implement the legislation. As Chapters 2 and 3 explain, the antiregulatory warriors of both political parties in the White House and in Congress, and often with the cooperation of the two, have imposed requirements that make it extraordinarily difficult for regulatory agencies to issue the rules they are required by legislation or by critical circumstances to produce. Often, indeed, they are barred by those very policies from meeting legislatively imposed deadlines for the issuance of rules. It is critical to eliminate policies that needlessly disable the regulators whose responsibility it is to protect the public as they are obliged by their legislative mandates to do. In truth, as Chapters 2 and 3 demonstrated, many of the procedural demands imposed by presidential directive and by legislation were not there to improve regulation but to block new regulations and to reduce new rules if possible as part of the war against regulation.

While in theory the idea that regulators should consider the impacts of the rules they are about to issue is certainly appropriate, there is no justification for the clear politicization of the process and the piling-on of manifold executive orders and OMB circulars and memoranda that create excessive and unreasonable cost/benefit and risk assessment requirements. The Office of Information and Regulatory Affairs (OIRA) was not created by Congress to be the executive branch command post in the war on regulation, but for much of the past three decades that has been its purpose. The Constitution obligates the president, and presumably the vice president, to take care that laws be faithfully executed, not to do all that they can to create barriers to their execution.

For all of its problems, the law that was created to govern those processes, the APA, was designed in an effort to instruct agencies as to how to promulgate rules in a manner that is open, orderly, and participative within the bounds of the requirements of agency operations under its governing legislation. These processes that have been imposed, such as regulatory review, cost/benefit evaluations, and risk assessments by the White House, not only to substantive rules but more recently even to guidance documents, have too often provided opportunities for political appeals outside the public eye that run counter to the purposes and intent of the APA and other legislation. The use of vice presidents in recent administrations to play a key role in leading the fight against these rulemaking processes and the rules they were designed to produce has undermined the effectiveness of the legal framework, and in a number of cases has violated it. Certainly, the role played by Vice President Quayle is a clear example.

An effort to ensure an effective legal foundation also requires an effort to enhance intergovernmental integration where that is appropriate. The previous chapters have demonstrated two realities of contemporary regulatory law. First, for a variety of reasons, much of the regulation that is done presently (though not all, to be sure) operates through a legal framework that is built on partial preemption, in which federal legislation provides an opportunity for the use of state standards if they meet or exceed federal standards and are approved by the relevant federal agency along with state level enforcement.

Second, as the previous chapters also explain, preemption has been repeatedly seen by the White House, the Congress, and the Supreme Court as an effective weapon in the war against regulation. Thus, the system sometimes leaves the states with responsibilities to act in some areas, but blocks them from taking aggressive actions to protect their citizens in related cases. That is true even where there have clearly been distinct local problems calling for tailored, and in some instances enhanced, regulatory responses, as in the case of Washington state's efforts to protect the Puget Sound and area residents. It has also been a problem where antiregulatory warriors at the federal level have removed protections and then prohibited states from stepping in even to protect their citizens in ways that have been traditional fields of regulation for state government. There has, as Chapter 4 explained, been little doubt that for some antiregulation warriors this has been part of an effort to reconstruct the laissez-faire era by ensuring a no-man's-land in which neither federal regulators nor state and local regulators may operate. That battle also employed limits on congressional authority under the commerce clause and the Eleventh Amendment and state authority by virtue of the regulatory takings doctrine as well as the preemption doctrine.

There has long been and probably will always be tension between state and federal policymakers. It is that system of federalism which, like the separation of powers at the federal level, provides for the kind of "hydraulic pressure" that is part of our frame of government.[43] That said, the warriors against regulation have emphasized the conflict and undermined the cooperation to a troublesome degree. A degree of cooperation and mutual support is essential to an effective regulatory framework.

Whatever the legal framework, a regulatory process cannot be effective if the agencies charged with its implementation and operation lack the essential resources to carry out the task. The earlier discussion of the ongoing problems of the FDA makes the point in clear terms, but so does the discussion of inadequate support for the Environmental Protection Agency (EPA) and other agencies. As Chapters 2 and 3 explained, it was not even necessary for antiregulatory warriors to cut funding for important agencies in order to ensure that they lacked the money and the people to do their jobs. It was sufficient to flat-fund those organizations at a time when their costs and their workloads were increasing. Of course, many state regulators found themselves in the same situation as antiregulatory warriors at that level were effective in reducing their resources.

At the same time, antiregulatory forces used antipersonnel attacks to eliminate staff and to drive away those who maintained a strong commitment to active and effective regulatory policymaking and enforcement. Efforts to muzzle regulatory administrators and to rein in those involved in enforcement activities, as described in Chapter 3, provide obvious examples of this very effective set of tactics.

The lack of resources was exacerbated by the continuing work of hollowing out government agencies by contracting out portions of their work rather than ensuring adequate in-house capabilities. Again, as earlier chapters explained, that not only made the agencies dependent upon contractors who might also work for regulated firms, but it also undermined the reputation of regulatory agencies as repositories of high levels of technical expertise in their policy domains.

The issue here is not alone one of expertise but also experience. As administrations of both political parties have made reductions in the size of government and the contracting out of what have long been regarded as important government positions, they have encouraged the departure of experienced professionals. While new and younger staff can be hired, many of whom bring strong educational backgrounds, that is no substitute for experience in these complex arenas. It takes a long time and a good deal of resources to bring these new regulators up to anything like the knowledge and experience levels of their predecessors and, in an environment in which they have enjoyed less security and professional respect and more private-sector opportunities with fewer burdens, there is every likelihood that those investments will pay off for regulated firms rather than for the public as those recently trained see greener pastures elsewhere.

Serious efforts at effective regulation require adequate resources measured against the scope and nature of the responsibilities of a given agency. While outside experts and personnel from other levels or parts of government may be helpful from time to time, they are not substitutes for an adequate basic complement of expert and experienced public service professionals in a regulatory agency. That is true at the state and local levels as well as in their federal counterparts.

The effort to recruit and retain well-qualified professionals to implement regulatory programs also requires assurance on their part—and for the rest of the society as well—that regulatory professionals will enjoy the proper level of independence from political interference. Chapter 3 stressed the increasing tendency to undermine that independence and the appearance of independence, which is perhaps as essential as the reality. If that independence is to be meaningful, it must be protected not only against political appointees or administration antiregulation forces, but also from outside regulated organizations and their lobbyists, who have too often been able to find backdoor opportunities through antiregulatory soldiers to undermine the independence of regulatory action.

Finally, accountability is essential, but that accountability cannot be established and operated in a manner that makes it part of the war against regulation rather than an important factor in the effort to make it operate more effectively and fairly. As long ago as the Ribicoff committee study, it was clear that too little attention has been paid to the people appointed by presidents to key positions in regulatory agencies and too little attention to the performance of those agencies unless and until a crisis occurs.

Too often the war on regulation has succeeded with serious casualties as a result because the legislature did not do its job. The first six years of the Bush administration perhaps marked a nadir in congressional oversight, as Republican members simply abandoned their responsibilities. One could argue as well that Democrats in Congress during the Clinton and Carter administrations did not carry out their responsibilities adequately, either, even if they did not go quite so far to the extreme as their Bush-era counterparts. In fact, congresses of both parties were too often allies in the war against regulation with the administrations over which they were supposed to conduct oversight to ensure regulatory effectiveness.

The media also own their share of responsibility. As the media have moved more and more to entertainment during the height of the war against regulation and to a kind of journalism, even in public affairs stories, based more in punditry and even sometimes ideology, there has been too little support for the kind of difficult and time-consuming research and reporting needed to address important regulatory issues. Reporters cannot effectively enlighten the public or policymakers about complex regulatory matters by interviewing each other on weekend televised panel discussions. Too often, the only reporting has come as media supported administrations in their battles against regulation and regulatory agencies. Ironically, many of those same media were quick to attack the embattled regulators when the inevitable occurred and a lapse in regulation contributed to an *E. coli* outbreak, an environmental crisis, or a mine disaster.

There have been exceptions to this criticism, such as Stephen Labaton of the *New York Times,* but they have been few and far between. However, one could with justification argue that the failure of the media to sound the alarm with the same fervor they afford to the domestic lives of entertainment celebrities when the regulatory agencies like the FDA and the EPA were under attack renders those media in some part responsible for the damage that came later. Too often, though, media criticism of government agencies has been more common than serious, systematic, in-depth, and careful reporting on the attacks directed at those agencies and their missions by presidents, their vice presidents, and their appointees, as well as their confederates in Congress.

At a minimum, effective accountability requires that there should not be political rewards for those who break the system and then blame it for being broken. To the degree that the public education system fails to train citizens to recognize that kind of behavior, the education system and the officials who dictate its curriculum and standards have failed the nation.

CONCLUSION

The war against regulation has indeed been the wrong war with the wrong enemy at the wrong time in the wrong place. It has produced a host of casualties, some of whom will not even feel the worst effects for years after they were subjected to environmental and safety hazards, and others will also take years to realize the damage done by abuses and fraudulent behavior to their economic well-being. Regulation is not the only answer to the problems facing society, but it is one possible policy response and one that has proven essential and effective across a wide range of policy domains over time. It is neither good nor bad in itself. It is not, and should not be, an enemy to be vanquished for political gain.

Regulation is not now and has not historically been primarily about economic choices aimed at efficiency, but primarily concerned with political choices about the public interest. In some instances, the two have been mutually supportive. In others they have been in tension. Many years ago, Aldo Leopold explained why it is unlikely that the effort to save a songbird would ever satisfy a cost/benefit analysis.[44] Today it would be difficult to convince the parent of a child disabled by exposure to high lead levels that regulation would create an excessive burden to the marketplace when a demanding cost versus risk assessment is required. While economics is one part of the decision process in the world of regulation, it is not and should not be more than that.

The fact that regulation has sometimes failed to protect those it was supposed to safeguard means that improvement is required, not that the war against regulation is justified. Too often the failures have come because that fight against regulation, by indirect as well as direct means, has been too successful. In order to be effective, regulatory policy, institutions, professionals, and operations require appropriate and consistent legal frameworks and adequate resources in terms of funds and institutional and political support. That includes the need for sufficient numbers of fully trained, expert, and experienced public service professionals to meet the level of responsibilities and the scope of coverage that the regulatory agency faces. Effective regulation also requires sufficient protection for the independence and integrity of the regulatory agencies and their people to prevent their work from being subverted or diverted by antiregulatory warriors inside government or outside it. Finally, it requires accountability, not only for the regulatory professionals but also for those who seek to make political capital by attacking the government of which they are a part. Accountability also applies to candidates who seek to use the war against regulation to win office where they are sworn to "take Care that the Laws be faithfully executed." Article II does not say to add to the duty-to-take-care clause the words, "except for regulatory laws." Congress has its own oversight obligations for which it has too seldom been held to account. Those obligations are not met merely by holding a hearing for the purposes of providing sound bites for the evening news in one's home district or state. The media and the educational system also have critical roles to play in ensuring regulatory accountability.

While those who have led the fight against regulation over the past three decades have won many battles, they have not ultimately won the war. Even so, they have done great damage. As noted earlier, those who wish to congratulate the antiregulatory warriors for their victories would do well to answer (with apologies to King Pyrrhus and Henry Clinton), "Another such victory and we are utterly undone."

Appendix
Sources and Methods

This research involved the use of policy tools analysis, a perspective that has been growing in importance in recent years. While the point here is not a separate article on the subject, but an indication of the approach taken in this study, it is nevertheless useful to consider the nature of policy tools analysis, the types of resources available, and the way the analysis of these tools can be effectively integrated. This study also used as an adjunct to the primary research analysis of the content of print media sources from the Carter administration through the George W. Bush years.

POLICY TOOLS RESEARCH:
A GROWING FIELD OF RESEARCH

The most recent round of discussions of policy tools analysis was encouraged by Lester M. Salamon's *The Tools of Government: A Guide to the New Governance* (Oxford: Oxford University Press, 2002). However, Salamon's book was by no means the first in the field. In fact Salamon and Michael S. Lund had several years earlier authored *Beyond Privatization: The Tools of Government Action* (Washington, D.C.: Urban Institute Press, 1989). Christopher Hood had even written a volume with the same main title as Salamon's in 1983, *The Tools of Government* (London: Macmillan, 1983).

Indeed, Hood published an excellent brief survey of the development of the policy tools literature in 2007 entitled, "Intellectual Obsolescence and Intellectual Makeovers: Reflections on the Tools of Government after Two Decades," 20 *Governance* 127 (2007). In the process, he acknowledged the contributions of such well-known works as Stephen H. Linder and B. Guy Peters, "Instruments of Government: Perceptions and Contexts," 9 *Journal of Public Policy* 35 (1989), and another piece by those authors, "The Study of Policy Instruments: Four Schools of Thought," in B. Guy Peters and Frans K. M. van Nispen, eds., *Public Policy Instruments: Evaluating the Tools of Public Administration* (Cheltenham, UK: Edward Elgar, 1998), 33–45, as well as Pierre Lascoumes and Patrick Le Galès's "Introduction: Understanding Public Policy through Its Instruments—From the Nature of Instruments to the Sociology of Public Policy Instrumentation," 20 *Governance* 22 (2007), and Richard Elmore's "Instruments and Strategy in Public Policy," 7 *Policy Studies Review* 174 (1987). Other frequently cited works include Anne Schneider and Helen Ingram, "Behavioral Assumptions of Policy Tools," 52 *Journal of Politics* 510 (1990), and Eugene Bardach, "Implementation Studies and the Study of Implements," paper presented to the annual meeting of the American Political Science Association, 1980. One source that is rarely credited as it should be for its brief but direct and clear presentation of what came to be called the policy tools perspective was a piece by Frederick C. Mosher in the *Public Administration Review* in 1980 entitled "The Changing Responsibilities and Tactics of the Federal Government," 40 *Public Administration Review* 541 (1980).

Much of the discussion among those who have written on policy tools focuses on the ways that various analysts classify and characterize the different types of policy tools. Central to that discussion has been the debate over the relative utility of market-based and incentive-driven policies as compared to other types. The other key set of questions concerns whether, how, and to what degree different types of policy tools actually affect behavior once policies are implemented.

Of course, policy tools are indeed tools that are used to construct policy mixes designed to address problems on the public agenda. And there have been policies and applied analyses done in recent years that draw explicitly on a policy tools perspective. Examples include Pat Cooke, "Building a Partnership Model to Manage Irish Heritage: A Policy Tools Analysis," 27 *Irish Journal of Management* 75 (2007); Annukka Berg, "European Forerunners of Sustainable Consumption and Production Programmes: Challenges and Possibilities in an Emerging Policy Field," Proceedings of the Nordic Consumer Policy Research Conference 2007, http://www.consumer2007 .info/wp-content/uploads/sustainability15-%20Berg.pdf (note: all Internet references in this appendix were valid as of February 22, 2009); and Poh Eng Hin, "Fiscal Misperceptions Associated with Tax Expenditure Spending: The Case of Pronatalist Tax Incentives in Singapore," 5 *eJournal of Tax Research* (2007), http://www.austlii.edu.au/ au/journals/eJTR/2007/1.html#Heading30.

The academic literature and practitioners tend to use the term "policy instruments" in place of the term "policy tools." Indeed, in Canada and some European countries, much of what is referred to in the United States as the New Public Management is addressed as the "instrument choice" model of governance. In Canada, this became the focus of the government's Policy Research Initiative (PRI) (http://www .policyresearch.gc.ca/page.asp?pagenm=rp_ora_index) and resulted in a conference and a volume on the subject. *Instrument Choice in Global Democracies: Conference Report,* September 26–28, 2002, Faculty of Law, McGill University, 2002 (Ottawa: Canada Department of Justice, 2002). See also Pearl Eliadis, Margaret M. Hill, and Michael Howlett, eds., *Designing Government: From Instruments to Governance* (Montreal: McGill-Queen's University Press, 2002).

POLICY TOOLS: MECHANISMS, INSTRUMENTS, AND POLICY SUPPORT MATERIALS

However, it is important at this point to address a problem in the language that is used in this field. The general term "policy tools" is certainly appropriate to capture the full range of policy devices of interest here. However, it is important to reconsider the use of the term "policy instruments." There are two types of devices involved in the general category that is termed "policy tools" and that should be recognized as distinct. First, there are devices that operate on the basis of some identifiable motive force that makes them attractive to use in certain circumstances. These are well summarized by the chapters in Salamon's *Tools of Government* and include such mechanisms as "direct action," "government corporations and government-sponsored enterprises," regulation, "government insurance," "public information," "corrective taxes, charges, and tradable permits," contracting, "grant programs," "loan and loan guarantees," "tax expenditures," and "vouchers." (See the table of contents in Salamon, *Tools of Government.*) There are others as well.

Second, there are authoritative policy documents and processes that put those devices into operation that are properly referred to as "policy instruments." The latter are legal instruments and formal processes that are intended to confer authority—legal, political, or both—on the policy mechanism and the agency charged with its implementation and to put it into operation. These instruments include, among others, statutes, administrative rules, treaties, executive agreements, interstate compacts, interjurisdictional agreements, executive orders, proclamations, presidential memoranda, national security directives, and judicial remedial decrees. The former are more properly termed "policy mechanisms," since, like machines, they function on different principles, differences already long recognized in the literature. See, e.g., Theodore Lowi, "Four Systems of Policy, Politics, and Choice," 32 *Public Administration Review* 298 (1972). See also the works by Mosher, Hood, and Elmore mentioned above.

The same policy mechanism may be put into operation in a policy mix by a variety of different policy instruments, and over time many important debates have turned not just on the mechanism that was selected to address a particular problem on the public policy agenda but also, and in some cases even primarily, on the type of instrument that was used to put that mechanism into operation. Thus, in recent decades there has been debate over the use and abuse of presidential directives of various kinds, ranging from executive orders to presidential memoranda to national security directives to presidential signing statements. The author has been a participant in the discussion of these policy instruments and their use and abuse. Phillip J. Cooper, *By Order of the President: The Use and Abuse of Presidential Direct Action* (Lawrence: University Press of Kansas, 2002); "The President as Judge: Signing Statements as Declaratory Judgments," 16 *William & Mary Bill of Rights Law Journal* 253 (2007); "George W. Bush, Edgar Allan Poe, and the Use and Abuse of Presidential Signing Statements," 35 *Presidential Studies Quarterly* 515 (2005); "Presidential Memoranda and Executive Orders: Of Patchwork Quilts, Trump Cards, and Shell Games," 31 *Presidential Studies Quarterly* 126 (2001); "By Order of the President: Administration by Executive Order and Proclamation," 18 *Administration & Society* 233 (1986); "Government Contracts in Public Administration: The Role and Environment of the Contracting Officer," 40 *Public Administration Review* 459 (1980). And see American Bar Association Task Force on Presidential Signing States and the Separation of Powers Doctrine (2006) at http://www.abanet.org/op/signingstatements/aba_final_signing_statements_recommendation-report_7-24-06.pdf; Coalition to Defend Checks and

Balances, The Constitution Project, "Statement on Presidential Signing Statements," http://www.constitutionproject.org/pdf/Statement_on_Presidential_Signing_Statement.pdf; T. J. Halstead, Congressional Research Service, Presidential Signing Statements: Constitutional and Institutional Implications (2007), at http://www.fas.org/sgp/crs/natsec/RL33667.pdf; Marc N. Garber and Kurt A. Wimmer, "Presidential Signing Statements as Interpretations of Legislative Intent: An Executive Aggrandizement of Power," 24 *Harvard Journal on Legislation* 363 (1987); William D. Popkin, "Judicial Use of Presidential Legislative History," 66 *Indiana Law Journal* 699 (1991); Kenneth R. Mayer, *With the Stroke of a Pen* (Princeton, N.J.: Princeton University Press, 2001).

The author has also written on a variety of other policy instruments, including contracts and remedial decrees: *Governing by Contract: Challenges and Opportunities for Public Managers* (Washington, D.C.: CQ Press, 2003); *Hard Judicial Choices: Federal District Judges and State and Local Officials* (New York: Oxford University Press, 1988).

ENHANCED CAPABILITIES IN POLICY TOOLS RESEARCH

As interest in policy instruments, and particularly executive direct action tools like executive orders, memoranda, and signing statements, has increased in recent years, and as Internet technology has expanded and become more readily available not only for users, but for operators of websites, the availability and ease of access to these instruments has improved dramatically. Sites like John T. Woolley and Gerhard Peters's "The American Presidency Project [online]" at the University of California Santa Barbara, http://www.presidency.ucsb.edu; Joyce Green's "Presidential Signing Statements," http://www.coherentbabble.com/; and the University of Michigan's "Federal Government Resources: President of the United States" http://www.lib.umich.edu/govdocs/fedprs.html are extremely useful. Similarly, executive orders are now available in an easy-to-use form through the National Archives and Records Administration, "Executive Orders Disposition Tables," http://www.archives.gov/federal-register/executive-orders/disposition.html, and national security directives are available by administration through the Federation of American Scientists, "Presidential Directives and Executive Orders," http://www.fas.org/irp/offdocs/direct.htm. The E-Government Act of 2002 and developments under the Freedom of Information Act have forced significant enhancement of resource availability and led to enhanced publication of material through agency websites, notwithstanding efforts by the George W. Bush administration to constrain the availability of some types of materials. Legislative sites have also improved significantly, in part because Congress and state legislatures are themselves using Internet tools for their work.

In addition to the instruments themselves, a broad class of what are appropriately termed "policy support materials" are also extremely useful in policy tools research and are increasingly available. They include legislative history and tracking materials, including hearing transcripts and witness testimony along with documentary evidence submitted in support of hearings. These hearings can produce far more than politically oriented testimony. It was the Iran/Contra hearings that resulted in the publications of large numbers of national security directives from the Reagan administration which, in turn, enhanced the effectiveness of various groups to access and publish such materials once they were no longer classified. These materials also include reports and testimony prepared by the Government Accountability Office (http://www.gao.gov/), the Congressional Research Service (increasingly available on the web through Open CRS and other organizations; http://opencrs.com/), and agency inspectors general. (See, e.g., the online site of the Special Inspector General for Iraq Reconstruction, http://www.sigir.mil/.) The materials provided with these documents often include memoranda and other relevant correspondence within agencies and among policymakers. Other organizations, like the Center for Regulatory Effectiveness, http://www.thecre.com/ombpapers/index.html, and OMB Watch, http://www.ombwatch.org/, also regularly and systematically post such working materials on their websites and archive those that are not current. Newspapers have also in a variety of cases posted such documents to their sites, including particularly sensitive materials leaked to the media by whistleblowers or provided to the media by officials of the administration as trial balloons. That said, where it was once possible to obtain such working documents only when they were matters of history, current practice and technology make it possible to obtain documents virtually in real time.

The ability to find, access, and use these policy support materials has been dramatically enhanced by the availability of increasingly sophisticated search engines. While it is true that it is necessary to exercise care to ensure the accuracy of materials, the ability to track those materials to official sources and to find copies of original documents scanned in and then posted makes it relatively easy to triangulate and cross-check materials. Also, once such documents become otherwise available, it is common practice for government agencies to post them on their sites to avoid confusion and accusations that they are hiding something. The same is true of news releases and transcripts of interviews that agencies prefer to publish themselves so as to ensure that the whole document reaches the public and not just the severely edited broadcast news clips of a statement.

That said, it is also now possible to do systematic searches of newspaper stories. While journalistic reports must always be used with considerable care and an awareness of their limits, it is now possible to check multiple outlets on the same story at any point in contemporary history, now reaching back several decades. Thus, it is relatively easy to cross-check reports and often quotations from public officials. In this way, it is possible to understand the context and stories as presented to the public on a particular issue at a moment in time. This research also gives an indication of the way in which policymakers seek to explain their positions and establish a favorable context for their proposals. A comparison of the subject matter that reached the public through media interest and those policy support materials that were being used internally during the same period provides insight into the use and abuse of policy tools.

As the presidential libraries have gone increasingly digital, they have offered not only online access to large volumes of documents, video, and audio but also online search capabilities for both posted and hard copy materials in their collections. Starting with the Clinton administration, they are also now serving as online digital archives for the web-based materials of presidential administrations. Thus, it is possible to search and access quickly materials that only a few years ago would have been available only by archival research on site.

On the judicial side, web access to materials has increased dramatically, with most courts now providing real-time access to orders and opinions. Additionally, and in the realm of policy support documents, it is now possible to access briefs and supporting record materials online and without subscription to proprietary databases, which for some time limited access to those at universities and law offices whose organizations had the resources to subscribe to them. Additionally, many organizations that file policy-oriented litigation now provide copies of the complaints and other relevant documents on their websites. In order to assist their case in the court of public opinion, government agencies now often post their working materials on the other side of the case. Thus, when the Congressional Research Service provided a strong report criticizing the Bush administration's National Security Agency domestic surveillance program, the Department of Justice (DOJ) promptly posted what amounted to a reply brief on its website. Indeed, the DOJ posts its briefs in major cases as well as Office of Legal Policy memoranda on the agency's website.

For all these reasons, it is now far simpler to do policy tools research with a range of materials about the mechanisms, the instruments, and the policy support materials never available before or at least not available until years or even decades had passed. In the past, such searches required researchers to travel extensively and expend weeks and months laboriously hand searching materials, even after the boxes of materials had been catalogued by hard-working archivists.

CONCLUSION

This study benefited from the use of all of these materials. It built on a broad base established during the preparation of the *By Order of the President* book, and the acquisition of materials by administration has continued since then.

It will be useful if, in the future, policy tools scholars and others will consider the mechanisms, the instruments, and the policy support materials as separate, but mutually interconnected categories for research. While they are certainly closely connected, they present different foci and offer lessons of different kinds. It is certainly important to understand whether a proposed policy is intended to operate by economic incentives, coercive action, subsidies, moral suasion or public embarrassment, or risk reduction, but it is also critical to know just how that proposal is to be put into operation. The instruments also are important. It makes considerable difference in a variety of ways whether the legislation, presidential directives, administrative rules, or judicial opinions are used in the effort to put a particular policy mechanism into place.

This study focused on regulation as a mechanism, but employed the full range of instruments used to change policy with respect to regulation, and to eliminate or reduce it where possible. It also utilized an analysis of print news articles from the Carter through the George W. Bush administrations.

Notes

PREFACE

1. See, e.g., Susan J. Tolchin and Martin Tolchin, *Dismantling America: The Rush to Deregulate* (New York: Oxford University Press, 1985); Michael Pertschuk, *Revolt against Regulation* (Berkeley: University of California Press, 1982); Mark J. Green, *The Other Government*, rev. ed. (New York: Norton, 1978).

2. Omar Bradley, quoted in David McCullough, *Truman* (New York: Simon & Schuster, 1992), 854.

3. Joseph E. Stiglitz, *The Roaring Nineties: A New History of the World's Most Prosperous Decade* (New York: W. W. Norton, 2003).

CHAPTER 1. CAN THERE REALLY BE AN
ATTACK ON REGULATION WHEN THERE
IS SO MUCH OF IT?

1. See, e.g., Sidney A. Shapiro and Robert L. Glicksman, *Risk Regulation at Risk* (Stanford, Calif.: Stanford University Press, 2003); Sidney A. Shapiro, "Outsourcing Government Regulation," 53 *Duke Law Journal* 389 (2003); Malcolm K. Sparrow, *The Regulatory Craft* (Washington, D.C.: Brookings Institution, 2000).

2. A tradition led by people like Friedrich von Hayek, *The Road to Serfdom* (Chicago: University of Chicago Press, 1944).

3. Omar Bradley, quoted in David McCullough, *Truman* (New York: Simon & Schuster, 1992), 854.

4. So much for Herbert Kaufman's famous question *Are Government Organizations Immortal?* (Washington, D.C.: Brookings Institution, 1976).

5. See, e.g., *Motor Vehicle Manufacturers Association v. State Farm Mutual*, 463 U.S. 29 (1983); *Federal Communications Commission v. WNCN Listeners Guild*, 450 U.S. 582 (1981).

6. *Morales v. TWA*, 504 U.S. 374 (1992).

7. *United States v. Locke*, 529 U.S. 89 (2000).

8. E. J. Mundell, "U.S. Food Safety: The Import Alarms Keep Sounding," Healthfinder.gov, January 15, 2008, Office of Disease Prevention and Health Promotion, Department of Health and Human Services, http://www.healthfinder.gov/news/newsstory.asp?docID=611280, accessed September 14, 2008.

9. See H. Brinton Milward, "Implication of Contracting Out: New Roles for the Hollow State," in Patricia W. Ingraham and Barbara S. Romzek, eds., *New Paradigms for Government* (San Francisco: Jossey-Bass, 1994), 41–62; H. Brinton Milward,

"Introduction to Symposium on the Hollow State: Capacity, Control, and Performance in Interorganizational Settings," 6 *Journal of Public Administration Research and Theory* 193 (1996); H. Brinton Milward, "The Changing Character of the Public Sector," in James Perry, ed., *Handbook of Public Administration,* 2nd ed. (San Francisco: Jossey-Bass, 1996).

10. This use of the phrase recalls the Watergate era.

11. This author developed this argument in *Government by Contract* (Washington, D.C.: CQ Press, 2003).

12. On this doctrine of deference, see *Chevron U.S.A. v. Natural Resources Defense Council,* 467 U.S. 837 (1984).

13. Mark J. Green, *The Other Government: The Unseen Power of Washington Lawyers,* rev. ed. (New York: Norton, 1978), 12–16.

14. See the Administrative Procedure Act, 5 U.S.C. §551 et seq.

15. On the developments in rulemaking generally, see Cornelius M. Kerwin, *Rulemaking,* 3rd ed. (Washington, D.C.: CQ Press, 2005).

16. Executive Order 13422, 72 Fed. Reg. 2763 (2007).

17. OMB, "Peer Review and Information Quality, Proposed OMB Bulletin under Executive Order 12866 and Supplemental Information Quality Guidelines," September 2003, http://www.whitehouse.gov/omb/inforeg/peer_review_and_info_quality.pdf, accessed September 14, 2008.

18. Mary Schiavo, *Flying Blind, Flying Safe* (New York: Avon Books, 1997), 18–33.

19. See, e.g., USDA, Food Safety and Inspection Service, "Prohibition of the Use of Specified Risk Materials for Human Food and Requirements for the Disposition of Non-Ambulatory Disabled Cattle," Interim Final Rule, 69 Fed. Reg. 1862 (2004).

20. See *McConnell v. FEC,* 540 U.S. 93 (2003); *Randall v. Sorrell,* 165 L. Ed. 2d 482 (2006).

21. *Federal Election Commission v. Wisconsin Right to Life,* 127 S. Ct. 2652 (2007).

22. *Food and Drug Administration v. Brown & Williamson Tobacco Corp.,* 529 U.S. 120 (2000).

23. FDA, "Draft Guidance for Industry on Good Reprint Practices for the Distribution of Medical Journal Articles and Medical or Scientific Reference Publications on Unapproved New Uses of Approved Drugs and Approved or Cleared Medical Devices; Availability," Docket No. FDA-2008-D-0053, February 15, 2008, http://www.fda.gov/oc/op/goodreprint.html, accessed September 14, 2008.

24. *Massachusetts v. EPA,* 549 U.S. 497 (2007).

25. See Green, *Other Government,* at 14–16.

26. Marver Bernstein, *Regulating Business by Independent Commission* (Princeton, N.J.: Princeton University Press, 1955), 90.

27. See James Q. Wilson, "The Politics of Regulation," in James Q. Wilson, ed., *The Politics of Regulation* (New York: Basic Books, 1980), 357–394.

28. Kenneth J. Meier, E. Thomas Garman, and Lael R. Keiser, *Regulation and Consumer Protection: Politics, Bureaucracy, and Economics,* 3rd ed. (Houston, Tex.: DAME Publications, 1998), 6.

29. The term "power law" is taken from Green, *Other Government,* 12–16.

30. See, e.g., Rosemary O'Leary, *Environmental Change: Federal Courts and the EPA* (Philadelphia: Temple University Press, 1993).

31. See Green, *Other Government,* 13–16.

CHAPTER 2. THE WAR AGAINST REGULATION
FROM JIMMY CARTER TO GEORGE H. W. BUSH

1. Bush used the language "the three generals in the war for regulatory reforms," but he meant war on regulation. He was referring to the leaders of the Council on Competitiveness, often known as the Quayle Commission, which was one of the leading combat units in that war. See George H. W. Bush, "Remarks on Regulatory Reform," 28 *Weekly Compilation of Presidential Documents* 726 (1992).

2. For those who were unaware of these commitments to deregulation, word first came in press reports early in his administration. See "Panel Changes Favor Gas Decontrol," *Washington Post,* February 11, 1977, Friday, Final Edition, A8.

3. Airline Deregulation Act of 1978, P.L. 95-504, 92 Stat. 1705.

4. Staggers Rail Act of 1980, P.L. 96-448, 94 Stat. 1895.

5. Motor Carrier Act of 1980, P.L. 96-296, 94 Stat. 793.

6. Quoted in William H. Jones, "Carter Deregulation Remarks Worry Trucking Spokesman; Truckers Fear Carter Proposal," *Washington Post,* March 18, 1977, D9.

7. Natural Gas Policy Act of 1978, P.L. 95-621, 92 Stat. 3351.

8. Depository Institute Deregulation and Monetary Control Act, P.L. 96-221, 94 Stat. 132 (1980).

9. Ward Sinclair, "The Battle for Big Bucks; Banking Deregulation: Battle for Bucks; Contrasting Banking Deregulation Bills Bring Immense Pressure on Congress," *Washington Post,* November 23, 1979, A1.

10. P.L. 96-354, 94 Stat. 1165 (1980).

11. Paperwork Reduction Act of 1980, P.L. 96-511, 94 Stat. 2826.

12. See James P. Pfiffner, *The Strategic Presidency,* 2nd ed., rev. (Lawrence: University Press of Kansas, 1996), 158; Glenn O. Robinson, "The Federal Communications Commission: An Essay on Regulatory Watchdogs," 64 *Virginia Law Review* 169, 183–85 (1978); and Henry J. Friendly, *The Federal Administrative Agencies* (Cambridge, Mass.: Harvard University Press, 1962), 142–43.

13. Robinson, "Federal Communications Commission," 188.

14. See, e.g., Robert F. Durant, *The Administrative Presidency Revisited: Public Lands, the BLM, and the Reagan Revolution* (Albany: State University of New York Press, 1992).

15. One of his best-known academic writings on the subject was *The Economics of Regulation: The Principles and Institutions* (New York: John Wiley & Sons, 1970).

16. Isaiah Sharfman, *The Interstate Commerce Commission* (New York: Commonwealth Fund, 1937).

17. Larry Kramer, "O'Neal Opens ICC's Battle for Trucking Deregulation; ICC Debates Deregulation," *Washington Post,* November 8, 1978, E1.

18. See, e.g., U.S. Regulatory Council, *Regulating with Common Sense: A Progress Report on Innovative Regulatory Techniques* (Washington, D.C.: U.S. Regulatory Council, 1980); and U.S. Regulatory Council Conference, *Innovative Techniques in Theory and Practice, Proceedings* (Washington, D.C.: U.S. Regulatory Council, 1980).

19. Ibid., 9.

20. See 5 U.S.C. §553.

21. See Cornelius M. Kerwin, *Rulemaking: How Government Agencies Write Law and Make Policy,* 3rd ed. (Washington, D.C.: CQ Press, 2003). I have explained this process in detail in *Public Law and Public Administration,* 4th ed. (Belmont, Calif.: Wadsworth/Thomson, 2007), ch. 5.

22. *Natural Resources Defense Council v. Nuclear Regulatory Commission,* 547 F.2d 633 (D.C.Cir. 1976); *Mobil Oil v. Federal Power Commission,* 483 F.2d 1238 (D.C.Cir. 1973); *International Harvester Co. v. Ruckelshaus,* 478 F.2d 615 (D.C.Cir. 1973); *Appalachian Power Co. v. Environmental Protection Agency,* 477 F.2d 495 (4th Cir. 1973); *Walter Holm & Co. v. Hardin,* 449 F.2d 1009 (D.C.Cir. 1971); *American Airlines v. Civil Aeronautics Board,* 359 F.2d 624 (D.C.Cir. 1966).

23. *Vermont Yankee Nuclear Power Corp. v. Natural Resources Defense Council,* 435 U.S. 519 (1978).

24. Executive Order 12044, 43 Fed. Reg. 12661 (1978).

25. Douglas M. Costle to William M. Nichols, November 16, 1977, http://www.thecre.com/pdf/Carter_EPA2OMBLet.PDF, accessed February 17, 2009, 3.

26. Ibid., 2.

27. Executive Order 12044.

28. U.S. Regulatory Council, *Regulatory Reform Highlights, 1978–80* (Washington, D.C.: U.S. Regulatory Council, 1980), 8.

29. Memorandum from George Eads to Regulatory Analysis Review Group Participants, "Executive Committee Membership," October 17, 1979, attachment 1, p. 1.

30. White House, "Preliminary Conference Report," The White House Conference on Small Business, January 13–17, 1980, http://www.thecre.com/pdf/Carter_WHConfSmBus0113-1780.PDF, accessed February 17, 2009, 13.

31. Paperwork Reduction Act of 1980.

32. Memorandum, John M. Harmon, Office of Legal Council, Department of Justice, to Sam Lazarus, Associate Director, Domestic Council, July 22, 1977, http://www.thecre.com/pdf/Carter_DOJOpinion072277.PDF, accessed February 17, 2009, 1.

33. Memorandum, William Nichols, General Counsel, OMB, to Deputy Director, OMB, February 1, 1977, http://www.thecre.com/pdf/Carter_OMBGenCounselMem0020179.PDF, accessed February 17, 2009, 1.

34. National Security Action Memorandum 2, February 3, 1961, @9D435253-7A2A-4B26-8712-94F6AD7C15F7:http://www.jfklibrary.org/Asset+Tree/Asset+Viewers/Image+Asset+Viewer.htm?guid=&type=Image, accessed February 17, 2009.

35. Quoted in Timothy B. Clark, "Carter's Assault on the Costs of Regulation," *National Journal,* August 12, 1978, 1282.

36. Quoted in Carole Shifrin, "House Votes To Ease Curbs On Airlines; House Overwhelmingly Backs Bill to Reduce Regulation of Airlines," *Washington Post,* September 22, 1978, A1.

37. Larry Kramer, "Carter Calls for an End to Wasteful Regulations," *Washington Post,* January 12, 1980, C7.

38. Quoted in Carole Shifrin, "President Signs Rail Industry Decontrol Bill; Carter Signs Rail Deregulation," *Washington Post,* October 15, 1980, E1.

39. Ernest Hosendolph, "The U.S. Drive for Regulation," *New York Times,* October 7, 1980, D1.

40. Ibid.

41. Ibid.

42. See, e.g., Roger E. Meiners and Bruce Yandle, "Regulatory Lessons from the Reagan Era: Introduction," in Roger E. Meiners and Bruce Yandle, eds., *Regulation and the Reagan Era: Politics, Bureaucracy, and the Public Interest* (New York: Holmes & Meier, 1989), 3–4.

43. Durant, *Administrative Presidency Revisited,* 52.

44. See, e.g., Murray Weidenbaum, *The Costs of Government Regulation of Business,* a study prepared for the use of the Subcommittee on Economic Growth and Stabilization of the Joint Economic Committee of the Congress; Murray Weidenbaum, *Business, Government and the Public* (Englewood Cliffs, N.J.: Prentice-Hall, 1977).

45. Ronald Brownstein and Nin Easton, *Reagan's Ruling Class* (New York: Pantheon Books, 1983), 297.

46. See, e.g., Martha Derthick and Paul J. Quirk, *The Politics of Deregulation* (Washington, D.C.: Brookings Institution, 1985).

47. See, generally, Stuart M. Butler, Michael Sanera, and W. Bruce Weinrod, *Mandate for Leadership II* (Washington, D.C.: Heritage Foundation, 1984).

48. Carolyn Ban and Patricia Ingraham, "Short-Timers: Political Appointee Mobility and Its Impact on Political/Career Relations in the Reagan Administration," 22 *Administration & Society* 106 (1990).

49. Quoted in Merrill Brown, "FCC Votes Major Radio Deregulation in Industry Victory," *Washington Post,* January 15, 1981, G1.

50. Quoted in Jerry Knight, "Mark Fowler Plans to Resign as FCC Chairman in Spring; Steered Communications Deregulation for 5 Years," *Washington Post,* January 17, 1987, A2.

51. *Pacific Legal Foundation v. DOT,* 593 F.2d 1338 (D.C.Cir. 1979); *Chrysler v. DOT,* 472 F.2d 659 (6th Cir. 1972).

52. 46 Fed. Reg. 12033 (1981).

53. 46 Fed. Reg. 21205 (1981).

54. *Motor Vehicle Manufacturers Association v. State Farm Mutual,* 463 U.S. 29, 42 (1983).

55. Ibid., 58, Rehnquist, J., dissenting.

56. Timothy B. Clark, "OMB to Keep Its Regulatory Powers in Reserve in Case Agencies Lag," *National Journal,* March 14, 1981, 426.

57. The president's memorandum, entitled "Postponement of Pending Regulations," was published on January 29, 1981, 46 Fed. Reg. 11227.

58. 46 Fed. Reg. 13193 (1981).

59. See, e.g., *Public Citizen Health Research Group v. Brock,* 823 F.2d 626 (D.C.Cir. 1987); *New York and Florida v. Reilly,* 969 F.2d 1147, 1149-1150 (D.C.Cir. 1992).

60. Memorandum, Christopher DeMuth, Administrator, OIRA, to Department and Agency Heads, "Regulatory Contacts," September 22, 1983.

61. *EDF v. Thomas,* 627 F. Supp. 566, 570-571 (D.D.C. 1986).

62. 50 Fed. Reg. 11036 (1986).

63. 21 *Weekly Compilation of Presidential Documents* 13 (1985).

64. *Dole v. United Steelworkers,* 494 U.S. 26 (1990).

65. "Inaugural Address," January 20, 1981, *Public Papers of the President of the United States, Ronald Reagan, 1981* (Washington, D.C.: Government Printing Office, 1982), 1.

66. "Memorandum Directing a Federal Employee Hiring Freeze," 17 *Weekly Compilation of Presidential Documents* 6–7 (1981).

67. The training was provided by the right-wing Heritage Foundation. See, generally, Butler, Sanera, and Weinrod, *Mandate for Leadership II.*

68. Durant, *Administrative Presidency Revisited,* 38.

69. See David A. Stockman, *The Triumph of Politics: Why the Reagan Revolution Failed* (New York: Harper & Row, 1986), 71–73.

70. Rosemary O'Leary, *Environmental Change: Federal Courts and the EPA* (Philadelphia: Temple University Press, 1993).

71. On the Nixon version of new federalism, see Michael D. Reagan, *The New Federalism* (New York: Oxford University Press, 1972).

72. U.S. General Accounting Office, *Block Grants: Characteristics, Experience, and Lessons Learned* (Washington, D.C.: GAO, 1995) 34.

73. Discussed in Phillip J. Cooper, Linda P. Brady, Olivia Hidalgo-Hardeman, Albert Hyde, Katherine C. Naff, J. Steven Otte, and Harvey White, *Public Administration in the Twenty-First Century* (Fort Worth, Tex.: Harcourt Brace, 1998), 128–129.

74. Mark J. Green, *The Other Government: The Unseen Power of Washington Lawyers,* rev. ed. (New York: Norton, 1978), 12–16.

75. The author has explained this concept in greater detail in *Public Law and Public Administration,* ch. 10.

76. P.L. 99-499, 100 Stat. 1613 (1986).

77. Balanced Budget and Emergency Deficit Control Act of 1985, P.L. 99-177, 99 Stat. 1038 (1985).

78. Nathaniel C. Nash, "Budget Curbs Bank Agencies," *Washington Post,* March 17, 1986, D2.

79. Quoted in Robert Pear, "In Bush Presidency, the Regulators Ride Again," *New York Times,* April 28, 1991, Section 4, p. 5.

80. P.L. 102-166, 105 Stat. 1071 (1991).

81. 27 *Weekly Compilation of Presidential Documents* 1701 (1991).

82. Americans with Disabilities Act, P.L. 101-336, 104 Stat. 327 (1990).

83. See, e.g., Kerwin, *Rulemaking.*

84. Quoted in Pear, "Regulators Ride Again," 5.

85. See Diane Alters, "Bush Blasted for Leading Safety Deregulation Bid," *Boston Globe,* October 12, 1988, Wednesday, National/Foreign Section, 16.

86. George Bush, "Address on Administration Goals before a Joint Session of Congress," February 9, 1989, http://bushlibrary.tamu.edu/research/papers/1989/89020900 .html, accessed June 19, 2004.

87. Barry D. Friedman, *Regulation in the Reagan-Bush Era: The Eruption of Presidential Influence* (Pittsburgh: University of Pittsburgh Press, 1995), 164.

88. "Statement by Press Secretary Fitzwater on the Review of Regulatory Issues by the Council on Competitiveness," June 15, 1990, Bush Library Public Papers, http:// bushlibrary.tamu.edu/research/papers/1990/90061507.html, accessed June 19, 2004.

89. Christine Triano and Nancy Watzman, *All the Vice President's Men* (Washington, D.C.: OMB Watch, 1991), i.

90. See Malcolm D. Woolf, "Clean Air or Hot Air?: Lessons from the Quayle Competitiveness Council's Oversight of EPA," 10 *Journal of Law & Public Policy* 97 (1993).

91. This was done in an October 1990 memorandum to members of the cabinet and agency heads. See Triano and Watzman, *All the Vice President's Men,* 7.

92. Weidenbaum's approach is discussed in Susan J. Tolchin and Martin Tolchin, *Dismantling America: The Rush to Deregulate* (New York: Oxford University Press, 1985).

93. "Memorandum from the Vice President to all Heads of Executive Departments and Agencies," March 22, 1991, quoted in Triano and Watzman, *All the Vice President's Men,* 7.

94. Congressman David E. Skaggs (D-Colo.), quoted in Keith Schneider, "Prominence Proves Perilous for Bush's Rule Slayer," *Washington Post,* June 30, 1992.

95. Christine Triano, "Quayle and Co.," *Government Information Insider,* June 1991, 8.

96. Don R. Clay, Assistant Administrator, EPA, to John D. Dingell, Chair, Subcommittee on Oversight and Investigations, September 1991.

97. Quoted in Friedman, *Regulation in Reagan-Bush Era,* 166.

98. Bob Woodward and David S. Broder, "Quayle's Quest: Curb Rules, Leave 'No Fingerprints,'" *Washington Post,* January 9, 1992, A1.

99. Friedman, *Regulation in Reagan-Bush Era,* 165, quoting Dana Priest, "Competitiveness Council Suspected of Unduly Influencing Regulators: Secrecy Foils Senate Panel's Attempt to Probe Vice President's Group," *Washington Post,* November 18, 1991, A19.

100. C. Boyden Gray, Counsel to the President, to John Conyers, Chairman, Committee on Government Operations, April 30, 1990.

101. Paperwork Reduction Act of 1995, P.L. 104-13, 109 Stat. 163, 44 U.S.C. §3501 et. seq.

102. Andrew Rosenthal, "The 1992 Campaign: Despite Grip on Nomination—Bush Still Gropes for Agenda," *New York Times,* April 30, 1992, A1.

103. "Memorandum for Certain Department and Agency Heads," "Memorandum on Reducing the Burden of Government Regulation," January 28, 1992, George Bush, *Public Papers of the Presidents of the United States* (Washington, D.C.: Government Printing Office, 1993), Book 1, 1992–1993, 166.

104. Ibid.

105. "Memorandum on Implementing Regulatory Reforms," 28 *Weekly Compilation of Presidential Documents* 728 (1992).

106. "Remarks on Regulatory Reform," 28 *Weekly Compilation of Presidential Documents* 726 (1992).

107. See Clement E. Vose, *Caucasians Only: The Supreme Court, the NAACP, and the Restrictive Covenant Cases* (Berkeley: University of California Press, 1959); Karen O'Connor and Lee Epstein, "Amicus Curiae Participation in U.S. Supreme Court Litigation," 16 *Law & Society Review* 311 (1981); Lee Epstein, "The Rise of Conservative Interest Group Litigation," 45 *Journal of Politics* 479 (1983); Lee Epstein, *Conservatives in Court* (Knoxville: University of Tennessee Press, 1985); Lee Epstein, "Interest Group Litigation during the Rehnquist Era," 9 *Journal of Law and Politics* 639 (1993); Jayanth K. Krishnan and Kevin R. den Dulk, "So Help Me God: A Comparative Study of Religious Interest Group Litigation," 30 *Georgia Journal of International and Comparative Law* 233 (2002).

108. See Dan Quayle, "Civil Justice Reform," 41 *American University Law Review* 559 (1992); Dan Quayle, "Proposed Civil Justice Reform Legislation: Proposed Legislation: Agenda for Civil Justice Reform in America," 60 *University of Cincinnati Law Review* 979 (1992).

109. Civil Justice Reform Act of 1990, 101-650, 28 U.S.C. 471-482.

110. 56 Fed. Reg. 55195 (1991).

111. Carl Tobias, "Executive Branch Civil Justice Reform," 42 *American University Law Review* 1521, 1523 n. 9 (1993).

112. See generally, U.S. House, Hearing before the Subcommittees on Human Rights and International Organizations, Western Hemisphere Affairs, and International Economic Policy and Trade of the Committee on Foreign Affairs, *The Enterprise for the Americas Initiative.* 101st Cong., 2nd Sess. (1990).

113. Joseph E. Stiglitz, *The Roaring Nineties: A New History of the World's Most Prosperous Decade* (New York: W. W. Norton, 2003), 23–24.

CHAPTER 3. THE WILLIAM CLINTON AND
GEORGE W. BUSH ADMINISTRATIONS

1. "Remarks on Regulatory Reform," 28 *Weekly Compilation of Presidential Documents* 726 (1992).

2. Joseph E. Stiglitz, *The Roaring Nineties: A New History of the World's Most Prosperous Decade* (New York: W. W. Norton, 2003), 89–91.

3. See Progressive Policy Institute, "About the Third Way," http://www.ppionline
.org/ppi_ci.cfm?knlgAreaID=87&subsecID=205&contentID=895, accessed November 4, 2007. See also Bob Woodward, *The Agenda: Inside the Clinton White House* (New York: Simon and Schuster, 1994).

4. Al Gore, *From Red Tape to Results: Creating a Government That Works Better and Costs Less,* Report of the National Performance Review (Washington, D.C.: Government Printing Office, 1993), 11–12.

5. Ibid., 6.

6. Ibid., 7.

7. Eugene Bardach, *The Implementation Game* (Cambridge, Mass.: MIT Press, 1977).

8. See, generally, Will Marshall and Martin Schram, eds., *Mandate for Change* (New York: Progressive Policy Institute, 1993).

9. Woodward, *Agenda,* 54.

10. See Stiglitz, *Roaring Nineties,* ch. 1. See also Woodward, *Agenda.*

11. See Steven Mufson, "Clinton Appointees Form a Collage of Varying Economic Views," *Washington Post,* December 11, 1992, A35.

12. Stiglitz, *Roaring Nineties,* chs. 1–3.

13. Executive Order 12839, 58 Fed. Reg. 8515 (1993).

14. Quoted in Keith Schneider, "E.P.A. Plans to Seek Loosening of a Law on Food Pesticides," *New York Times,* February 2, 1993, A1.

15. Paul Farhi, "Gore Urges Phone, Cable Deregulation; Plan Requires Firms to Forgo Monopolies," *Washington Post,* January 12, 1994, F1.

16. Sandra Sugawara and Paul Farhi, "Cable, TV Deregulation Plan on Way; Gore Calls Executives to the White House Tuesday," *Washington Post,* January 4, 1994, E1.

17. Farhi, "Gore Urges Phone, Cable Deregulation."

18. P.L. 103-305, 108 Stat. 1569 (1994).

19. Ibid., Sections 601(c) and 601(b).

20. *Morales v. TWA,* 504 U.S. 374 (1992).

21. P.L. 103-328, 103 P.L. 328; 108 Stat. 2338 (1994).

22. "Remarks on Signing the Riegle-Neal Interstate Banking and Branching Efficiency Act of 1994, September 29, 1994, 30 *Weekly Compilation of Presidential Documents,* 1896–1897 (1994).

23. "Remarks by the President to the City Club of Cleveland," October 24, 1994, http://www.ibiblio.org/pub/archives/whitehouse-papers/1994/Oct/1994-10-24-Remarks-by-the-President-at-Cleveland-City-Club, accessed February 17, 2009.

24. Dennis B. Roddy, "A GOP President with My Job Record Would Get a Statue, Clinton Tells Press," *Pittsburgh Post-Gazette,* November 1, 1994, A1.

25. "The President's News Conference with President Kuchma of Ukraine," November 22, 1994, 30 *Weekly Compilation of Presidential Documents,* 2424–2425 (1994).

26. Quoted in "Clinton Calls for a Centrist 'Social Compact,'" *Washington Post,* January 25, 1995, A1.

27. Editorial, "Aftershocks from the Baring Crash," *Atlanta Journal and Constitution,* March 1, 1995, 10A.

28. Herbert Kaufman, *Are Government Organizations Immortal?* (Washington, D.C.: Brookings Institution, 1976).

29. David E. Sanger, "A U.S. Agency, Once Powerful, Is Dead at 108," *New York Times,* January 1, 1996, 1.

30. Telecommunications Act of 1996, P.L. 104-104; 110 Stat. 56 (1996).

31. Edmund L. Andrews, "Communications Bill Signed, and the Battles Begin Anew," *New York Times,* February 9, 1996, A1.

32. U.S. Senate, Report of the Committee on the Judiciary together with Additional and Supplemental Views, *The Comprehensive Regulatory Reform Act of 1995—S. 343,* 104th Cong., 1st Sess. (1995), 151.

33. Title II of P.L. 104-121, 110 Stat. 847. (1996).

34. Ibid., Sec. 251, Congressional Review of Agency Rulemaking, which adds §§ 800 et. seq. outlining the process for legislative review.

35. See *INS v. Chadha,* 462 U.S. 919 (1983); *Consumer Energy Council v. Federal Energy Regulatory Commission,* 673 F.2d 425 (D.C.Cir. 1982).

36. Equal Access to Justice Act, P.L. 104-121, Sec. 231, 232.

37. 60 Fed. Reg. 41314 (1995).

38. 61 Fed. Reg. 44396 (1996).

39. Mary Schiavo, *Flying Blind, Flying Safe* (New York: Avon Books, 1997).

40. *FDA v. Brown & Williamson Tobacco Corp.,* 529 U.S. 120 (2000).

41. This was the basis for close regulation of public utilities since *Munn v. Illinois,* 94 U.S. 113 (1876).

42. See, e.g., *Pacific Gas & Electric v. State Energy Resources Conservation and Development Commission,* 461 U.S. 190 (1983).

43. Quoted in Agis Salpukas, "Power Deregulation: Shadow, Substance and Politics," *New York Times,* March 26, 1998, D3.

44. P.L. 106-102, 113 Stat. 1338 (1999).

45. See Stiglitz, *Roaring Nineties,* 19–24.

46. Ibid., 35.

47. Ibid., 90–91.

48. This transformation is the central theme of Woodward, *Agenda.*

49. Stiglitz, *Roaring Nineties,* 91.

50. Gore, *From Red Tape to Results.*

51. Al Gore to the President, September 7, 1993, letter of transmittal, in Gore, *From Red Tape to Results.*

52. Gore, *From Red Tape to Results.*

53. OMB Director Leon E. Panetta, quoted in John H. Cushman, "President Moves to Loosen Grip of White House on Regulations," *New York Times,* October 1, 1993, A-16.

54. David Osborne and Ted Gaebler, *Reinventing Government* (New York: Penguin, 1993).

55. For an excellent contemporary discussion of the New Public Management and its development from a European perspective, see Christopher Pollitt, "Management Techniques for the Public Sector: Pulpit and Practice," in B. Guy Peters and Donald J. Savoie, eds., *Governance in a Changing Environment* (Ottawa: McGill/Queens University Press, 1995), 203–238.

56. Gore, *From Red Tape to Results,* see the lists of recommendations at the end of each chapter.

57. 58 Fed. Reg. 48255.

58. 58 Fed. Reg. 48257.

59. 58 Fed. Reg. 51735.

60. U.S. General Accounting Office, *Regulatory Reform: Implementation of the Regulatory Review Executive Order* (Washington, D.C.: GAO, 1996), 5–6.

61. See, e.g., the report of the National Academy of Science published in 1994 that discussed the fact that while risk assessment is important to do, it remained a complex and challenging enterprise. National Research Council, *Science and Judgment in Risk Assessment* (Washington, D.C.: National Academy Press, 1994).

62. 5 U.S.C. §706.

63. Quoted in Steven Greenhouse, "Administration Completing Plan to Ease Rules on Bank Lending," *New York Times,* February 24, 1993, A-1.

64. Office of the Vice President, Memorandum for Heads of Executive Departments and Agencies, "Memo Announcing Phase II of NPR," January 3, 1995, http://govinfo.library.unt.edu/npr/library/direct/memos/266e.html, accessed February 17, 2009.

65. William Jefferson Clinton, Memorandum for Heads of Departments and Agencies: Regulatory Reinvention Initiative, March 4, 1995, Released by the Office of the White House Press Secretary March 6, 1995, http://govinfo.library.unt.edu/npr/library/direct/memos/reinvent.html, accessed February 17, 2009.

66. U.S. General Accounting Office, *Regulatory Reform: Implementation of the Regulatory Review Executive Order* (Washington, D.C.: GAO, 1996), 15.

67. Ibid., 16.

68. Quoted in John H. Cushman, "Proposed Changes Simplify Rules on Pollution Control," *New York Times,* March 17, 1995, A20.

69. "Remarks to the National Conference of the Building and Construction Trades Department of the AFL-CIO," 31 *Weekly Compilation of Presidential Documents* 544 (1996).

70. Paul Basken, "FDA to Ease Drug, Device Requirements," United Press International, April 6, 1995.

71. AFL-CIO, "Chronology of OSHA's Ergonomics Standard and the Business Campaign Against It," http://www.aflcio.org/issues/safety/ergo/upload/chrono2004.pdf, accessed February 17, 2009.

72. *Cooley v. Board of Wardens of Port of Philadelphia,* 53 U.S. 299 (1852).

73. See *International Association of Independent Tanker Owners (INTERTANKO) v. Lowry,* 947 F. Supp. 1484, 1488-1489 (WDWA 1996), and *International Association of Independent Tanker Owners (INTERTANKO) v. Locke,* 148 F.3d 1053 (9th Cir. 1998).

74. "Note Verbale from the Royal Danish Embassy to the U.S. Department of State 1 (June 14, 1996), quoted in *United States v. Locke,* infra at 98.

75. *United States v. Locke,* 529 U.S. 89 (2000).

76. *Crosby v. National Foreign Trade Council,* 530 U.S. 363 (2000).

77. Executive Order 13083, 63 Fed. Reg. 27651 (1998).

78. Executive Order 13095, 63 Fed. Reg. 42565 (1998). See David S. Broder, "Executive Order Urged Consulting, but Didn't," *Washington Post,* July 16, 1998, A15.

79. Robert Nakamura, Thomas Church, and Phillip Cooper, "Environmental Dispute Resolution and Hazardous Waste Cleanups: A Cautionary Tale of Policy Implementation," 10 *Journal of Policy Analysis and Management* 204 (1991).

80. Office of the Vice President, National Performance Review, "Improving Regulatory Systems: REG06: Encourage Alternative Dispute Resolution When Enforcing Regulations," 1993, http://govinfo.library.unt.edu/npr/library/reports/rego6.html, accessed January 5, 2008.

81. Supra note 65.

82. 101 P.L. 552, 104 Stat. 2736 (1990).

83. Supra note 65.

84. P.L. 101-648 amended the APA by adding sections 581 et. seq. Originally, the statute required periodic reauthorization but it was made permanent by P.L. 104-320, 110 Stat. 3870 (1996).

85. 5 U.S.C. §563.

86. 5 U.S.C. §570.

87. Chip Cameron, Philip J. Harter, Gail Bingham, and Neil R. Eisner, "Alternative Dispute Resolution with Emphasis on Rulemaking Negotiations," 4 *Administrative Law Journal* 83, 87–88 (1990).

88. 5 U.S.C. §582(b).

89. Office of the Vice President, For Immediate Release September 18, 1995, "President, Vice President Release Regulatory Reform Reports, DOA, FCC, SEC, FCA Unveil Regulatory Highlights, Improved Customer Service," http://govinfo.library.unt.edu/npr/library/news/26ae.html, accessed February 17, 2009.

90. See Phillip J. Cooper and Claudia María Vargas, *Implementing Sustainable Development: From Global Policy to Local Action* (Lanham, Md.: Rowman & Littlefield, 2004), 195. These programs and results were developed from an author interview with Jinnan Wang, April 23, 1996, Chinese Research Academy of Environmental Sciences. Wang produced such papers as "Pollution Charges and Environmental Taxes in China," Chinese Research Academy of Environmental Sciences, November 17, 1995; "The Framework of Environmental Economic Policies in Transition Economy in China," Chinese Research Academy of Environmental Sciences, 1995.

91. See, e.g., John H. Cushman, "Gore Orders Changes in E.P.A. Procedures," *New York Times,* April 8, 1998, A13.

92. Vice President Al Gore, "Memorandum for [Agriculture] Secretary Daniel R. Glickman and [EPA] Administrator Carol M. Browner: Food Quality Protection," April 8, 1998, http://www.aenews.wsu.edu/May98AENEWS/Goreaddress.html, accessed February 17, 2009.

93. Cushman, "Gore Orders Changes."

94. Ibid.

95. The memorandum indicates that this document was to be published in the *Federal Register.* The author did not find a citation for the document in the *Register.*

96. Office of Management and Budget, *Budget of the United States, Fiscal Year 1996* (Washington, D.C.: OMB, 1995), 3.

97. Office of Management and Budget, *Budget of the United States, Fiscal Year 2001* (Washington, D.C.: OMB, 2000), 4.

98. Stiglitz, *Roaring Nineties,* chs. 4 and 5.

99. See Cindy Skrzycki, "Slowing the Flow of Federal Rules; New Conservative Climate Chills Agencies' Activism," *Washington Post,* February 18, 1996, A01. This article was the first in a three-part series.

100. See Schiavo, *Flying Blind, Flying Safe.*

101. Adam Bryant, "F.A.A. Struggles as Airlines Turn to Subcontracts," *New York Times,* June 2, 1996, 1.

102. Andrew H. Card, Jr., to the Heads and Acting Heads of Executive Departments and Agencies, "Regulatory Review Plan," January 20, 2001, http://www.georgewbush-whitehouse.archives.gov/news/releases/print/20010123-4.html, accessed May 30, 2009.

103. 65 Fed. Reg. 68261 (2000).

104. P.L. 107-5, signed by George W. Bush on March 20, 2001. "Statement on Signing Legislation to Repeal Federal Ergonomics Regulations," 37 *Weekly Compilation of Presidential Documents* 477 (2001).

105. Andrew H. Card, Jr., to the Heads and Acting Heads of Executive Departments and Agencies, "Government Hiring Controls," January 20, 2001, http://www.georgewbush-whitehouse.archives.gov/news/releases/20010123-3.html, accessed May 30, 2009.

106. P.L. 107-396, 116 Stat. 2135 (2002), Section 841.

107. Department of Homeland Security, "Human Resources Management System," Final Rule. 70 Fed. Reg. 5272 (2005).

108. National Defense Authorization Act for FY 2004, 108 P.L. 136; 117 Stat. 1392, Codified as 5 U.S.C. §9902.

109. Office of Management and Budget, The President's Management Agenda, Fiscal Year 2002, http://www.georgewbush-whitehouse.archives.gov/omb/budget/fy2002/mgmt.pdf, accessed May 30, 2009.

110. Commercial Activities Panel, Final Report, *Improving the Sourcing Decisions of the Government, Final Report* (Washington, D.C.: GAO, 2002), 118.

111. 106 P.L. 398; 114 Stat. 1654, Section 832.

112. E. C. Aldridge, Jr., who was Under Secretary of Defense for Acquisition, Technology and Logistics, formerly of LTV Aerospace Corporation and before that the McDonnell Douglas Electronic Systems Company, had been secretary of the Air Force under Reagan. Kay Coles James, who was then the director of the Office of Personnel Management in the Executive Office of the President, was formerly of the Heritage Foundation and before that a dean at Regents University and the Family Research Council. Sean Okeefe was administrator of NASA, before that Deputy Director of the Office of Management and Budget under George W. Bush. Angela Styles was administrator of the White House Office of Federal Procurement Policy. David Pryor was director of the Institute of Politics at Harvard University and before that a Democratic Senator from Arkansas. Frank A. Camm, Jr., was at the RAND Corporation and held a Ph.D. in Economics from the University of Chicago. Mark C. Filteau was president of the Johnson Controls corporations. Stephen Goldsmith was senior vice president at Affiliated Computer Services corporation and formerly an Indianapolis, Indiana, mayor who made contracting out as much as possible a focus of his two terms and who included in his biographical statement his success in eliminating regulations. Stan Z. Soloway was president of the Professional Services Council, a trade association with a strong advocacy position on outsourcing. There were three employee union representatives on the panel: Bobby L. Harnage, Sr., national president of the American Federation of Government Employees, AFL-CIO; Colleen M. Kelley, national president of the National Treasury Employees Union; and Robert M. Tobias, a distinguished adjunct professor at American University, who formerly served for thirty-one years, including as its president, with the National Treasury Employees Union (NTEU).

113. Competitive Activities Panel, *Improving the Sourcing Decisions of the Government, Final Report,* "Statements of Individual Panelists," 56–78.

114. See, e.g., Gansler Commission, *Report of the Commission on Army Acquisition and Program Management in Expeditionary Operations,* issued in the fall of 2007 at http://www.army.mil/docs/Gansler_Commission_Report_Final_071031.pdf, accessed May 30, 2009, as well as several GAO reports on major contracting problems at the DHS that arose in the wake of Hurricane Katrina.

115. Phillip J. Cooper, "George W. Bush, Edgar Allan Poe, and the Use and Abuse of Presidential Signing Statements," 35 *Presidential Studies Quarterly* 515 (2005); see also American Bar Association Task Force on Presidential Signing Statements and the Separation of Power Doctrine, "Report to the House of Delegates," incorporated into American Bar Association Resolution 304, August 7–8, 2006; http://www.abavideo news.org/ABA374/media/304.pdf (accessed July 28, 2007); Constitution Project, Coalition to Defend Checks and Balances, "Statement on Presidential Signing Statements, http://www.constitutionproject.org/pdf/Statement_on_Presidential_Signing_ Statement.pdf (accessed July 28, 2007); T. J. Halstead, "Presidential Signing Statements: Constitutional and Institutional Implications," CRS Report for Congress, September 20, 2006 (updated September 17, 2007), at http://www.fas.org/sgp/crs/natsec/ RL33667.pdf, accessed May 30, 2009.

116. Cooper, "George W. Bush, Edgar Allan Poe," 522.

117. Explained in greater detail in Cooper, "George W. Bush, Edgar Allan Poe." See also Phillip J. Cooper, "Signing Statements as Declaratory Judgments: The President as Judge," 16 *William & Mary Bill of Rights Journal* 253 (2007).

118. E.O. 13258, 67 Fed. Reg. 9385 (February 26, 2002).

119. See *Cheney v. U.S. District Court,* 542 U.S. 367 (2004).

120. 5 U.S.C. App. 1.

121. *Cheney v. U.S. District Court,* 542 U.S. 367 (2004).

122. *Walker v. Cheney,* 230 F. Supp. 2d 51 (D.D.C. 2002).

123. P.L. 109-58, 119 Stat. 594 (2005).

124. *Citizens for Responsibility and Ethics in Washington v. Department of Homeland Security,* Civil Action No. 06-0883, https://ecf.dcd.uscourts.gov/cgi-bin/show_public _doc?2006cv0883-79, accessed February 17, 2009.

125. OMB, "OMB Regulatory Review: Principles and Procedures," September 20, 2001, followed later by OMB Circular, A-4, "Regulatory Analysis," September 17, 2003, http://www.georgewbush-whitehouse.archices.gov/omb/circulars/a004/a-4.pdf, accessed May 30, 2009.

126. OMB, "Final Information Quality Bulletin for Peer Review," December 15, 2004, http://www.georgewbush-whitehouse.archives.gov/omb/memoranda/fy2005/ m05-03.pdf, accessed May 30, 2009. On this tradition of judicial deference, see *Chevron U.S.A. v. Natural Resources Defense Council,* 467 U.S. 837 (1984).

127. OMB, "Draft Office of Management and Budget Good Guidance Practices Bulletin and Request for Comment," November 23, 2005, http://www.whitehouse.gov/ omb/inforeg/good_guid/good_guidance_preamble.pdf, accessed May 30, 2009.

128. 72 Fed. Reg. 2763 (2007). The APA had specifically avoided treating interpretive rules like substantive rules, exempting the interpretive rules from the requirements for rulemaking set forth in statute 5 U.S.C. §553(b)(A).

129. Ibid., Sec. 5(b).

130. OMB, "Proposed Risk Assessment Bulletin," January 9, 2006, http://www .georgewbush-whitehouse.archives.gov/omb/inforeg/proposed_risk_assessment_ bulletin_010906.pdf, accessed May 30, 2009.

131. National Academy of Sciences, *Scientific Review of the Proposed Risk Assessment Bulletin from the Office of Management and Budget* (Washington, D.C.: National Academies Press, 2007), 3.

132. Ibid., 6.

133. Ibid., 3.

134. Ibid., 4.

135. Ibid.

136. Ibid., 5.

137. Ibid.

138. Ibid., 8.

139. Ibid., 6.

140. Memorandum, Susan E. Dudley, Administrator, Office of Information and

Regulatory Affairs, Office of Management and Budget, and Sharon L. Hays, Associate Director and Deputy Director for Science, office of Science and Technology Policy, for Heads of Executive Departments and Agencies, "Updated Principles for Risk Assessment," September 19, 2007.

141. Thomas O. McGarity, Sidney Shapiro, and David Bollier, *Sophisticated Sabotage: The Intellectual Games Used to Subvert Responsible Regulation* (Washington, D.C.: Environmental Law Institute, 2004).

142. See, e.g., William C. Powers, Jr., Chair, Raymond S. Troubh, and Herbert S. Winokur, Jr., Report of Investigation by the Special Investigative Committee of the Board of Directors of Enron Corp., February 1, 2002, http://news.findlaw.com/hdocs/docs/enron/sicreport/sicreport020102.pdf, accessed February 17, 2009. This report focuses on the manipulations of the company's earnings reports, but, in the process, explains the structure and processes by which the firm manipulated pricing and obligations.

143. Senate Governmental Affairs Committee, Majority Staff, "Committee Staff Investigation of the Federal Energy Regulatory Commission's Oversight of Enron Corporation," November 12, 2002, Congressional Information Service, Inc., Committee Prints, 107th Congress; 2nd Session, 2003 S-402-5, 2003 CIS S. Print 4025. See also Minority Staff Special Investigations Division Committee on Government Reform, U.S. House of Representatives, "Bush Administration Contacts with Enron," May 2002, http://oversight.house.gov/documents/20040817122823-67561.pdf, accessed February 17, 2009.

144. OMB Watch, *Special Interest Takeover: The Bush Administration and the Dismantling of Public Safeguards* (Washington, D.C.: OMB Watch & Citizens for Sensible Safeguards Coalition, 2004), 28.

145. Ibid., 104.

146. Ibid., 13.

147. Ibid., 40.

148. Ibid., 78.

149. Quoted in Paul Davidson, "New FCC Chief Stresses Deregulation for TV, Phone," *USA Today,* February 7, 2001, 1B.

150. Quoted in Neda Ulaby, "Kevin Martin's Contentious Turn at Helm of FCC," *All Things Considered,* National Public Radio, February 5, 2008, http://www.npr.org/templates/story/story.php?storyId=18711487, accessed February 10, 2008.

151. After her departure, her frustration with the extreme move to the right by the administration prompted her to write a book on the problem as she saw it. Christine Todd Whitman, *It's My Party Too: The Battle for the Heart of the GOP and the Future of America* (New York: Penguin, 2005).

152. U.S. Senate, Hearings before the Committee on Commerce, Science and Transportation, *Nomination of Mary Sheila Gall to Be Chairman of the Consumer Product Safety Commission,* 107th Cong., 1st Sess. (2001). She addressed this in her testimony at pp. 31–32. Her use of the concept was the subject of criticism throughout the hearing.

153. Ibid.

154. A major article in the *New York Times* by Stephen Labaton, part of a series on Bush administration deregulation, reported these connections as well as the levels of campaign funding from the trucking industry and the later rollback of trucking regulations. Stephen Labaton, "As Trucking Rules Are Eased, a Debate on Safety Intensifies," *New York Times,* December 3, 2006, 1. However, there was surprisingly little reporting by broadcast media and surprisingly little public attention in the aftermath of the reports.

155. The backgrounds of a good number of these officials are described in OMB Watch, *Special Interest Takeover: The Bush Administration and the Dismantling of Public Safeguards* (Washington, D.C.: OMB Watch, 2004), http://www.ombwatch.org/regs/2004/sitreport.pdf, accessed February 10, 2008.

156. Press Release, Statement of Inspector General Nikki L. Tinsley on the Office of Inspector General Report *Additional Analyses of Mercury Emissions Needed before EPA Finalizes Rules for Coal-Fired Electric Utilities,* dated February 3, 2005, http://www.epa.gov/oig/reports/2005/20050203-2005-P-00003_Statement.pdf, accessed February 17, 2009.

157. Office of the Inspector General, U.S. Environmental Protection Agency, *Evaluation Report, Additional Analyses of Mercury Emissions Needed before EPA Finalizes Rules for Coal-Fired Electric Utilities,* Report No. 2005-P-00003, February 3, 2005, http://www.epa.gov/oig/reports/2005/200 50203-2005-P-00003.pdf, accessed February 19, 2009, Report Summary, p. 1. (Hereafter cited as EPA IG Report.)

158. U.S. Environmental Protection Agency, "Study of Hazardous Air Pollutant Emissions from Electric Utility Steam Generating Units—Final Report to Congress, EPA-453/R-98-004a, February 1998, volumes provided at http://www.epa.gov/ttn/caaa/t3/meta/m28497.html. The fact sheet for the report is at http://www.epa.gov/ttn/oarpg/t3/fact_sheets/utilfs.pdf, accessed February 19, 2009.

159. EPA IG Report, 37.

160. See H.R. Rep. No. 769, 105th Cong., 2d Sess. (1998), 281–282.

161. Ibid.

162. Ibid., 1–2.

163. Ibid., 2.

164. *Natural Resources Defense Council v. EPA,* D.C. Cir., No. 92-1415, 4/15/98, cited in EPA IG Report, p. 7, n. 6.

165. EPA IG Report, 9.

166. Ibid.

167. Ibid.

168. Ibid., 15.

169. 68 Fed. Reg. 52922 (2003).

170. 42 U.S.C. § 7602(h).

171. See, e.g., *Whitman v. American Trucking Ass'ns,* 531 U.S. 457 (2001); *Ethyl Corp. v. EPA,* 541 F.2d 1 (D.C. Cir. 1976).

172. *Commonwealth of Massachusetts v. EPA,* No. 05-1120, Petition for Writ of Certiorari.

254 Notes to Pages 118–124

173. *Commonwealth of Massachusetts v. EPA,* No. 05-1120, "Brief of Former EPA Administrators Carol M. Browner, William K. Reilly, Douglas M. Costle, and Russell E. Train as Amici Curiae in Support of Petitioners," 2.

174. Ibid., 2–3.

175. *Massachusetts v. EPA,* 127 S. Ct. 1438, 1462 (2007).

176. Ibid., 1463.

177. U.S. House, Committee on Oversight and Government Reform, *Political Interference with Climate Change Science under the Bush Administration,* December 2007, http://oversight.house.gov/documents/20071210101633.pdf, accessed February 19, 2009.

178. Ibid., i–ii.

179. Ibid.

180. See Stiglitz, *Roaring Nineties,* 112–134.

181. P.L.107-204, 116 Stat. 745 (2002).

182. Stephen Labaton, "S.E.C.'s Chairman Stepping Down from Split Panel," June 2, 2005, *New York Times,* A1; Deborah Solomon, "Cox's Nomination to Run SEC Signals a Regulatory Shift," *Wall Street Journal,* June 3, 2005, A1.

183. Quoted in Floyd Norris, "Panel of Executives and Academics to Consider Regulation and Competitiveness," *New York Times,* September 13, 2006, C3.

184. Ibid.

185. Stephen Labaton, "Bush Aides and Business Meet on Shift in Regulation," *New York Times,* March 13, 2007, C1.

186. U.S. Department of Agriculture, "Transcript of News Conference with Agriculture Secretary Ann M. Veneman on BSE," December 23, 2003, p. 1, http://www.usda.gov/wps/portal/!ut/p/_s.7_0_A/7_0_1OB/.cmd/ad/.ar/sa.retrievecontent/.c/6_2_1UH/.ce/7_2_5JM/.p/5_2_4TQ/.d/3/_th/J_2_9D/_s.7_0_A/7_0_1OB?PC_7_2_5JM_contentid=2003/12/0433.html&PC_7_2_5JM_navtype=RT&PC_7_2_5JM_parentnav=TRANSCRIPTS_SPEEC, accessed September 6, 2005.

187. 69 Fed. Reg. 1862 (2004).

188. 69 Fed. Reg. 1874 (2004).

189. 69 Fed. Reg. 1885 (2004).

190. 69 Fed. Reg. 42256 (2004).

191. U.S. Department of Agriculture, Food Safety and Inspection Service, "Recall Release: California Firm Recalls Beef Products Derived from Non-Ambulatory Cattle without the Benefit of Proper Inspection," February 17, 2008, http://www.fsis.usda.gov/pdf/recall_005-2008_Release.pdf, accessed February 19, 2009.

192. U.S. Department of Agriculture, Food Safety and Inspection Service, "Prohibition of the Use of Specified Risk Materials for Human Food and Requirements for the Disposition of Non-Ambulatory Disabled Cattle; Prohibition of the Use of Certain Stunning Devices Used to Immobilize Cattle during Slaughter: Affirmation of Interim Final Rules with Amendments," 72 Fed. Reg. 38700 (2007).

193. Ibid.

194. Ibid., 38701.

195. See, e.g., *Public Citizen v. Federal Motor Carrier Safety Administration,* 374 F.3d

1209 (D.C.Cir. 2004), concerning relaxation of driver hours rules; *Center for Biological Diversity v. Kempthorne,* 2008 U.S. Dist. LEXIS 4866 (NDCA 2008); *Center for Biological Diversity v. Kempthorne,* 2008 U.S. Dist. LEXIS 17517 (DAZ 2008), concerning the Endangered Species Act.

196. Eric V. Schaeffer, EPA Director, Office of Regulatory Enforcement, to Christine Whitman, Administrator, U.S. EPA, February 27, 2002, at http://www.4cleanair .org/, accessed June 2, 2009.

197. John W. Kingdon, *Agendas, Alternatives, and Public Policies,* 2nd ed. (New York: Longman, 1995), 204.

198. See Federal Energy Regulatory Commission, Order Granting Authority under Section 3 of the Natural Gas Act and Issuing Certificates, September 18, 2008, http://www .ferc.gov/whats-new/comm-meet/2008/091808/C-1.pdf, accessed February 19, 2009.

199. 508 F.Supp.2d 295 (D.VT 2007).

200. 2008 U.S. Dist. LEXIS 23909 (EDCA 2008).

201. U.S. Senate, Committee on Environment and Public Works, "Internal EPA Documents on California Waiver Request," http://epw.senate.gov/public/index.cfm ?FuseAction=Files.View&FileStore_id=7da5ce50-92bd-4443-bcd4-0f006309f172, accessed February 19, 2009.

202. *Wyeth v. Levine,* No. 06-1249, "Brief of Amici Curiae Former FDA Commissioners Dr. Donald Kennedy and Dr. David A. Kessler," U.S. Supreme Court, October Term 2008, p. 8.

203. *Levine v. Wyeth,* 2006 VT 107 (2006), affm'd in *Wyeth v. Levine,* 129 S.Ct. 1187 (2009).

204. U.S. House of Representatives, Committee on Oversight and Government Reform, Majority Staff Report, *FDA Career Staff Objected to Agency Preemption Policies,* October 2008, http://oversight.house.gov/documents/20081029102934.pdf, accessed February 17, 2009.

205. *Wyeth v. Levine,* No. 06-1249, "Brief of Amici Curiae Former FDA Commissioners Dr. Donald Kennedy and Dr. David A. Kessler."

206. Federal Activities Inventory Reform Act, P.L. 105-270, 112 Stat. 2382 (1998).

207. See, e.g., Report of the Commission on Army Acquisition and Program Management in Expeditionary Operations (Gansler Commission), *Urgent Reform Required: Army Expeditionary Contracting* (Washington, D.C.: Department of the Army, 2007), Executive Summary, Report pp. 1–12, http://www.army.mil/docs/Gansler_ Commission_Report_Final_071031.pdf, accessed February 19, 2009.

208. *Center for Biological Diversity v. Kempthorne,* 2008 U.S. Dist. LEXIS 4866 (NDCA 2008).

209. Office of Management and Budget, *Budget of the United States Government, Fiscal Year 2007* (Washington, D.C.: OMB, 2006), 63.

210. Ibid., 2.

211. Supra note 196.

212. "Stronger Rules and More Oversight for Produce Likely after Outbreaks of E. Coli," *New York Times,* December 11, 2006, 23.

213. *FDA Science and Mission at Risk: Report of the Subcommittee on Science and Technology,* http://www.fda.gov/ohrms/dockets/AC/07/briefing/2007-4329b_02_01_ FDA%20Report%20on%20Science%20and%20Technology.pdf, accessed February 19, 2009. See also U.S. Senate, Finance Committee, *FDA, Merck, and Vioxx,* 108th Cong., 2d Sess. (2004).

214. Ibid., 6.

215. Ibid., 9.

216. Ibid., 4.

217. Ibid., 7.

218. Joshua B. Bolten to Heads of Executive Departments and Agencies, Issuance of Agency Regulations at the End of the Administration, May 9, 2008, http://www .ombwatch.org/files/regs/PDFs/BoltenMemo050908.pdf, accessed February 14, 2009.

219. 5 U.S.C. §800 et. Seq.

220. *Motor Vehicle Manufacturers Assn. v. State Farm Mutual,* 463 U.S. 29 (1983).

221. Testimony of Curtis W. Copeland, Specialist in American National Government, Congressional Research Service, Hearings before the Committee on the Judiciary Subcommittee on Commercial and Administrative Law, House of Representatives, February 4, 2009, *Midnight Rulemaking: Shedding Some Light,* 111th Cong., 1st Sess., http://judiciary.house.gov/hearings/pdf/Copeland090204.pdf, accessed February 15, 2009, 6–7.

222. Bolten, to Heads of Executive Departments and Agencies, 1.

223. Curtis W. Copeland, "Midnight Rulemaking: Considerations for Congress and a New Administration." Updated November 24, 2008, Congressional Research Service, http://www.fas.org/sgp/crs/misc/RL34747.pdf, accessed February 15, 2009.

224. OMB Watch, "After Midnight: The Bush Legacy of Deregulation and What Obama Can Do" (Washington, D.C.: OMB Watch, 2009), http://www.ombwatch.org/ files/regs/aftermidnight.pdf, accessed February 15, 2009.

225. Testimony of Copeland, 3.

226. Testimony of Gary D. Bass, Ph.D., Executive Director, OMB Watch, before the Subcommittee on Commercial and Administrative Law Committee on the Judiciary U.S. House of Representatives, on Midnight Rulemaking: Shedding Some Light, 111th Cong., 1st Sess., February 4, 2009, http://judiciary.house.gov/hearings/pdf/Bass090204 .pdf, accessed February 15, 2009, 3.

227. Testimony of Copeland, 3–7. See also OMB Watch, "After Midnight," 1.

228. "Legislative Proposal for Treasury Authority to Purchase Mortgage-Related Assets," September 21, 2008, http://www.nytimes.com/2008/09/21/business/21draftcnd .html?_r=1&pagewanted=print, accessed February 15, 2009, 2.

229. She was referring to the General Accounting Office, *Financial Derivatives: Actions Needed to Protect the Financial System* (Washington, D.C.: GAO, 1994), http:// archive.gao.gov/t2pbat3/151816.pdf, accessed February 17, 2009.

230. Committee Holds Hearing on the Role of Federal Regulators in the Financial Crisis, http://oversight.house.gov/story.asp?ID=2256, accessed February 17, 2009.

231. Committee Holds Hearing on Causes and Effects of the Lehman Brothers Bankruptcy, http://oversight.house.gov/story.asp?ID=2208, accessed February 17, 2009.

232. Committee Holds Hearing on the Causes and Effects of the AIG Bailout, http://oversight.house.gov/story.asp?ID=2211, accessed February 17, 2009.

233. Committee Holds Hearing on Collapse of Fannie Mae and Freddie Mac, http://oversight.house.gov/story.asp?ID=2252, accessed February 17, 2009.

234. P.L. 110-343, 122 Stat. 3765 (2008).

235. Congressional Review Panel, Accountability for the Troubled Asset Relief Program: The Second Report of the Congressional Oversight Panel, http://cop.senate .gov/documents/cop-010909-report.pdf, accessed February 17, 2009, 3.

236. Ibid., 5.

237. The TARP legislation also created a Special Inspector General for the TARP, but he was not in place until late December 2008 and did not issue his first report until early January 2009, by which time the Bush administration was leaving office and had already spent the first half of the funds. See Special Inspector General for the TARP, Initial Report to Congress, January 9, 2009, http://www.sigtarp.gov/reports/ congress/2009/SIGTARP_Initial_Report_to_the_Congress.pdf, accessed February 17, 2009.

238. "Opening Statement of Congressman Paul E. Kanjorski, Committee on Financial Services, Hearing on TARP Accountability: Use of Federal Assistance by the First TARP Recipients, February 11, 2009, http://www.house.gov/apps/list/hearing/ financialsvcs_dem/kanjorski021109.pdf, accessed February 17, 2009, 1.

239. U.S. Attorney for the Southern District of New York, Press Release, "Investment Advisor and Former Chairman of NASDAQ Stock Exchange Arrested for Multibillion Dollar Ponzi Scheme," http://www.usdoj.gov/usao/nys/pressreleases/ December08/madoffarrestpr.pdf, accessed February 17, 2009, 1 (emphasis in original).

240. Subcommittee on Capital Markets, Insurance, and Government Sponsored Enterprises Hearing, Assessing the Madoff Ponzi Scheme and Regulatory Failures, February 4, 2009, http://www.house.gov/apps/list/hearing/financialsvcs_dem/ hr020409.shtml, accessed February 17, 2009.

241. Testimony of Harry Markopolos, CFA, CFE, Chartered Financial Analyst, Certified Fraud Examiner, before the U.S. House of Representatives, Committee on Financial Services, February 4, 2009, http://financialservices.house.gov/markopolos 020409.pdf, accessed February 17, 2009.

CHAPTER 4. THE BATTLE AGAINST
REGULATION IN THE COURTS

1. *Lochner v. New York,* 198 U.S. 45, 54 (1905), Holmes, J., dissenting.

2. See *NLRB v. Jones & Laughlin Steel,* 301 U.S. 1 (1937) [rvd *United States v. E.C. Knight,* 156 U.S. 1 (1895)]; *Steward Machine Co. v. Davis,* 301 U.S. 548 (1937) [rvd *Bailey*

v. Drexel 259 U.S. 20 (1922)]; *United States v. Darby,* 312 U.S. 100 (1941) [rvd *Hammer v. Dagenhart,* 247 U.S. 251 (1918)]; *Wickard v. Filburn,* 317 U.S. 111 (1942) [rvd *United States v. Butler,* 297 U.S. 1 (1936)]; *Nebbia v. New York,* 291 U.S. 502 (1934); *West Coast Hotel Co. v. Parrish,* 300 U.S. 379 (1937) [rvd *Adkins v. Children's Hospital,* 261 U.S. 525 (1923)]; *Phelps Dodge v. NLRB,* 312 U.S. 669 (1941) [rvd *Coppage v. Kansas,* 236 U.S. 1 (1915)]; *Olsen v. Nebraska,* 313 U.S. 236 (1941) [rvd *Ribnick v. McBride,* 277 U.S. 350 (1928)]; and *Lincoln Union v. Northwestern Co.,* 335 U.S. 525 (1949).

3. *National League of Cities v. Usery,* 426 U.S. 833 (1976).

4. *United States v. Darby,* 312 U.S. 100 (1941); *Maryland v. Wirtz,* 392 U.S. 183 (1968).

5. *McCulloch v. Maryland,* 17 U.S. (4 Wheat.) 316 (1819); *Gibbons v. Ogden,* 22 U.S. (9 Wheat.) 1 (1824).

6. U.S. Constitution, Article I, §8, cl. 18.

7. Ibid., Article VI, §2.

8. *National League of Cities v. Usery,* 426 U.S. 833, 840 (1976).

9. Ibid., 859, Brennan, J., dissenting.

10. U.S. Constitution, Amendment X.

11. See, e.g., *United States v. California,* 297 U.S. 175 (1936); *New York v. United States,* 326 U.S. 572 (1946).

12. *Hodel v. Virginia Surface Mining & Reclamation Assoc.,* 452 U.S. 264, 288 (1981).

13. *National League of Cities v. Usery,* 426 U.S. 833, 856 (1976), Blackmun, J., concurring.

14. *Gibbons v. Ogden,* 22 U.S. (9 Wheat.) 1 (1824).

15. *McCulloch v. Maryland,* 17 U.S. (4 Wheat.) 316 (1819).

16. *National League of Cities v. Usery,* 426 U.S. 833, 876 (1976), Brennan, J., dissenting.

17. Ibid., 880.

18. Ibid., 881, Stevens, J., dissenting.

19. Ibid.

20. *Hodel v. Virginia Surface Mining & Reclamation Assoc.,* 452 U.S. 264, 288 (1981); *Hodel v. Indiana,* 452 U.S. 314 (1981).

21. *Federal Energy Regulatory Commission v. Mississippi,* 456 U.S. 742 (1982).

22. *EEOC v. Wyoming,* 460 U.S. 226 (1983).

23. Ibid., 239.

24. Ibid., 248–249, Stevens, J., concurring.

25. *Garcia v. San Antonio Metropolitan Transit Authority,* 469 U.S. 528 (1985).

26. Ibid., 531.

27. Ibid., 580, Rehnquist, J., dissenting.

28. *Dred Scott v. Sanford,* 60 U.S. 393 (1857).

29. *Slaughter-House Cases,* 83 U.S. 36 (1873); *Bradwell v. State,* 83 U.S. 130 (1873); *Minor v. Happersett,* 88 U.S. 162 (1874).

30. *Civil Rights Cases,* 109 U.S. 3 (1883).

31. See *E. C. Knight v. United States,* 156 U.S. 1 (1895); *Hammer v. Dagenhart,* 247

U.S. 251 (1918); *United States v. Butler,* 297 U.S. 1 (1936), later reversed by the cites cited in note 2 supra.

32. See *Adkins v. Children's Hospital,* 261 U.S. 525 (1923); *Coppage v. Kansas,* 236 U.S. 1 (1915); *Ribnick v. McBride,* 277 U.S. 350 (1928), later reversed by the cites cited in note 2 supra. And see the cases rejected in Justice Black's opinion in *Lincoln Union v. Northwestern Co.,* 335 U.S. 525 (1949).

33. See, e.g., *Bailey v. Drexel,* 259 U.S. 20 (1922).

34. See *NLRB v. Jones & Laughlin Steel,* 301 U.S. 1 (1937); *Steward Machine Co. v. Davis,* 301 U.S. 548 (1937); *United States v. Darby,* 312 U.S. 100 (1941); *Wickard v. Filburn,* 317 U.S. 111 (1942).

35. *Wickard v. Filburn,* 317 U.S. 111 (1942).

36. *Heart of Atlanta Motel v. United States,* 379 U.S. 241, 258 (1964).

37. See ibid.; *Katzenbach v. McClung,* 379 U.S. 294 (1964).

38. *United States v. Lopez,* 514 U.S. 549 (1995).

39. Ibid., 551.

40. Ibid., 614–615, Souter, J., dissenting.

41. *United States v. Morrison,* 529 U.S. 598 (2000).

42. Ibid., 601.

43. Ibid., 610.

44. Ibid., 611–612.

45. Ibid.

46. Ibid.

47. Ibid., 617–618.

48. Ibid.

49. Ibid., 629, Souter, J., dissenting.

50. Ibid., 637.

51. *Seminole Tribe of Florida v. Florida,* 517 U.S. 44 (1996).

52. *Pennsylvania v. Union Gas Co.,* 491 US 1 (1989).

53. *Seminole Tribe of Florida v. Florida,* 517 U.S. 44, 77 (1996).

54. Ibid., at p. 100, Souter, J., dissenting.

55. *City of Boerne v. Flores,* 521 U.S. 507, 520 (1997).

56. *Florida Prepaid Postsecondary Ed. Expense Bd. v. College Savings Bank,* 527 U.S. 627 (1999).

57. *Alden v. Maine,* 527 U.S. 706 (1999).

58. *Kimel v. Florida Bd. of Regents,* 528 U.S. 62 (2000).

59. *Bd. of Trustees of the University of Alabama v. Garrett,* 531 U.S. 356 (2001).

60. *Kimel v. Florida Bd. of Regents,* 528 U.S. 62, 67 (2000).

61. Ibid., 82–83.

62. Ibid., 89.

63. *Kimel v. Florida Bd. of Regents,* 528 U.S. 62, 93 (2000), Stevens, J., dissenting.

64. *Bd. of Trustees of the University of Alabama v. Garrett,* 531 U.S. 356, 367–368 (2001).

65. Ibid., 377–378, Breyer, J., dissenting.

66. Ibid., 379.

67. Ibid., 387–388.

68. *Federal Maritime Commission v. South Carolina State Ports Authority,* 535 U.S. 743, 761 (2002).

69. Ibid., 772, Breyer, J., dissenting.

70. Ibid., 788.

71. *New York v. United States,* 505 U.S. 144, 160 (1992).

72. Ibid., 189, White, J., concurring in part and dissenting in part.

73. Ibid.

74. Ibid., 210.

75. Ibid., 211, Stevens, J., concurring in part and dissenting in part.

76. *Printz v. United States,* 521 U.S. 898 (1997).

77. Ibid., 935.

78. Ibid., 955, Steven, J., dissenting.

79. *Prudential Insurance Co. v. Benjamin,* 328 U.S. 408 (1946).

80. And indeed this model was recognized by the Supreme Court in *Hodel v. Virginia Surface Mining & Reclamation Assoc.,* 452 U.S. 264, 288 (1981).

81. *Euclid v. Ambler,* 272 U.S. 365 (1926). On the modern debate on regulatory takings, see William A. Fischel, *Regulatory Takings: Law, Economics, and Politics* (Cambridge, Mass.: Harvard University Press, 1995).

82. Ibid., 387.

83. Ibid., 395.

84. *Day-Brite Lighting v. Missouri,* 342 U.S. 421 (1952).

85. Ibid., 424–425.

86. Ibid., 423.

87. "*Lochner v. New York,* 198 U.S. 45, which invalidated a New York law prescribing maximum hours for work in bakeries; *Coppage v. Kansas,* 236 U.S. 1, which struck down a Kansas statute outlawing 'yellow dog' contracts; *Adkins v. Children's Hospital,* 261 U.S. 525," ibid.

88. See *West Coast Hotel Co. v. Parrish,* 300 U.S. 379 (1937); *Nebbia v. New York,* 291 U.S. 502 (1934); *Olsen v. Nebraska,* 313 U.S. 236 (1941). See also *Lincoln Union v. Northwestern Co.,* 335 U.S. 525 (1949); *California Auto. Assn. v. Maloney,* 341 U.S. 105 (1951).

89. *Nollan v. California Coastal Commission,* 483 U.S. 825, 866 (1987), Blackmun, J., dissenting.

90. *Lucas v. South Carolina Coastal Commission,* 505 U.S. 1003 (1992).

91. Ibid., 1031–1032.

92. See *Euclid v. Ambler,* 272 U.S. 365 (1926). See also Ernst Freund, *Standards of American Legislation* (Chicago: University of Chicago Press, 1917), ch. 3.; Roscoe Pound, *Administrative Law: Its Growth, Procedure and Significance* (Pittsburgh, Pa.: University of Pittsburgh Press, 1942); James M. Landis, *The Administrative Process* (New Haven, Conn.: Yale University Press, 1938); Walter Gellhorn, *Federal Administrative Proceedings* (Baltimore, Md.: Johns Hopkins University Press, 1941).

93. *Lucas v. South Carolina Coastal Commission,* 505 U.S. 1003, 1060 (1992), Blackmun, J., dissenting.

94. Ibid., 1046.

95. Ibid., 1052.

96. Ibid., 1060.

97. Ibid.

98. Ibid., 1061.

99. *Dolan v. Tigard,* 512 U.S. 374 (1994).

100. Ibid., 386.

101. Ibid., 388–389.

102. Ibid., 391–396.

103. Ibid., 394–395.

104. Ibid., 405, Stevens, J., dissenting.

105. Ibid., 410.

106. *City of Monterrey v. Del Monte Dunes,* 526 U.S. 687 (1999).

107. Ibid., 733, Souter, J., dissenting.

108. Ibid., 755.

109. *FMC Corp. v. Holliday,* 498 U.S. 52 (1990).

110. *Prudential Insurance Co. v. Benjamin,* 328 U.S. 408 (1946).

111. *FMC Corp. v. Holliday,* 498 U.S. 52, 67 (1990), Stevens, J., dissenting.

112. *Morales v. TWA,* 504 U.S. 374, 383 (1992).

113. Ibid., 424, Stevens, J., dissenting.

114. *Gade v. National Solid Wastes Management Assn,* 505 U.S. 88 (1992).

115. Ibid., 116, Souter, J., dissenting, citing *Rice v. Santa Fe Elevator Corp.,* 331 U.S. 218, 230 (1947).

116. Ibid., 109, Kennedy, J., concurring in part and concurring in the judgment.

117. *United States v. Locke,* 529 U.S. 89 (2000).

118. Quoted in Eric Nalder, "Oil-Spill Draft Report: States Need More Clout—Federal Oil-Shipping Rules Called Insufficient," *Seattle Times,* January 2, 1990, B1.

119. *Ray v. Atlantic Richfield,* 435 U.S. 151 (1978).

120. *Cooley v. Board of Wardens of Port of Philadelphia,* 53 U.S. 299 (1852).

121. *Kotch v. Bd. of River Port Pilot Commissioners,* 330 U.S. 552 (1947). This was not a preemption case, but one that faced a challenge under the equal protection clause of the Fourteenth Amendment because of the manner in which river pilots were trained, licensed, and regulated.

122. 33 U.S.C. § 2718.

123. *International Association of Independent Tanker Owners (INTERTANKO) v. Lowry,* 947 F. Supp. 1484 (WDWA 1996).

124. *International Association of Independent Tanker Owners (INTERTANKO) v. Locke,* 148 F.3d 1053 (9th Cir. 1998).

125. "Note Verbale from the Royal Danish Embassy to the U.S. Department of State," 1 (June 14, 1996), quoted in *United States v. Locke,* 529 U.S. 89, 98 (2000).

126. *Cooley v. Board of Wardens of Port of Philadelphia,* 53 U.S. 299 (1852).

127. *United States v. Locke,* 529 U.S. 89, 98 (2000).

128. Ibid., at 116.

129. See, e.g., *White v. Massachusetts Council of Construction Workers,* 460 U.S. 204 (1983).

130. *Crosby v. Nat'l Foreign Trade Council,* 530 U.S. 363 (2000).

131. Ibid., 381.

132. *American Ins. Ass'n v. Garamendi,* 539 U.S. 396, 401 (2003).

133. Ibid., 421.

134. Ibid., 427.

135. Ibid., 439, Ginsburg, J., dissenting.

136. *Rowe v. New Hampshire Motor Transport Association,* 128 S. Ct. 989 (2008).

137. *Riegel v. Medtronic, Inc.,* 128 S. Ct. 999 (2008).

138. Ibid., at 1018, Ginsburg, J., dissenting.

139. *Preston v. Ferrer,* 128 S. Ct. 978 (2008).

140. *Air Transport Association of American v. Cuomo,* 520 F.3d 218 (2nd Cir. 2008).

141. Ibid., 222.

142. Ibid., 223–224.

143. See Richard Kluger, *Simple Justice* (New York: Knopf, 1975). There is a literature on this civil rights policy development through legal action that traces back to Clement E. Vose, *Caucasians Only: The Supreme Court, the NAACP, and the Restrictive Covenant Cases* (Berkeley: University of California Press, 1959).

144. P.L. 101-336; 104 Stat. 327 (1990).

145. P.L. 90-202, 81 Stat. 602 (1967).

146. P.L. 103-3; 107 Stat. 6 (1993).

147. *Massachusetts v. EPA,* 127 S. Ct. 1438 (2007).

148. See the discussion of *Morales v. TVA* earlier in this chapter.

149. See, e.g., *State of North Carolina v. TVA,* 439 F. Supp. 2d 486 (WDNC 2006); *California v. General Motors,* 2007 U.S. Dist. LEXIS 68547 (NDCA 2007); *Rhode Island v. Lead Paint Association,* 2007 R.I. Super. LEXIS 32 (Superior Ct., RI 2007).

150. State Attorneys General, *Multistate Settlement with the Tobacco Industry,* http://www.library.ucsf.edu/tobacco/litigation/msa.pdf, accessed September 14, 2008. See also Symposium: "State Attorney General Litigation: Through Litigation and the Separation of Powers," 31 *Seton Hall Law Review* 612 (2001). See also Graham Kelder and Patricia Davidson, eds., for the Tobacco Control Resource Center, Northwestern University School of Law, *The Multistate Master Settlement Agreement and the Future of State and Local Tobacco Control* (Chicago: Tobacco Control Resource Center, 1999). Also available at http://www.tobacco.neu.edu/tobacco_control/resources/msa/msa_analysis.pdf, accessed September 14, 2008.

151. See, e.g., Peter Schuck, *Agent Orange on Trial,* rev. ed. (Cambridge, Mass.: Belknap Press, 2006).

152. These are discussed at length in Phillip J. Cooper, *Public Law and Public Administration,* 4th ed. (Belmont, Calif.: Wadsworth/Thomson Learning, 2007), ch. 7.

153. See *Middlesex County Sewage Authority v. National Sea Clammers Association,* 453 U.S. 1 (1981); *Gonzaga University v. Doe,* 536 U.S. 273 (2002).

154. See *Alexander v. Sandoval,* 532 U.S. 275 (2001), denying an implied right of action under Title VI of the Civil Rights Act of 1964.

155. *Heckler v. Chaney,* 470 U.S. 821, 832 (1985).

156. *Amchem Products, Inc. v. Windsor,* 138 L.Ed.2d 689 (1997); *General Telephone Co. of the Southwest v. Falcon,* 457 U.S. 147 (1982); *Eisen v. Carlisle & Jacquelin,* 417 U.S. 156 (1974); and *Zahn v. International Paper Co.,* 414 U.S. 291 (1973).

157. *Exxon v. Baker,* 128 S. Ct. 2605, 2621 (2008).

158. See, e.g., *State Farm Mut. Automobile Ins. Co. v. Campbell,* 538 U. S. 408, 425 (2003).

159. *Exxon v. Baker,* 128 S. Ct. 2605, 2634 (2008).

160. Ibid., 2614.

161. Ibid., 2634.

162. Exxon Mobil, "Exxon Mobil Corporation Announces Estimated Second Quarter 2008 Results," Press Release, July 31, 2008, http://www.businesswire.com/portal/site/exxonmobil/index.jsp?ndmViewId=news_view&ndmConfigId=1001106&newsId=20080731005690&newsLang=en, accessed September 14, 2008.

163. See W. Kip Viscusi, *Regulation through Litigation* (Washington, D.C.: American Enterprise Institute, 2002).

164. Ibid., ch. 1.

CHAPTER 5. "THE WRONG WAR IN THE WRONG PLACE AT THE WRONG TIME WITH THE WRONG ENEMY"

1. Linda L. Emanuel, *Regulating How We Die* (Cambridge, Mass.: Harvard, 1999).

2. See Edmund S. Morgan, *The Puritan Dilemma: The Story of John Winthrop* (Boston: Little, Brown, 1958), for the classic discussion of Winthrop's governance efforts.

3. The author has addressed these criticisms and their significance for the development of rulemaking in *Public Law and Public Administration,* 4th ed. (Belmont, Calif.: Wadsworth/Thomson Learning, 2007), chs. 4 and 5.

4. See, generally, Kenneth Culp Davis, *Discretionary Justice: A Preliminary Inquiry* (Baton Rouge: Louisiana State University Press, 1969).

5. All but the last of these make up the core elements of the scope of judicial review in administrative law outlined in the Administrative Procedure Act, 5 U.S.C. §706.

6. The author has dealt with these cases in greater detail in *Hard Judicial Choices: Federal District Judges and State and Local Officials* (New York: Oxford University Press, 1988).

7. The actual quoted language comes from Clinton's memoirs, Henry Clinton, *The*

American Rebellion: Sir Henry Clinton's Narrative of His Campaigns, 1775–1782, William B. Willcox, ed. (New Haven, Conn.: Yale University Press, 1954), 19.

8. See Ernst Freund, *Standards of American Legislation* (Chicago: University of Chicago Press, 1917), ch. 3; Roscoe Pound, *Administrative Law: Its Growth, Procedure and Significance* (Pittsburgh, Pa.: University of Pittsburgh Press, 1942), 113. See also Ernst Freund, *Administrative Powers over Persons and Property: A Comparative Survey* (Chicago: University of Chicago Press, 1928).

9. See *Lucas v. South Carolina Coastal Commission,* 505 U.S. 1003 (1992); *Nollan v. California Coastal Commission,* 483 U.S. 825 (1987); *Dolan v. Tigard,* 512 U.S. 374 (1994), and the discussion of these rulings in Chapter 4.

10. See, e.g., *Shelley v. Kraemer,* 334 U.S. 1 (1948).

11. See the discussion of the so-called civil justice reform effort in Chapters 2–4.

12. See, e.g., *In the Matter of Baby M,* 537 A.2d 1227, 1246-1248 (NJ 1988).

13. Discussed by the author in more detail in Phillip J. Cooper, *Governing by Contract: Challenges and Opportunities for Public Managers* (Washington, D.C.: CQ Press, 2003).

14. See, generally, W. Noel Keyes, *Government Contracts: Under the Federal Acquisition Regulation,* 2nd ed. (St. Paul, Minn.: West Publishing, 1996).

15. Inspector General Act of 1978, P.L. 95-452, 92 Stat. 1101.

16. See, e.g., U.S. General Accounting Office, *Worker Protection: Federal Contractors and Violations of Labor Law* (Washington, D.C.: GAO, 1995).

17. On the presumptive unreviewability of enforcement discretion, see *Heckler v. Chaney,* 470 U.S. 821 (1985).

18. See, generally, Steven Kelman, *Procurement and Public Management: The Fear of Discretion and the Quality of Government Performance* (Washington, D.C.: AEI Press, 1990), and Donald F. Kettl, *Sharing Power* (Washington, D.C.: Brookings Institution, 1993).

19. U.S. Constitution, Article I, §8, Cl. 3.

20. Ibid., cl. 18.

21. Article I, §4, cl. 2; Article I, §5, cl. 2; Article I, §7, cl. 3; Article I, §8, cl. 4; Article I, §8, cl. 5; Article I, §8, cl. 11; Article I, §8, cl. 14; Article I, §8, cl. 18; Article I, §9, cl. 6; Article III, §2; Article IV, §2, cl. 3; Article IV, §3, cl. 2; Amendment 2; Amendment 7.

22. Federalist, numbers 4–7, 10–13, 15–17, 19–23, 28–29, 33, 36, 38–46, 49, 52–56, 58–62, 64, 69, 72, 75, 78, 82–84, and that does not count 51 in which Madison discusses the need to regulate the governed and then to have the government regulated.

23. Alexander Hamilton, James Madison, and John Jay, *The Federalist Papers* (New York: Mentor, 1961), Federalist 10, 79.

24. Milton M. Carrow, *The Background of Administrative Law* (Newark, N.J.: Associated Lawyers, 1948), 6.

25. Ernst Freund, *Administrative Powers over Persons and Property: A Comparative Survey* (Chicago: University of Chicago Press, 1928), p. 145.

26. Ibid., 143–144.

27. Carrow, *Background of Administrative Law,* 6.

28. Lester M. Salamon, ed., *The Tools of Government: A Guide to the New Governance* (New York: Oxford University Press, 2002).

29. U.S. Regulatory Council, *Regulatory Reform Highlights: An Inventory of Initiatives, 1978–1980* (Washington, D.C.: U.S. Regulatory Council, 1980), 9.

30. The sad state of affairs that led to the creation of the Food and Drug Administration was presented in Upton Sinclair's classic, *The Jungle* (New York: Airmont, 1965 [1906]).

31. See *United States v. Rutherford,* 442 U.S. 544 (1979); *Abigail Alliance for Better Access to Developmental Drugs v. von Eschenbach,* 495 F.3d 695 (D.C. Cir. 2007) for discussion of the history of this problem, including more recent versions of the problem.

32. See Louis D. Brandeis, *Other People's Money* (New York: Harper & Row, 1967); John Kenneth Galbraith, *The Great Crash* (Boston: Houghton-Mifflin, 1961); Ralph DeBedts, *The New Deal's SEC: The Formative Years* (New York: Columbia University Press, 1964); William O. Douglas, *Democracy and Finance* (Port Washington, N.Y.: Kennikat Press, 1940).

33. See the legislative histories of the National Traffic and Motor Vehicle Safety Act of 1966, P.L. 89-563, 80 Stat. 718, and the Highway Safety Act of 1966, P.L. 89-564, 80 Stat. 731, in 1966 *U.S. Code Congressional and Administrative News* 2709, 2741 (1966).

34. These are results of the study by the National Commission on Product Safety, cited in Kenneth Culp Davis, *Administrative Law: Cases—Text—Problems,* 6th ed. (St. Paul, Minn.: West, 1977), 9.

35. U.S. Senate, Subcommittee on Labor of the Committee on Labor and Public Welfare, *Legislative History of the Occupational Safety and Health Act of 1970,* 92nd Cong., 1st Sess. (1971), 142.

36. See, e.g., Federal Election Commission, *Legislative History of Federal Election Campaign Act Amendment of 1974* (Washington, D.C.: Government Printing Office, 1977).

37. See, e.g., U.S. Senate, Subcommittee on Labor of the Committee on Human Resources, *Legislative History of the Federal Mine Safety and Health Act of 1977,* 95th Cong., 2d Sess. (1978).

38. U.S. Senate, Committee on Governmental Affairs, *Study on Federal Regulation,* 95th Cong., 2d Sess. (1978), vol. 6, chap. 2.

39. Wilson, "Politics of Regulation," 358–363.

40. Ibid., 362–363.

41. Kenneth J. Meier, E. Thomas Garman, and Lael R. Keiser, *Regulation and Consumer Protection: Politics, Bureaucracy, and Economics,* 3rd ed. (Houston, Tex.: DAME Publications, 1998), 6–7.

42. Ibid.

43. *INS v. Chadha,* 426 U.S. 919, 951 (1983).

44. Aldo Leopold, *A Sand County Almanac with Essays on Conservation from Round River* (New York: Ballantine, 1970 [1949]), 246–251.

Bibliography

American Bar Association Task Force on Presidential Signing Statements and the Separation of Power Doctrine. "Report to the House of Delegates," incorporated into American Bar Association Resolution 304, August 7–8, 2006, at http://www.abanet .org/leadership/2006/annual/dailyjournal/20060823144113.pd; http://www.aba videonews.org/ABA374/media/304.pdf, accessed July 28, 2007.

Ban, Carolyn, and Patricia Ingraham. "Short-Timers: Political Appointee Mobility and Its Impact on Political/Career Relations in the Reagan Administration." 22 *Administration & Society* 106 (1990).

Bardach, Eugene. *The Implementation Game.* Cambridge, Mass.: MIT Press, 1977.

Bernstein, Marver. *Regulating Business by Independent Commission.* Princeton, N.J.: Princeton University Press, 1955.

Brandeis, Louis D. *Other People's Money.* New York: Harper & Row, 1967.

Breyer, Stephen. *Regulation and Its Reform.* Cambridge, Mass.: Harvard University Press, 1982.

Burton, Lloyd. "Ethical Discontinuities in Public-Private Sector Negotiation." 9 *Journal of Policy Analysis and Management* 23 (1990).

Butler, Stuart M., Michael Sanera, and W. Bruce Weinrod. *Mandate for Leadership II.* Washington, D.C.: Heritage Foundation, 1984.

Cameron, Chip, Philip J. Harter, Gail Bingham, and Neil R. Eisner. "Alternative Dispute Resolution with Emphasis on Rulemaking Negotiations." 4 *Administrative Law Journal* 83 (1990).

Carrow, Milton M. *The Background of Administrative Law.* Newark, N.J.: Associated Lawyers, 1948.

Commercial Activities Panel. *Improving the Sourcing Decisions of the Government, Final Report.* Washington, D.C.: GAO, 2002.

Commission on Army Acquisition and Program Management in Expeditionary Operations (Gansler Commission). *Urgent Reform Required: Army Expeditionary Contracting.* Washington, D.C.: Department of the Army, 2007.

Constitution Project, Coalition to Defend Checks and Balances, "Statement on Presidential Signing Statements," at http://www.constitutionproject.org/pdf/Statement _on_Presidential_Signing_Statement.pdf, accessed July 28, 2007.

Cooper, Phillip J. *By Order of the President: The Use and Abuse of Presidential Direct Action.* Lawrence: University Press of Kansas, 2002.

———. "George W. Bush, Edgar Allan Poe, and the Use and Abuse of Presidential Signing Statements." 35 *Presidential Studies Quarterly* 515 (2005).

———. *Government by Contract.* Washington, D.C.: CQ Press, 2003.

———. *Hard Judicial Choices: Federal District Judges and State and Local Officials.* New York: Oxford University Press, 1988.

————. *Public Law and Public Administration,* 4th ed. Belmont, Calif.: Wadsworth/ Thomson Learning, 2007.

————. "Signing Statements as Declaratory Judgments: The President as Judge." 16 *William & Mary Bill of Rights Journal* 253 (2007).

Cooper, Phillip J., and Claudia María Vargas. *Implementing Sustainable Development: From Global Policy to Local Action.* Lanham, Md.: Rowman & Littlefield, 2004.

Davis, Kenneth Culp. *Discretionary Justice: A Preliminary Inquiry.* Baton Rouge: Louisiana State University Press, 1969.

DeBedts, Ralph. *The New Deal's SEC: The Formative Years.* New York: Columbia University Press, 1964.

Derthick, Martha, and Paul J. Quirk. *The Politics of Deregulation.* Washington, D.C.: Brookings Institution, 1985.

Douglas, William O. *Democracy and Finance.* Port Washington, N.Y.: Kennikat Press, 1969.

Durant, Robert F. *The Administrative Presidency Revisited: Public Lands, the BLM, and the Reagan Revolution.* Albany: State University of New York Press, 1992.

Emanuel, Linda L. *Regulating How We Die.* Cambridge, Mass.: Harvard University Press, 1998.

Epstein, Lee. *Conservatives in Court.* Knoxville: University of Tennessee Press, 1985.

————. "Interest Group Litigation during the Rehnquist Era." 9 *Journal of Law and Politics* 639 (1993).

————. "The Rise of Conservative Interest Group Litigation." 45 *Journal of Politics* 479 (1983).

Freund, Ernst. *Administrative Powers over Persons and Property: A Comparative Survey.* Chicago: University of Chicago Press, 1928.

————. *Standards of American Legislation.* Chicago: University of Chicago Press, 1917.

Friedman, Barry D. *Regulation in the Reagan-Bush Era: The Eruption of Presidential Influence.* Pittsburgh: University of Pittsburgh Press, 1995.

Friendly, Henry J. *The Federal Administrative Agencies.* Cambridge, Mass.: Harvard University Press, 1962.

Galbraith, John Kenneth. *The Great Crash.* Boston: Houghton-Mifflin, 1961.

Gore, Al. *From Red Tape to Results: Creating a Government That Works Better and Costs Less.* Report of the National Performance Review. Washington, D.C.: Government Printing Office, 1993.

Green, Mark J. *The Other Government,* rev. ed. New York: Norton, 1978.

Halstead, T. J. "Presidential Signing Statements: Constitutional and Institutional Implications," CRS Report for Congress, September 20, 2006 (updated September 17, 2007), at http://www.fas.org/sgp/crs/natsec/RL33667.pdf, accessed May 30, 2009.

Hamilton, Alexander, James Madison, and John Jay. *The Federalist Papers.* New York: Mentor, 1961.

Hofstadter, Richard. *The Age of Reform.* New York: Random House, 1955.

Kaufman, Herbert. *Are Government Organizations Immortal?* Washington, D.C.: Brookings Institution, 1976.

Kelder, Graham, and Patricia Davidson, eds., for the Tobacco Control Resource Center, Northwestern University School of Law. *The Multistate Master Settlement Agreement and the Future of State and Local Tobacco Control.* Chicago: Tobacco Control Resource Center, 1999.

Kelman, Steven. *Procurement and Public Management: The Fear of Discretion and the Quality of Government Performance.* Washington, D.C.: AEI Press, 1990.

Kerwin, Cornelius M. *Rulemaking: How Government Agencies Write Laws and Make Policy,* 3rd ed. Washington, D.C.: CQ Press, 2003.

Kettl, Donald F. *Sharing Power.* Washington, D.C.: Brookings Institution, 1993.

Keyes, W. Noel. *Government Contracts: Under the Federal Acquisition Regulation,* 2nd ed. St. Paul, Minn.: West Publishing, 1996.

Kingdon, John W. *Agendas, Alternatives, and Public Policies.* New York: Longman, 1995.

Kluger, Richard. *Simple Justice.* New York: Knopf, 1975.

Krishnan, Jayanth K., and Kevin R. den Dulk. "So Help Me God: A Comparative Study of Religious Interest Group Litigation." 30 *Georgia Journal of International and Comparative Law* 233 (2002).

Leopold, Aldo. *A Sand County Almanac with Essays on Conservation from Round River.* New York: Ballantine, 1970 [1949].

Marshall, Will, and Martin Schram, eds. *Mandate for Change.* New York: Progressive Policy Institute, 1993.

McCullough, David. *Truman.* New York: Simon & Schuster, 1992.

McGarity, Thomas O., Sidney Shapiro, and David Bollier. *Sophisticated Sabotage: The Intellectual Games Used to Subvert Responsible Regulation.* Washington, D.C.: Environmental Law Institute, 2004.

Meier, Kenneth J., E. Thomas Garman, and Lael R. Keiser. *Regulation and Consumer Protection: Politics, Bureaucracy, and Economics,* 3rd ed. Houston, Tex.: DAME Publications, 1998.

Meiners, Roger E., and Bruce Yandle, eds. *Regulation and the Reagan Era: Politics, Bureaucracy, and the Public Interest.* New York: Holmes & Meier, 1989.

Milward, H. Brinton. "The Changing Character of the Public Sector," in James Perry, ed. *Handbook of Public Administration,* 2nd ed. San Francisco: Jossey-Bass, 1996.

———. "Implication of Contracting Out: New Roles for the Hollow State," in Patricia W. Ingraham and Barbara S. Romzek, eds. *New Paradigms for Government.* San Francisco: Jossey-Bass, 1994: 41–62.

———. "Introduction to Symposium on the Hollow State: Capacity, Control, and Performance in Interorganizational Settings." 6 *Journal of Public Administration Research and Theory* 193 (1996).

Nakamura, Robert, Thomas Church, and Phillip Cooper. "Environmental Dispute Resolution and Hazardous Waste Cleanups: A Cautionary Tale of Policy Implementation." 10 *Journal of Policy Analysis and Management* 204 (1991).

National Academy of Sciences. *Scientific Review of the Proposed Risk Assessment Bulletin from the Office of Management and Budget.* Washington, D.C.: National Academies Press, 2007.

National Performance Review. *Improving Regulatory Systems,* Washington, D.C.: Office of the Vice President, 1993, at http://govinfo.library.unt.edu/npr/library/reports/rego6.html, accessed January 5, 2008.

National Research Council. *Science and Judgment in Risk Assessment.* Washington, D.C.: National Academy Press, 1994.

O'Connor, Karen, and Lee Epstein. "Amicus Curiae Participation in U.S. Supreme Court Litigation." 16 *Law & Society Review* 311 (1981).

Office of the Inspector General, U.S. Environmental Protection Agency. *Evaluation Report, Additional Analyses of Mercury Emissions Needed before EPA Finalizes Rules for Coal-Fired Electric Utilities.* Report No. 2005-P-00003, February 3, 2005, at http://www.epa.gov/oig/reports/2005/200 50203-2005-P-00003.pdf, accessed February 19, 2009.

Office of Management and Budget. The President's Management Agenda, Fiscal Year 2002, at http://www.whitehouse.gov/omb/budget/fy2002/mgmt.pdf, accessed March 29, 2008.

O'Leary, Rosemary. *Environmental Change: Federal Courts and the EPA.* Philadelphia: Temple University Press, 1993.

OMB Watch. *Special Interest Takeover: The Bush Administration and the Dismantling of Public Safeguards.* Washington, D.C.: OMB Watch & Citizens for Sensible Safeguards Coalition, 2004.

Osborne, David, and Ted Gaebler. *Reinventing Government.* New York: Penguin, 1993.

Pertschuk, Michael. *Revolt against Regulation.* Berkeley: University of California Press, 1982.

Pfifnner, James P. *The Strategic Presidency,* 2nd ed., rev. Lawrence: University Press of Kansas, 1996.

Pollitt, Christopher. "Management Techniques for the Public Sector: Pulpit and Practice," in B. Guy Peters and Donald J. Savoie, eds. *Governance in a Changing Environment.* Ottawa: McGill/Queens University Press, 1995: 203–238.

Pound, Roscoe. *Administrative Law: Its Growth, Procedure and Significance.* Pittsburgh, Pa.: University of Pittsburgh Press, 1942.

Reagan, Michael D. *The New Federalism.* New York: Oxford University Press, 1972.

Robinson, Glenn O. "The Federal Communications Commission: An Essay on Regulatory Watchdogs." 64 *Virginia Law Review* 169 (1978).

Salamon, Lester M., ed. *The Tools of Government: A Guide to the New Governance.* New York: Oxford University Press, 2002.

Schiavo, Mary. *Flying Blind, Flying Safe.* New York: Avon Books, 1997.

Schuck, Peter. *Agent Orange on Trial,* rev. ed. Cambridge, Mass.: Belknap, 2006.

Shapiro, Sidney A., and Robert L. Glicksman. *Risk Regulation at Risk.* Stanford, Calif.: Stanford University Press, 2003.

———. "Outsourcing Government Regulation." 53 *Duke Law Journal* 389 (2003).

Sharfman, Isaiah. *The Interstate Commerce Commission.* New York: Commonwealth Fund, 1937.

Sparrow, Malcolm K. *The Regulatory Craft.* Washington, D.C.: Brookings Institution, 2000.

Stiglitz, Joseph E. *The Roaring Nineties: A New History of the World's Most Prosperous Decade.* New York: W. W. Norton, 2003.

Symposium: "State Attorney General Litigation: Through Litigation and the Separation of Powers." 31 *Seton Hall Law Review* 612 (2001).

Tolchin, Susan J., and Martin Tolchin. *Dismantling America: The Rush to Deregulate.* New York: Oxford University Press, 1985.

Triano, Christine, and Nancy Watzman. *All the Vice President's Men.* Washington, D.C.: OMB Watch, 1991.

U.S. Federal Election Commission. *Legislative History of Federal Election Campaign Act Amendment of 1974.* Washington, D.C.: Government Printing Office, 1977.

U.S. General Accounting Office (now Government Accountability Office). *Implementation of the Regulatory Review Executive Order.* Washington, D.C.: GAO, 1996.

———. *Worker Protection: Federal Contractors and Violations of Labor Law.* Washington, D.C.: GAO, 1995.

U.S. House, Committee on Oversight and Government Reform. *Political Interference with Climate Change Science under the Bush Administration,* December 2007, at http://oversight.house.gov/documents/20071210101633.pdf, accessed February 19, 2009.

———. Hearing before the Subcommittees on Human Rights and International Organizations, Western Hemisphere Affairs, and International Economic Policy and Trade of the Committee on Foreign Affairs. *The Enterprise for the Americas Initiative.* 101st Cong., 2nd Sess. (1990).

U.S. Regulatory Council. *Innovative Techniques in Theory and Practice, Proceedings.* Washington, D.C.: U.S. Regulatory Council, 1980.

———. *Regulating with Common Sense: A Progress Report on Innovative Regulatory Techniques.* Washington, D.C.: U.S. Regulatory Council, 1980.

———. *Regulatory Reform Highlights: An Inventory of Initiatives, 1978–1980.* Washington, D.C.: U.S. Regulatory Council, 1980.

U.S. Senate, Committee on Finance. *FDA, Merck, and Vioxx.* 108th Cong., 2d Sess. (2004).

———. Committee on Governmental Affairs. *Study on Federal Regulation.* 95th Cong., 2d Sess. (1978).

———. Hearings before the Committee on Commerce, Science and Transportation. *Nomination of Mary Sheila Gall to Be Chairman of the Consumer Product Safety Commission.* 107th Cong., 1st Sess. (2001).

———. Report of the Committee on the Judiciary together with Additional and Supplemental Views. *The Comprehensive Regulatory Reform Act of 1995—S. 343.* 104th Cong., 1st Sess. (1995).

———. Subcommittee on Labor of the Committee on Human Resources. *Legislative History of the Federal Mine Safety and Health Act of 1977.* 95th Cong., 2d Sess. (1978).

————. Subcommittee on Labor of the Committee on Labor and Public Welfare. *Legislative History of the Occupational Safety and Health Act of 1970.* 92nd Cong., 1st Sess. (1971).

Viscusi, W. Kip. *Regulation through Litigation.* Washington, D.C.: American Enterprise Institute, 2002.

von Hayek, Friedrich. *The Road to Serfdom.* Chicago: University of Chicago Press, 1944.

Vose, Clement E. *Caucasians Only: The Supreme Court, the NAACP, and the Restrictive Covenant Cases.* Berkeley: University of California Press, 1959.

Weidenbaum, Murray. *The Costs of Government Regulation of Business,* in Murray Weidenbaum, *Business, Government and the Public.* Englewood Cliffs, N.J.: Prentice-Hall, 1977.

Wilson, James Q. "The Politics of Regulation," in James Q. Wilson, ed. *The Politics of Regulation.* New York: Basic Books, 1980: 357–394.

Woodward, Bob. *The Agenda: Inside the Clinton White House.* New York: Simon and Schuster, 1994.

Woolf, Malcolm D. "Clean Air or Hot Air?: Lessons from the Quayle Competitiveness Council's Oversight of EPA." 10 *Journal Law & Public Policy* 97 (1993).

Cases Cited

Adkins v. Children's Hospital, 261 U.S. 525 (1923)

Air Transport Association of American v. Cuomo, 520 F.3d 218 (2nd Cir. 2008)

Alden v. Maine, 527 U.S. 706 (1999)

Alexander v. Sandoval, 532 U.S. 275 (2001)

Amchem Products, Inc. v. Windsor, 138 L.Ed.2d 689 (1997)

American Airlines v. Civil Aeronautics Board, 359 F.2d 624 (D.C.Cir. 1966)

American Ins. Ass'n v. Garamendi, 539 U.S. 396 (2003)

Appalachian Power Co. v. Environmental Protection Agency, 477 F.2d 495 (4th Cir. 1973)

Bailey v. Drexel, 259 U.S. 20 (1922)

Bd. of Trustees of the University of Alabama v. Garrett, 531 U.S. 356 (2001)

Bradwell v. State, 83 U.S. 130 (1873)

California v. General Motors, 2007 U.S. Dist. LEXIS 68547 (NDCA 2007)

Carter v. Carter Coal Co., 298 U.S. 238 (1936)

Center for Biological Diversity v. Kempthorne, 2008 U.S. Dist. LEXIS 4866 (NDCA 2008)

Center for Biological Diversity v. Kempthorne, 2008 U.S. Dist. LEXIS 17517 (DAZ 2008)

Cheney v. U.S. District Court, 542 U.S. 367 (2004)

Chevron U.S.A. v. Natural Resources Defense Council, 467 U.S. 837 (1984)

Chrysler v. DOT, 472 F.2d 659 (6th Cir. 1972)

City of Boerne v. Flores, 521 U.S. 507 (1997)

City of Monterrey v. Del Monte Dunes, 526 U.S. 687 (1999)

Civil Rights Cases, 109 U.S. 3 (1883)

Cohens v. Virginia, 6 Wheat. 264 (1821)

Consumer Energy Council v. Federal Energy Regulatory Commission, 673 F.2d 425 (D.C.Cir. 1982)

Cooley v. Board of Wardens of Port of Philadelphia, 53 U.S. 299 (1852)

Coppage v. Kansas, 236 U.S. 1 (1915)

Crosby v. National Foreign Trade Council, 530 U.S. 363 (2000)

Day-Brite Lighting v. Missouri, 342 U.S. 421 (1952)

Dolan v. Tigard, 512 U.S. 374 (1994)

Dole v. United Steelworkers, 494 U.S. 26 (1990)

Dred Scott v. Sanford, 60 U.S. 393 (1857)

E.C. Knight v. United States, 156 U.S. 1 (1895)

EDF v. Thomas, 627 F. Supp. 566 (D.D.C. 1986)

EEOC v. Wyoming, 460 U.S. 226 (1983)

Eisen v. Carlisle & Jacquelin, 417 U.S. 156 (1974)

Ethyl Corp. v. EPA, 541 F.2d 1 (D.C. Cir. 1976)

Euclid v. Ambler, 272 U.S. 365 (1926)

Exxon v. Baker, 128 S. Ct. 2605 (2008)

Federal Communications Commission v. WNCN Listeners Guild, 450 U.S. 582 (1981)

Federal Election Commission v. Wisconsin

Index